I0813045

IMAGES
of America

SAN JUAN BAUTISTA

ON THE COVER: This "modern" incarnation of the mission and its bell tower was commissioned by Rev. Cipriano Rubio, who came to the mission as pastor in 1856. The Victorian-style bell tower consisted of two rooms, one on top of the other, and its bell-ringing system replaced an earlier method: a crossbeam in front of the church with bells hanging from it. (Courtesy San Juan Bautista State Historic Park.)

IMAGES
of America

SAN JUAN BAUTISTA

Joseph McMahon, Carla Hendershot,
and the Plaza History Association

ARCADIA
PUBLISHING

ISBN 978-0-7385-4773-2

PPublished by Arcadia Publishing
Charleston, South Carolina

Printed in the United States of America

Library of Congress Control Number: 2007923836

For all general information, please contact Arcadia Publishing:
Telephone 843-853-2070
Fax 843-853-0044
E-mail sales@arcadiapublishing.com
For customer service and orders:
Toll-Free 1-888-313-2665

Visit us on the Internet at www.arcadiapublishing.com

CONTENTS

ACKNOWLEDGMENTS

The authors would like to thank the California State Parks and San Juan Bautista State Historic Park, as well as the San Juan Bautista Historical Society and the Plaza History Association. These organizations graciously provided many of the magnificent images in this volume. Special thanks must go to Henrietta Patino, curator of the San Juan Bautista State Historic Park archives, whose amazing generosity and assistance made exploration through the archives possible, and to Mark McMahon, who photographed many of the interior images of the mission. We would also like to thank Pat Hathaway for the images he graciously allowed us to use, and a very special thank you to all who contributed their knowledge and expertise to this book: Mary Anzar, Debbie Cable, Georgana Gularte, and Anna Winn.

BIBLIOGRAPHY

Clough, Charles W. *San Juan Bautista: The Town, the Mission, and the Park.* Fresno, CA: Word Dancer Press, 1996.

Crimes and Careers of Tiburcio Vasquez. Hollister, CA: Evening Free Lance, 1927.

Egan, Ferol. *Fremont: Explorer for a Restless Nation.* Reno: University of Nevada Press, 1977.

Engelhard, Zephyrin, OFM. *Mission San Juan Bautista.* Santa Barbara, CA: The Shauer Printing Studio, Inc., 1931.

Flint, Dorothy and Marjorie Flint. *Escarpment on the San Andreas.* Hollister, CA: Evening Free Lance, 1978.

Geiger, Maynard, OFM. *Franciscan Missionaries in Hispanic California: 1769–1848.* San Marino, CA: The Huntington Library, 1969.

King, Joseph A. *Winter of Entrapment.* Toronto: P. D. Meany Publishers, 1992.

Martin, John M, MM. *Indian Legends from Mission San Juan Bautista.* Monterey, CA: Angel Press, 1977.

Milliken, Ralph LeRoy. *California Dons.* Fresno, CA: Academy Library Guild, 1956.

Mylar, Issac L. *Early Days at the Mission San Juan Bautista.* Watsonville, CA: Evening Pajaronian, 1929.

Roddy, William Crane. *The Sanchez File.* San Juan Bautista, CA: The History Company, 1995.

Thomas, Mark. *Wielding the Gavel.* San Jose, CA: Alma Press, 1996.

INTRODUCTION

Faced with the greatest obstacles of any California mission town, San Juan Bautista has survived—and flourished—against all odds. Periods of economic, civic, and environmental turbulence have shaken the town to its very foundations frequently throughout its history and prehistory. The lean times that ceased missions' services and turned other thriving frontier villages forever into ghost towns riddled San Juan Bautista but never defeated it. From its natural environment, wrought by the dramatic shifting of the San Andreas Fault, to its place today as one of the most pristinely preserved California State Historic Parks, San Juan Bautista carries on, as spectacularly as its very beginnings.

The earth's crust is broken into several sections called tectonic plates floating on hot magma. The great San Andreas Fault, which runs most of the length of California, is the juncture of two plates, the American Plate to the east and the Pacific Plate to the west. The movement of these two plates has created the unique geography of the San Juan Bautista area. The northerly movement of the Pacific Plate, locked deep underground just north of San Juan Bautista, has caused an uplift of the earth's surface, thus creating a bulge or knoll above a valley. It was on this high knoll that the mission was built. As along most large earthquake faults, the dramatic shifting of the environment resulted in a spectacular landscape that was a natural choice for the mission's location.

The first human inhabitants, the Mutsuns, were hunter-gatherers whose villages, some 25 family groups, extended as far south as Pinnacles National Monument, as far east as the foot of the Pacheco Pass, north along the Pajaro River, and west to near the junction of Highways 101 and 129. Each village spoke its own dialect of a common language and gathered annually to trade, hunt, and harvest the region's many resources together. The nearest village was located about a half-mile south of the mission, nestled in a canyon of oak trees, and consisted of 150 to 200 people. In November 1795, Spanish explorers arrived in the area to select a site for the mission, and as soon as it was chosen, a cross was erected. All of these villages were under the jurisdiction of the mission.

Mission San Juan Bautista's location was determined by Gov. Diego Borica in October 1795, when he decided that it would be a great convenience to travelers if missions along the El Camino Real were only one day's journey apart. This was not possible between Missions San Carlos and Santa Clara, so a party left Monterey on November 15, 1795, to find a suitable spot for a new mission. Led by Ens. Hermenegildo Sal and Fr. Antonio Danti, they arrived at a plateau west of the Rio San Benito, where they found an American Indian village called Papeloutchom. Two natural springs below a high knoll provided fresh water. Redwood timber, tulles or rushes for roofing, and sandstone and limestone for foundations were in abundant supply. It took many months before permission was given to start the new mission's construction; during that time, a garrison of soldiers was assigned to protect the new site and give assistance to the builders. By June 17, 1797, soldiers, two carpenters, and native workers had completed a church, a house for the padres, and a guardhouse. The following week, Fr. Fermin de Lasuen arrived, and on June 24, 1797, the feast of St. John the Baptist, the 15th in the chain of California missions was dedicated.

Immediately after the dedication, two Franciscan padres, six Spanish soldiers, and skilled workers from Mexico began construction of necessary mission buildings. Men skilled in farming began planting crops, fruit trees, and vineyards. Others set about raising cattle, sheep, and horses. These skilled workers, under the direction of the padres, began training the Native American men. Their wives trained the women in weaving, candle making, and other domestic skills. The mission prospered until Mexico revolted against Spain in 1815. Supplies from Mexico would not reach the mission for months, sometimes years, during this period. Lack of material and financial support left all California missions in dire straits. Mexico then won its independence in 1821. A series of incompetent governors were sent to California, and in 1824, the Mexican Congress decreed that all Spaniards must swear allegiance to Mexico, or leave California. That order devastated older padres who had been born and raised in Spain. Many were driven out of the missions they had served for years.

In 1834, the California territorial government ordered the confiscation of all mission properties and buildings and their contents, livestock, crops, and tools. Left with only the church building, the missions could no longer provide employment or support for the native population. Secularization of the missions resulted in the abandonment of many of these sites. San Juan Bautista was the only mission to maintain services and employ a padre, because the local population continued to support the church and provide for the care of the buildings. Due to this, San Juan Bautista still holds services today.

In response to lackadaisical rule from California's governors, the Californios began a plot in 1844 to make the area independent. With General Castro selected as governor, the unsuccessful revolt ended in less than nine months, and none of the conspirators were given more than a reprimand. In 1846, the United States declared war on Mexico. It was during this war that Lt. John C. Fremont and his American survey party arrived in California. They came to San Juan and were told by General Castro to leave the area. Instead they proceeded into the hills south of town, spying on the troops. By the time Castro decided to go after them, Fremont's party had already left the area, skirting confrontation.

With the signing of the Treaty of Guadalupe Hidalgo in 1848, the border between Mexico and the United States was established. General Castro fled to Mexico, but most of the Californios stayed, becoming American citizens. Some of the more prominent citizens in the area were members of the Larios, Castro, Anzar, and Sanchez families.

After California statehood in 1850, some gold seekers disembarked in Monterey, heading east to the goldfields. The only settlement on their journey was San Juan Bautista. The town grew quickly, and stores opened to accommodate the miners. San Juan became an important stop for miners and settlers, and many would return, purchasing property with their newfound wealth. New businesses opened and cattle ranches spread through the valley. The face of San Juan had changed forever. In 1853, three years after statehood, the United States Government Board of Land Commissioners settled all missions' property claims. In 1859, the claim for Mission San Juan Bautista property was finally settled, and its ownership returned to the Catholic Church.

During the late 1800s, San Juan Bautista experienced a series of devastating events. An early contender for San Benito County seat, a great fire destroyed much of the downtown business area and that governmental distinction was shifted elsewhere. In the 1870s, the town was bypassed by the railroad, forcing many businesses to move to Hollister, where the station had been built.

San Juan Bautista was a survivor. By the 20th century, the remaining businesses were determined to bring the town back from the edge. When the California State Parks Department bought all the buildings on the historic plaza except for the mission, the town once again began to prosper. San Juan had become the home to one of the state's major historic parks. Today San Juan Bautista State Historic Park and Mission draws thousands of visitors yearly.

One

THE NATIVE AMERICANS

The many villages of the Mutsun Indians gathered together once or twice each year for trading and collecting acorns, pine nuts, and seeds gathered from the hills surrounding the valley. For thousands of years, the Mutsuns had developed skills in making just about everything they needed for survival. What they did not have on hand they sought through trade with neighboring villages. The trading of shell beads, feathers, and seafood was carried out with the coastal Native Americans; the trading of minerals and timber occurred with the tribes of the San Joaquin Valley. Strong, straight branches were needed for making arrows and obsidian and chert for points. These materials came from the Central Valley and the foothills of the Sierras.

The San Juan Valley included many freshwater ponds fed by rivers and streams. Mutsuns fished these pools using woven nets filled with yorbe del pescado, an herbal mixture that acted as an opiate, stunning the fish, which then floated to the surface to be gathered. Another way of catching fish was to stretch a net filled with leaves across a narrow part of a pond and have the children get into the water and scare the fish to the net.

In addition to fish, the meat of deer, rabbits, and other small game were sources of food. Bears were believed to be sacred and were therefore seldom killed. The tree squirrel, considered a delicacy, was caught by locating its nest, putting mud over the upper hole, and starting a smoky fire in the lower hole. The asphyxiated animal was then removed, cleaned, and roasted. The skins and fur were made into clothing and the bones were used for tools to cut and sew.

The Mutsuns lived in thatched huts made from tulles that grew near the many ponds and streams. Grasses, thin tree branches, and pine needles were woven into baskets for cooking, storing food, and carrying goods. Gift baskets were often decorated with abalone shells from the coast. Few baskets have survived; however, two Mutsun baskets are presently in the collections of the mission museum.

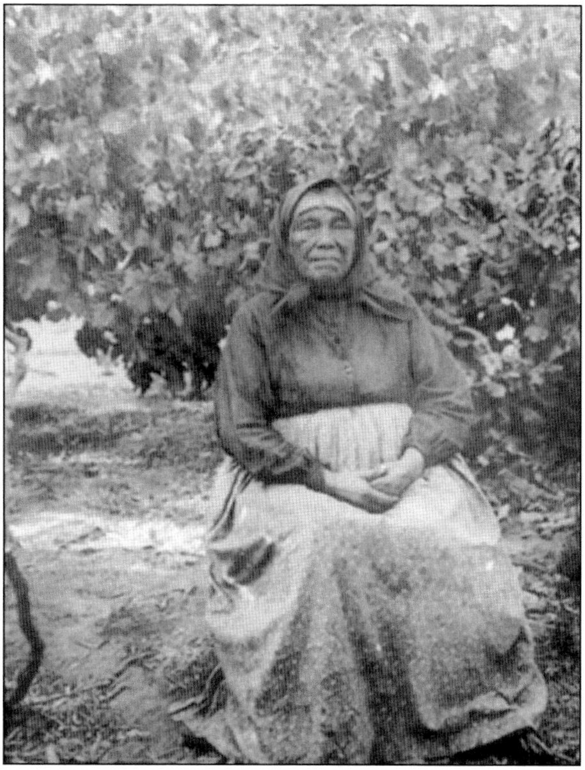

This photograph, on exhibit at the state park, depicts Barbara Serra Solarsano, a Mutsun Indian. Baptized at the mission, she was given the name Barbara after an early saint. Her maiden name, Serra, was given to her in honor of Padre Junipero Serra, founder of the California missions.

Doña Ascension Solarsano de Cervantes, daughter of Barbara Serra, was born in 1855 and baptized at the mission. When she died in 1930, she was buried along the church wall in the American Indian cemetery. Prior to her death, ethnologist and linguist John Peabody Harrington spent some months with her gathering the language, stories, and songs of her Mutsun heritage. Harrington made many recordings of the language, as well copious written notes. Unfortunately the records were accidentally broken before arrival at the Smithsonian. Harrington's notes, however, are stored there.

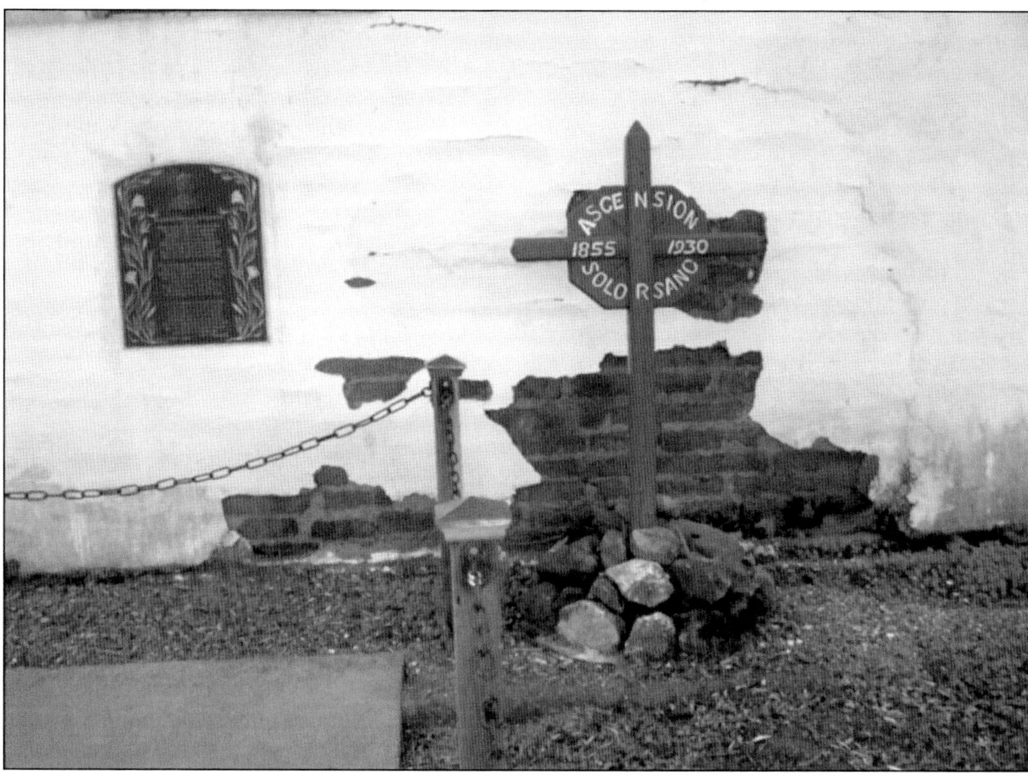

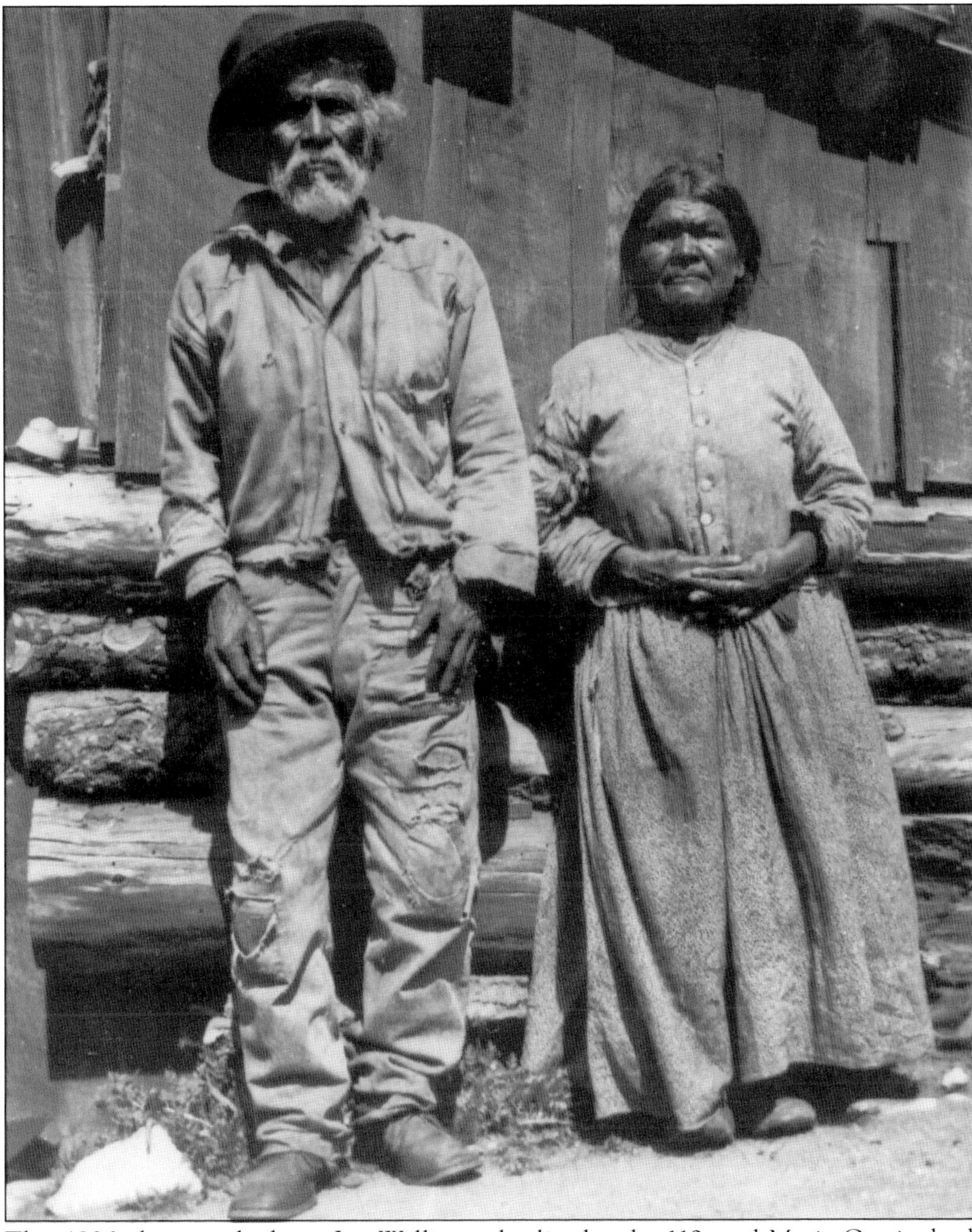

This 1906 photograph shows Joe Wellina, who lived to be 110, and Maria Garcia, both Mutsun Indians.

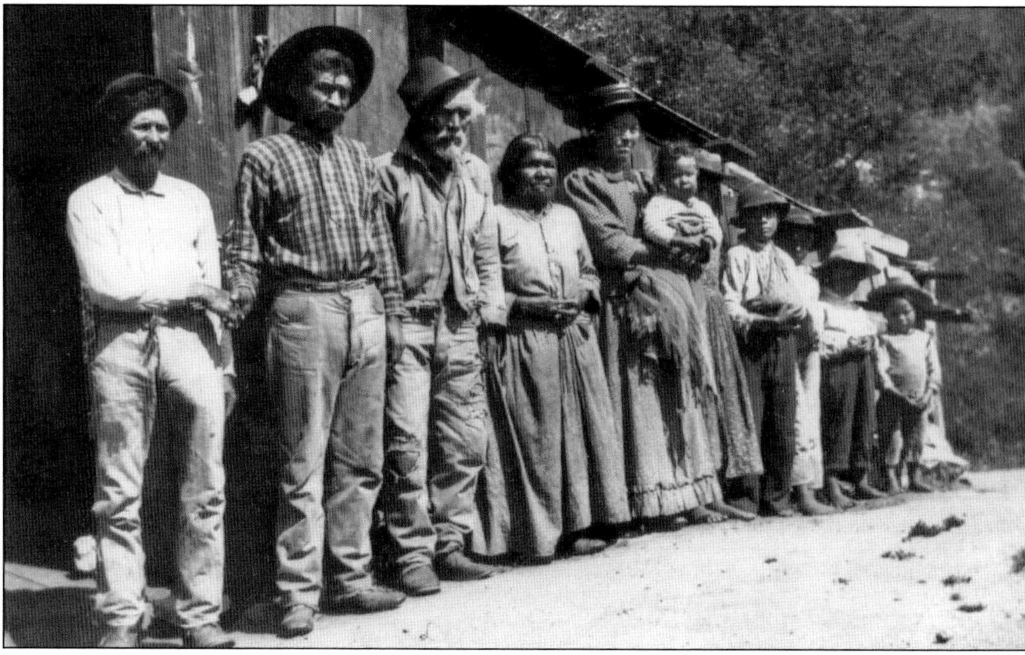

Mutsun Indians, pictured in 1906, stand in front of a building constructed after their home burned. The man in the plaid shirt is Sebastian Garcia, husband of Maria Garcia, fourth from the left. Between them is Joe Wellina. Next to Maria are some of her 12 children

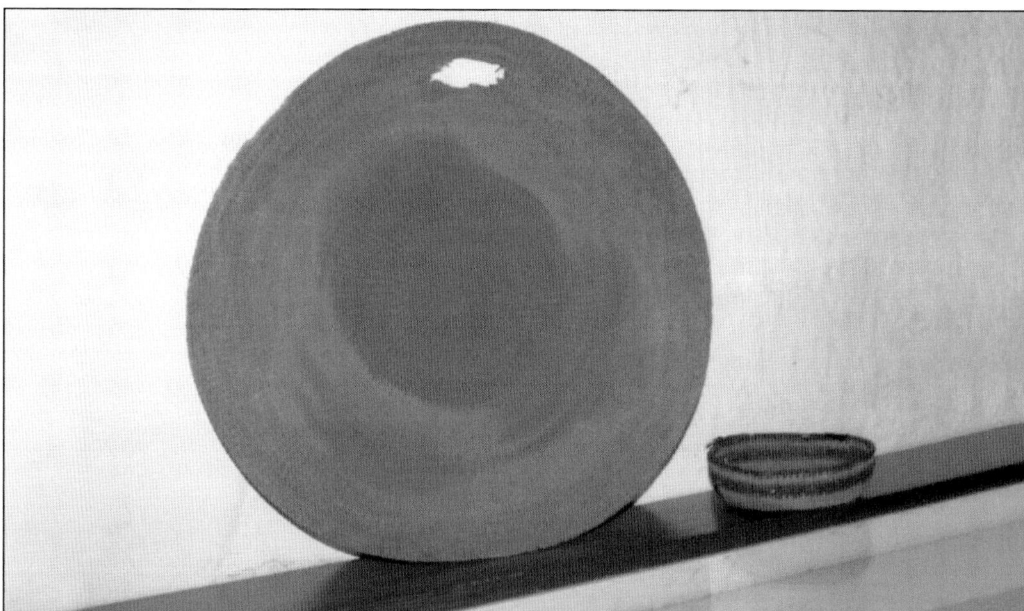

These baskets, made by Barbara Serra, were donated to the mission by her great-grandson Tony Corona. According to Tony, his grandmother Ascension used them. The large, almost flat winnowing basket helped in gleaning dried beans from the fields. He said, "Grandma Ascension kept her tobacco in the small basket." Small baskets were traditionally used as gift baskets containing something of value such as feathers or beads. The hole in the large basket was caused by mice while in storage.

Two

The Spanish Mission Period

After the location for the San Juan Bautista Mission was chosen in 1795 and permission was given to begin construction, the plaza at the heart of town was the first thing to take shape. Adobe buildings were constructed around a central courtyard. These buildings housed work and storage rooms, residences for the padres, and barracks for the soldiers. Construction progressed smoothly until October 1800. That month, there were, on average, six earthquakes a day for 30 days. The buildings that had been erected since 1797 were destroyed or so severely damaged that officials decided to rebuild the entire complex. Construction of the new church began in 1803 and was completed nine years later. When finished, it was the largest of all the California mission churches.

The mission prospered because the land was fertile and crops and herds increased. However, disease decimated the Mutsun Indian population over the first 20 years of the 19th century. During these years, the population of the mission and the town was reduced by some 70 percent. This created a shortage of laborers to maintain the mission complex. European diseases were the principle causes of death, but gastric diseases also killed many.

From the beginning, unmarried women were required to live in a special building called a *convento*. During the day, these women were allowed to work and move throughout the community, but at night, they were required to return to the convento, where they were locked in. When a young man wanted to marry, he would tell the name of his intended to the padre. Announcements of the intended marriage were made on Sunday at mass and preparations were made for the wedding. After the wedding, the couple was given a house and each was welcomed as an adult member of the Mutsun Indian community.

The Mutsuns were very fond of music and learned new songs with little effort. Because of this, San Juan Bautista became known as the "mission of music." Fr. Estevan Tapis, who was assigned to the mission in 1815, developed a unique method of writing music. He used large sheets and made the notes in different shapes and in four colors: red, yellow, black, and white. Mutsun groups learned to sing their color-designated notes in this fashion and were so renowned that they would travel from mission to mission giving recitals.

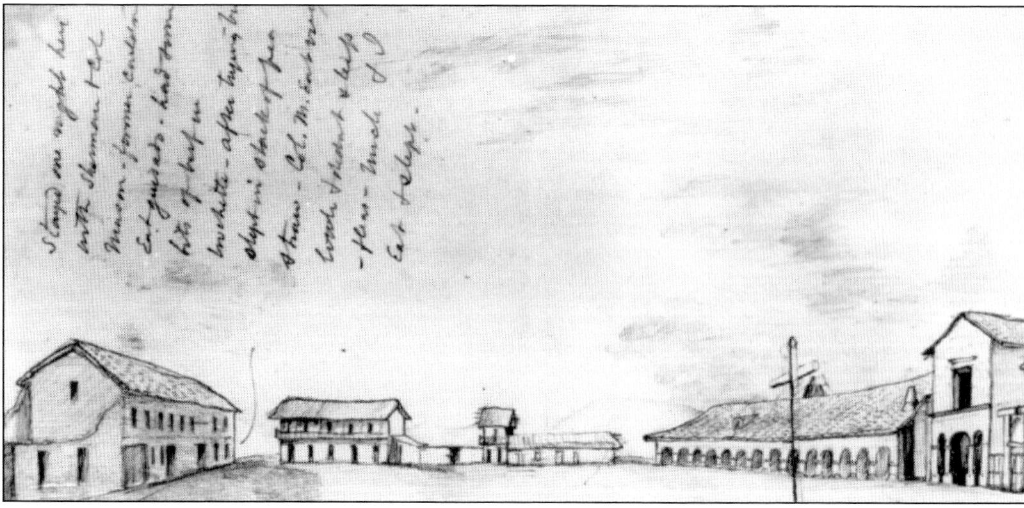

William R. Hutton created the earliest known sketch of the plaza on June 20, 1847, a year after the United States declared war on Mexico. The buildings, identified from left to right, are the nunnery, or home for single Mutsun girls; the Castro Adobe, built for Mexican general Jose M. Castro and his officers; the guardhouse; and the barracks constructed for the Spanish soldiers. The mission appears on the right.

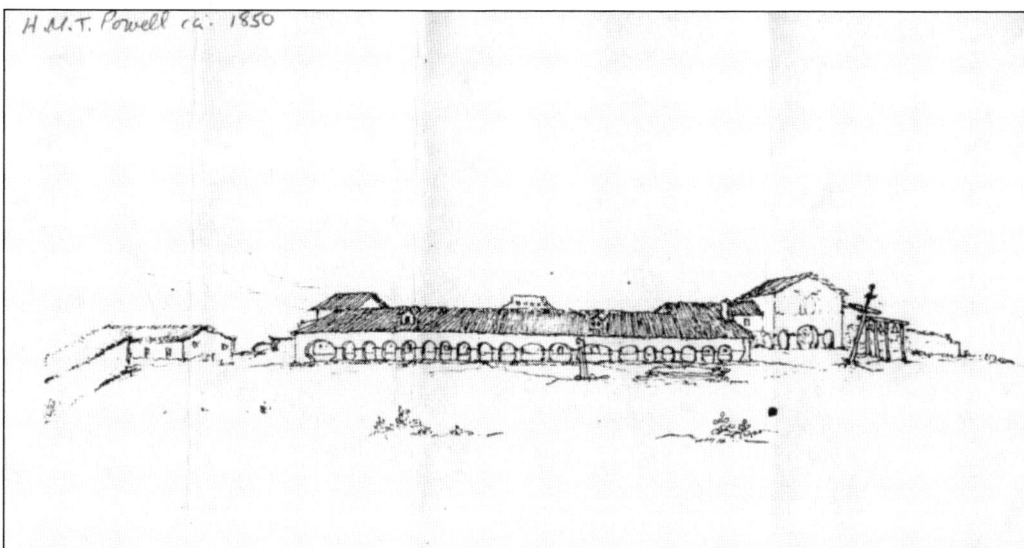

H. M. T. Powell made this sketch of the mission in 1850, two years after the United States won the war with Mexico. It was drawn shortly before California became a state on September 9, 1850. The sketch shows the three mission bells hung in the right in front of the church. To the far right is the wall around the Mutsun Indian cemetery. The original chimney for the kitchen is visible above the roof line in the middle of the convento wing.

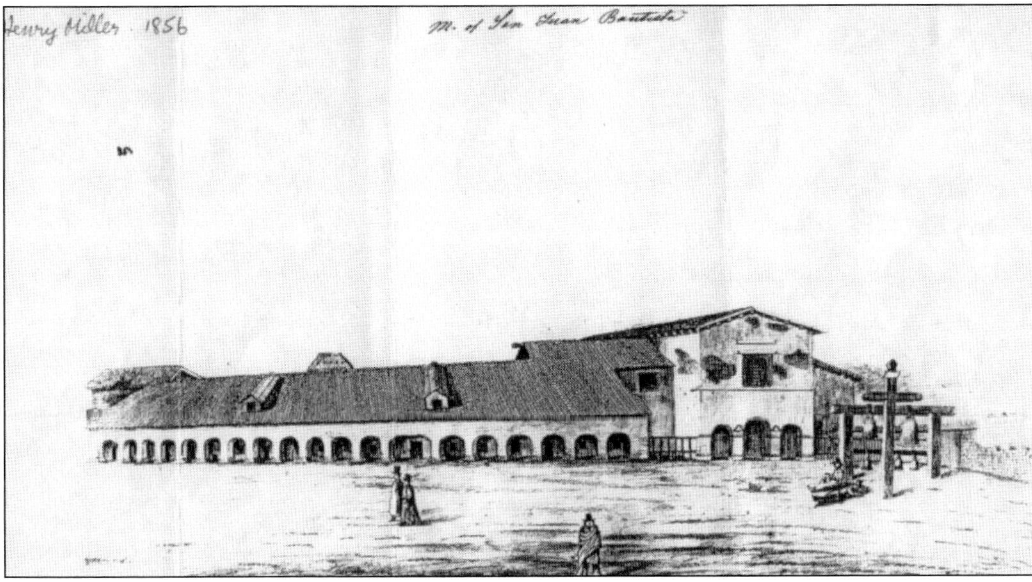

In 1853, the United States government established a board of land commission to settle all the land claims of the California missions. This sketch, drawn by Henry Miller in 1856, shows the sad condition of the mission buildings. Since the secularization of the properties and the dispersal of the Mutsun Indians, little or no maintenance was performed on the adobe structures. Plaster was falling off and all the original quadrangle buildings behind the mission were gone, leaving only the church and the convento wing.

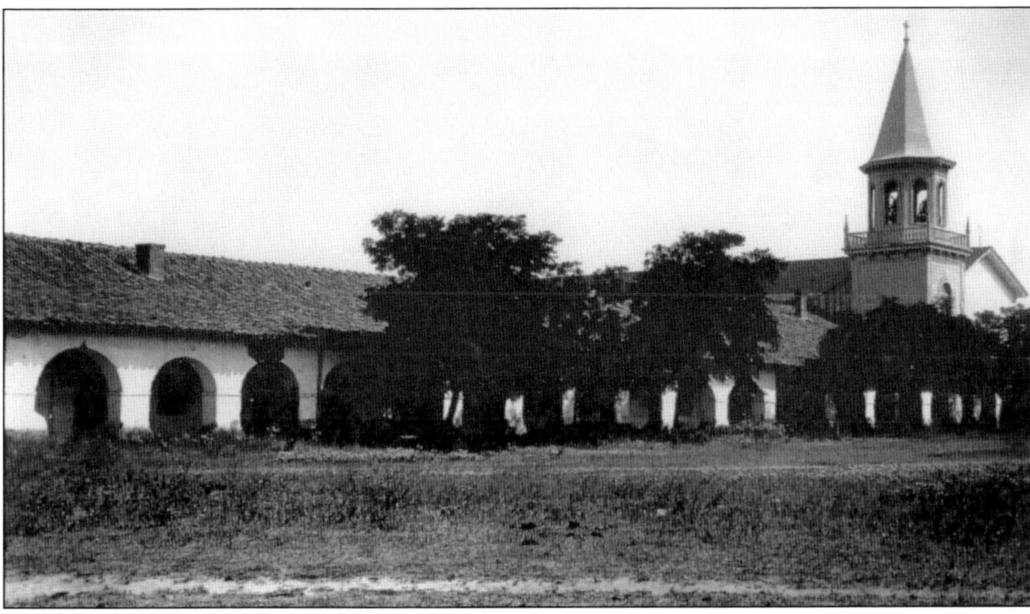

Rev. Cipriano Rubio arrived as pastor in 1856 and distinguished himself by modernizing the mission. Under his leadership in 1868, a bell tower was built of Victorian design. Prior to this time, the bells had been hung on a crossbeam in front of the church. This tower consisted of two rooms: the ground-floor sitting room and the second-floor bedroom and study. A rope for the bells extended through the ceiling and floor of the bedroom down to the ground floor so Reverend Rubio or a bell ringer from either floor could ring the bells for services.

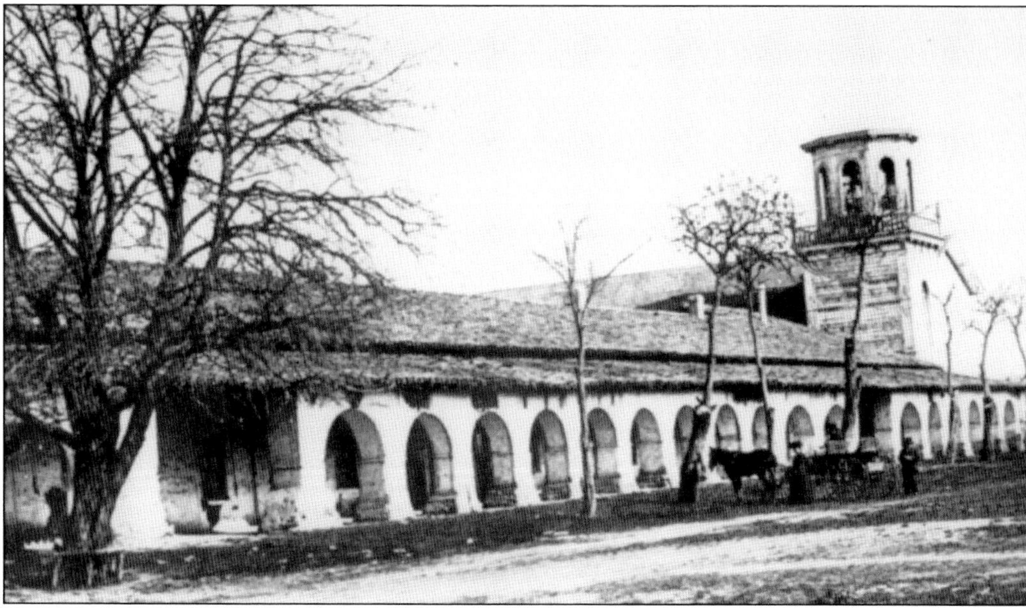

When Reverend Rubio was transferred in 1878, his successor, Fr. Ricardo Valentin Closa, decided to reside in the convento wing rather than in the tower. In 1897, a strong wind blew off the spire of the bell tower. This photograph, taken around 1900, shows the tiled roof and the absence of the original chimney. Three smaller chimneys can be seen on the convento wing much closer to the church. These chimneys indicate the rooms used for the priest's residence.

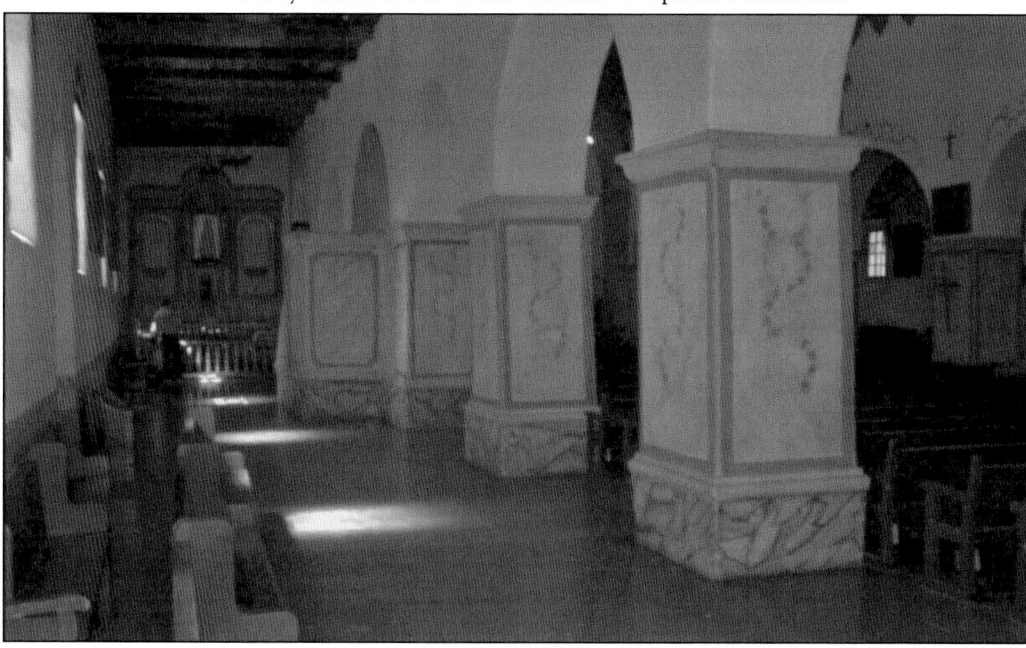

Construction of the present church building began in 1803 and was completed by 1812. The church was built with three naves, making it the largest of all the California mission churches. Redwood for the ceiling beams, door, and window frames came from a grove of trees about six miles west. Sandstone for the foundations was hauled from a large quarry four miles west. The painted ceiling was created while Father Rubio was pastor.

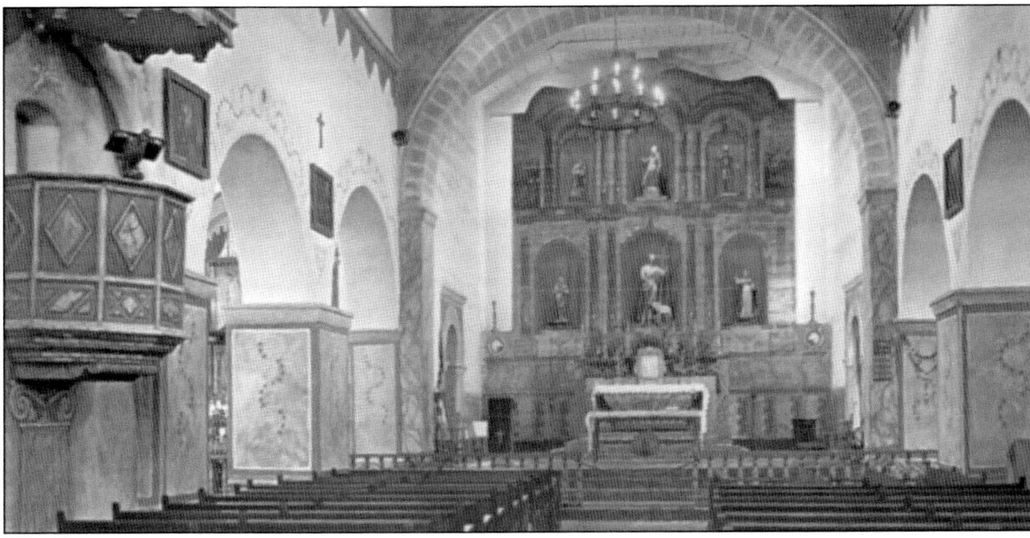

The reredos, the large structure behind the altar, holds six statues carved in Mexico. St. John the Baptist, below center, arrived in 1806. Thomas Doak, a sailor and ship's carpenter from Boston, left his ship in Monterey in 1816 and came to San Juan Bautista. In return for room and board, he constructed the reredos from redwood and, under the direction of Padre Tapis, painted the structure. Protruding from the wall on the left of the altar is the pulpit, accessed from a stairway in the back. The pulpit was situated along the side of the church so that all could hear the gospel. In the early mission period, the congregation sat on mats on the floor because there were no pews.

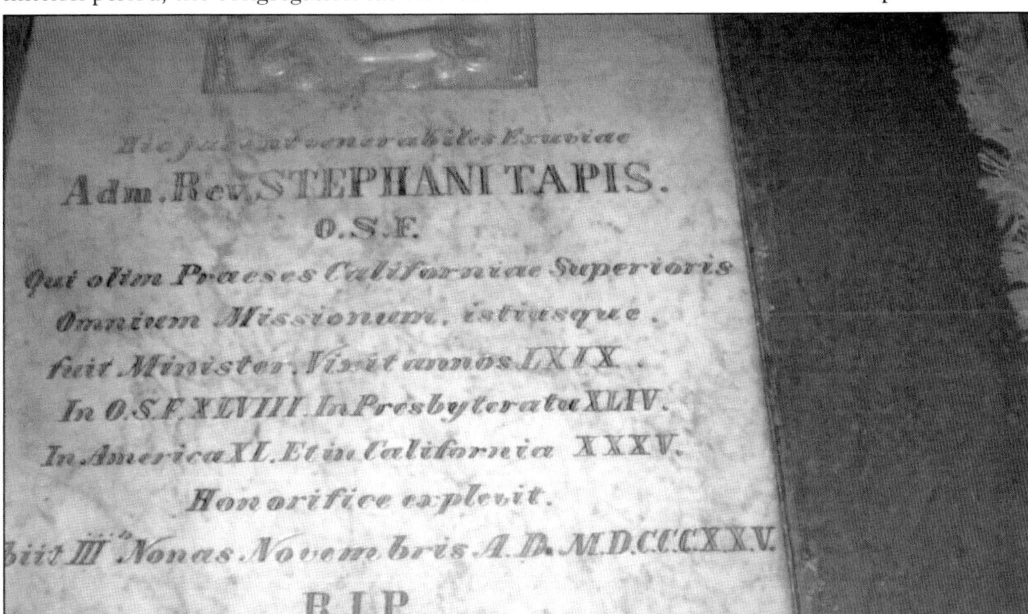

In 1825, Padre Estevan Tapis, born in Catalonia, Spain, died and was buried in the sanctuary of the church. He came to California in 1790 and served at various missions. An able administrator, while at Mission Santa Barbara, he was responsible for the construction of many buildings. When Padre Lasuen, president of the California missions, died in 1803, Padre Tapis was appointed as successor. In 1812, he retired from the presidency and became an ordinary missionary at San Juan Bautista. He remained there until his death.

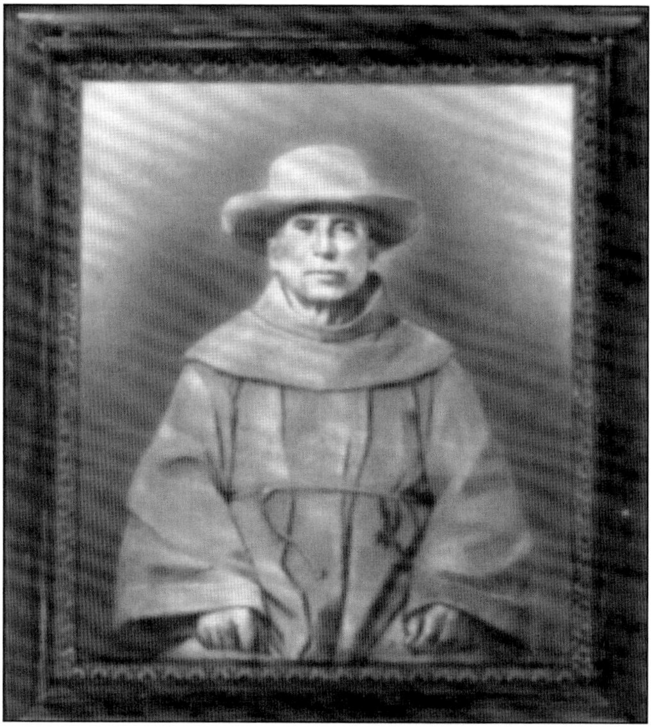

Padre Jose Antonio Anzar was born in Mexico in 1792. He came to Mission San Juan Bautista in 1833 and served until 1854, when he returned to Mexico. Father Anzar had the sad misfortune to see the mission through secularization and the sale of the church properties in 1834. Because of this, the church could no longer support or provide aid for the few Mutsun Indians who lived in the area. Those who could not find work from the Mexican families moved away while the mission continued its decline.

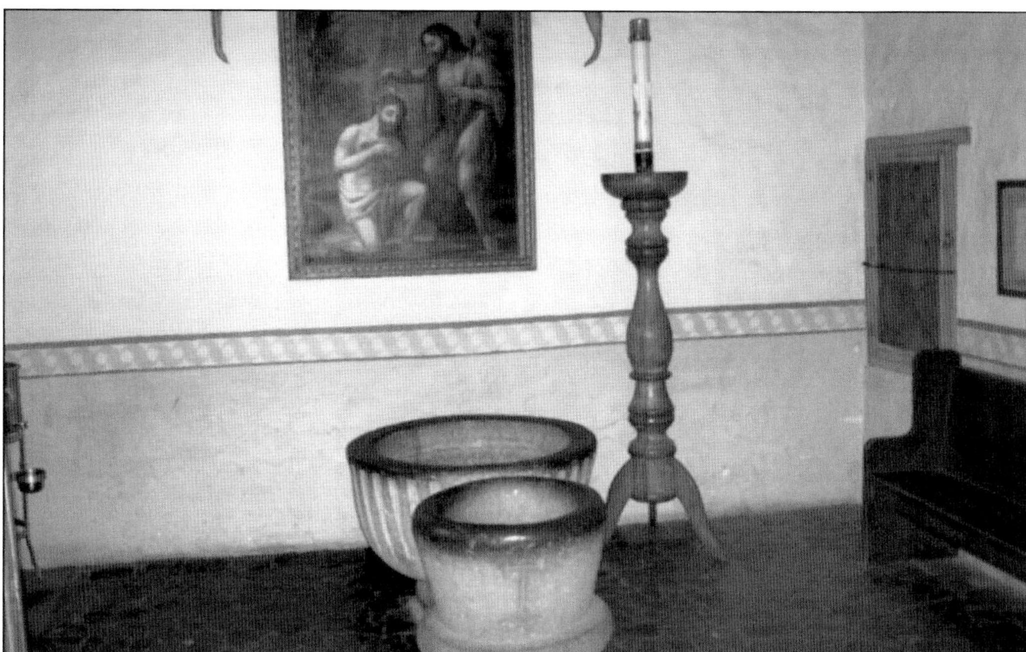

The baptismal fonts were carved from native sandstone and were installed during construction of the building. The larger of the two stored the water used in rites. The smaller font was used to carry off the water poured over the heads of the Mutsun Indians during baptism. Over 4,000 Mutsuns were baptized here, many at the same time, with males being baptized in the morning and females in the afternoon.

The old vestments, called "fiddlebacks" because of their shape, were created in Mexico and Peru. Made of damask or heavy silk, they were elaborately embroidered after patterns common to the Spanish. It was common for these vestments to be ordered from Mexico in exchange for the sale of tallow and hides.

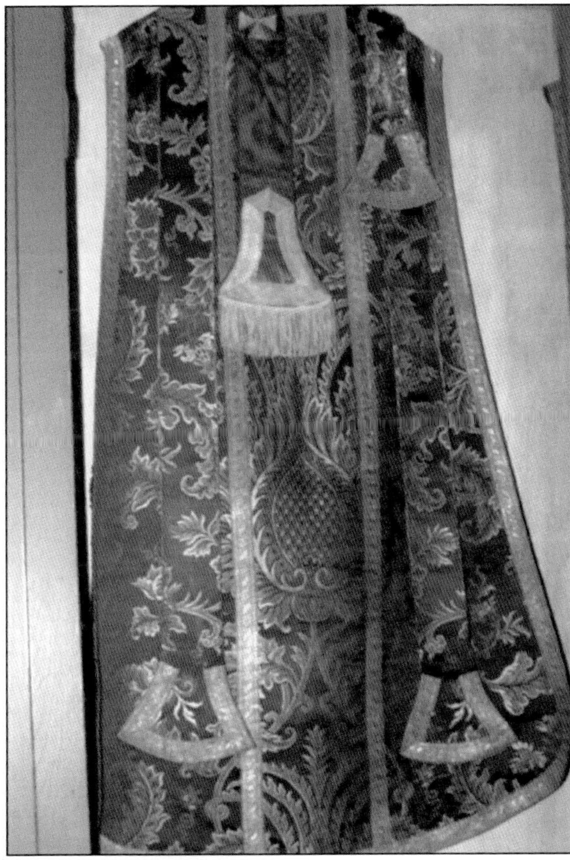

Santos, or small statues of saints, were often made locally as a thanksgiving to that saint for prayers answered. All were hand carved and painted with glass eyes embedded in the faces. Small cupboards were built for sacred vessels and often painted with religious symbols. Seen in the left center is a door from such a cupboard. The image on the right depicts Our Lady of Guadalupe. It has been painted on tin.

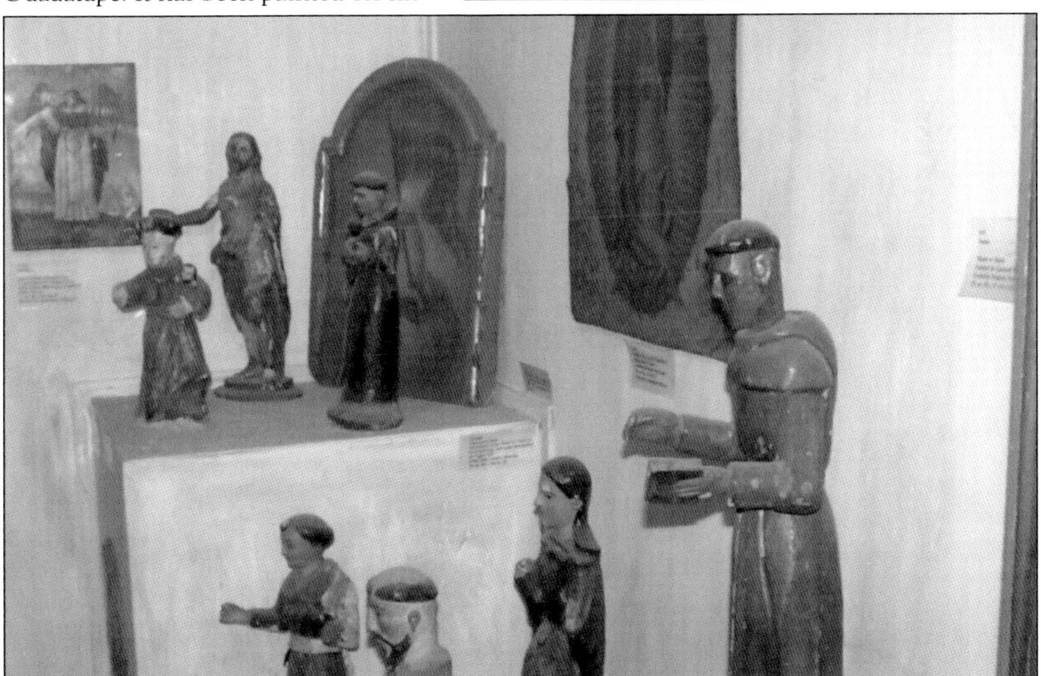

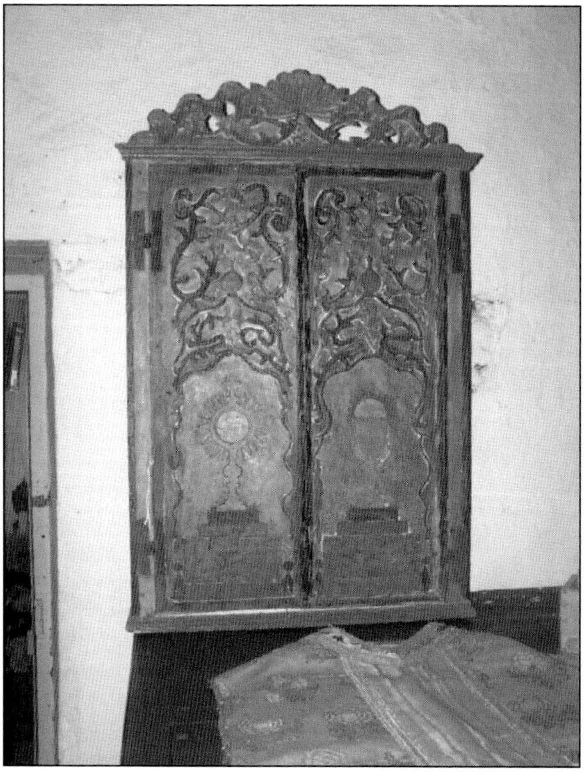

This cupboard was created from redwood with decoration carved in relief. The symbols on the doors indicate that this was a tabernacle used to store the sacred hosts. A local blacksmith made the hinges from iron.

The walls of the church and other rooms around the mission quadrangle were often decorated with designs found in pattern books that circulated throughout the missions. Paint was made from ground minerals, soot or charcoal, and powdered indigo. In recent years, many of the original decorations have been uncovered in the existing rooms. The cross above the window indicates that this served as the first chapel while the main building was being constructed.

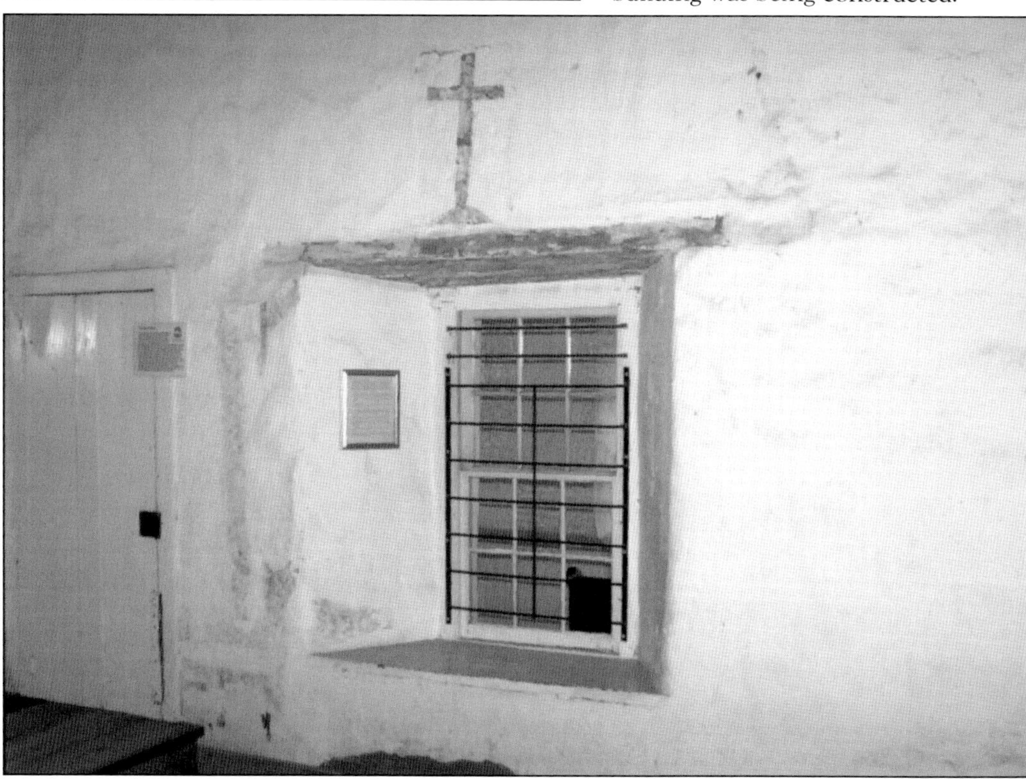

The barrel organ was made in England in 1829 and given to the mission. The false pipes in the front hid the fact that the instrument was actually a grind organ with a handle. Wooden drums with metal pins like a music box revolved to create the music. This organ was given to the padres in Monterey. The music was to entertain the sailors and was not designed for a church. Song titles included "White Cockade," "The College Hornpipe," and "Go to the Devil." Padre Arroyo de la Cuesta brought the organ to San Juan Bautista for the enjoyment of the Mutsun Indians.

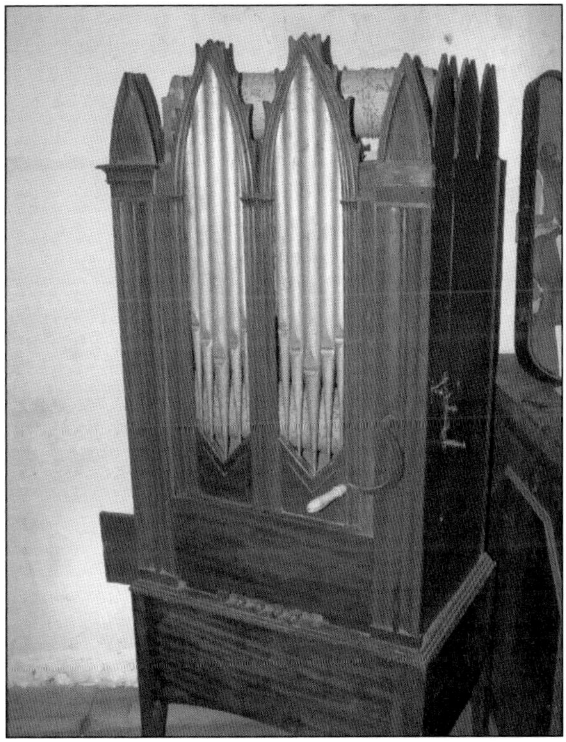

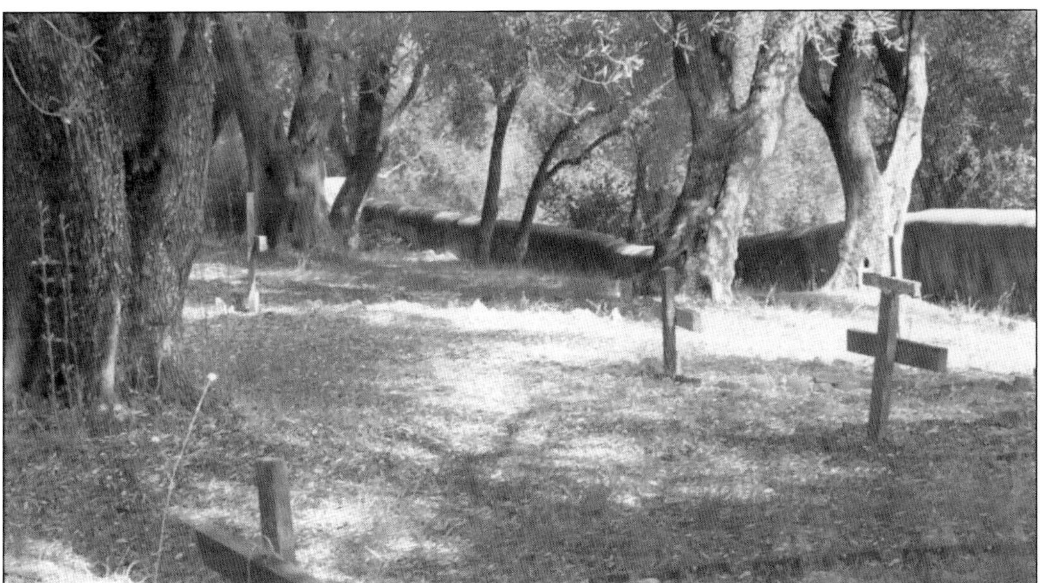

The cemetery on the north side of the church opened in 1797. The first burial, a child of a soldier, occurred on September 23, 1797. During the mission period, over 4,000 Mutsuns were buried here. As the cemetery filled, the wall was raised and new soil was brought in for fill. The last person to be interred was Ascension Solarsano, a direct descendant of the Mutsun Indians, who died in 1930. Fr. Antonio Anzar wrote in 1838, "On October 24, 1838, I blessed a new cemetery west of town because the church cemetery could hold no more bodies." Most of the Spanish and Mexican settlers of the period were buried in this new town cemetery.

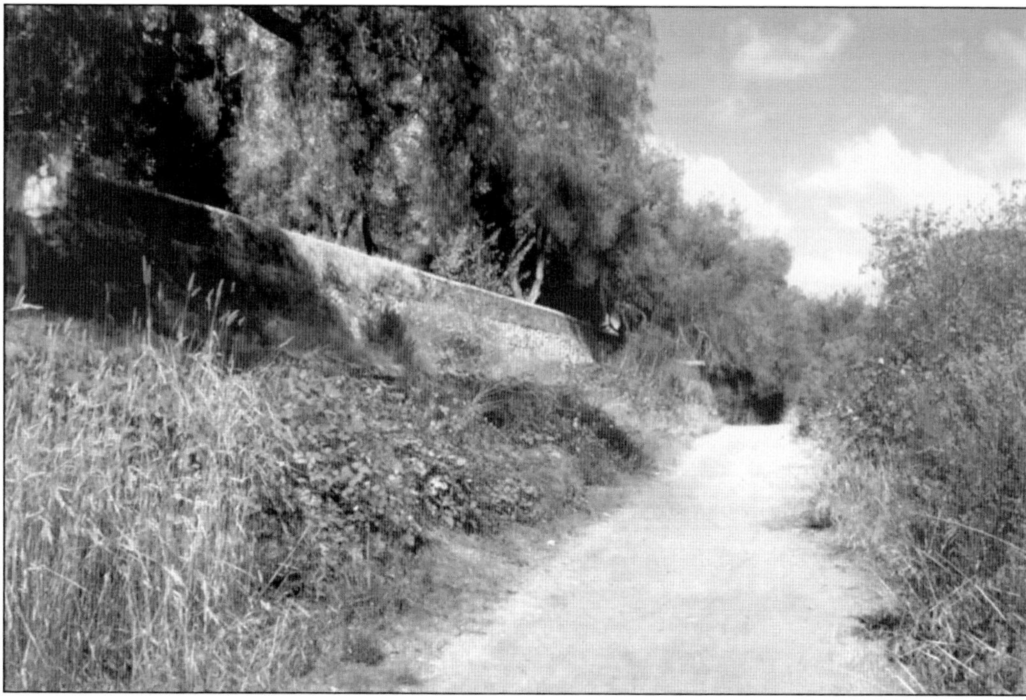

The Camino Real, or "Highway of the King," ran along the cemetery wall and up to the plaza in front of the mission. Connecting all the California missions, it was little more than a trail, just wide enough for horsemen and pack animals. The photograph below shows the original section of the Camino as it runs along the cemetery wall, while the photograph above shows changes in the wall as it was heightened to make room for more burials.

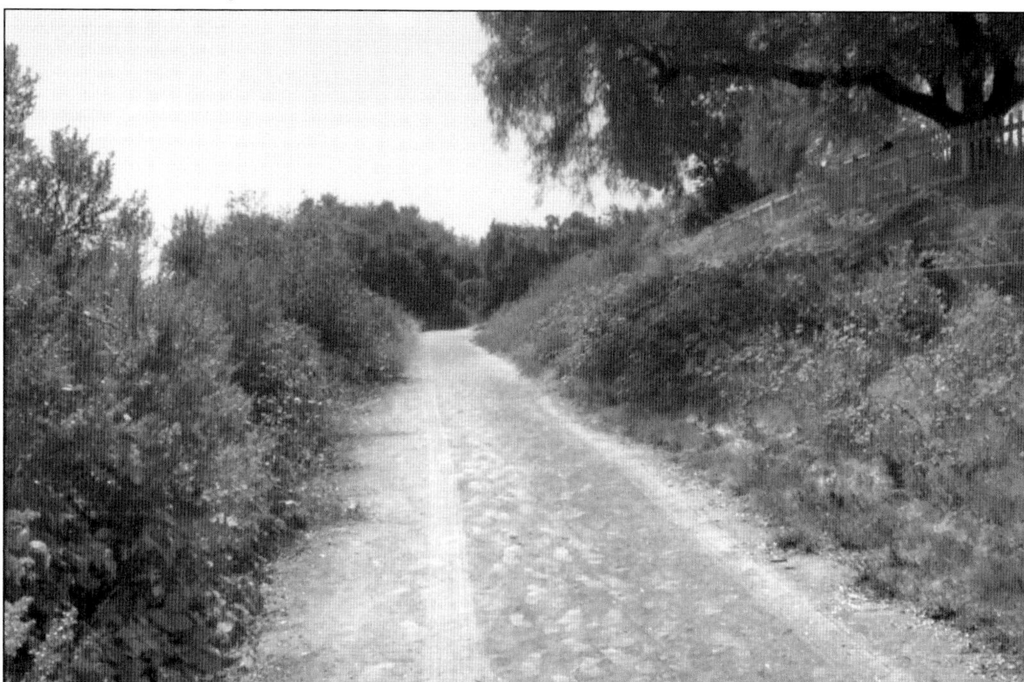

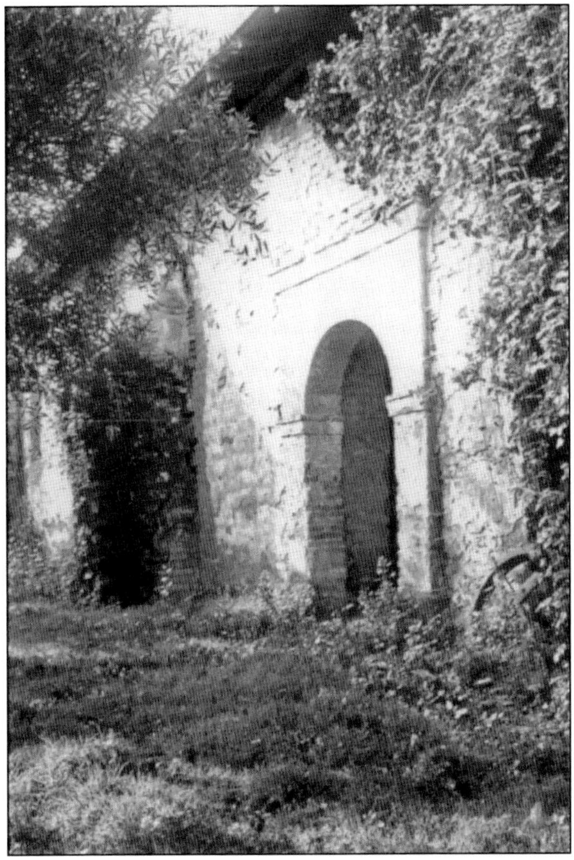

The church was built just a few feet from the San Andreas Fault, and since its founding, earthquakes have been a frequent occurrence. In October 1800, an average of six earthquakes a day was felt for 30 days. The quakes caused serious damage to the early buildings, resulting in the complete rebuilding of the mission. Padre Pedro Martinez was so terrified that he refused to sleep indoors and requested to be transferred to another mission. By the time the new church was completed in 1812, buttresses had been built along the outer wall to provide added support.

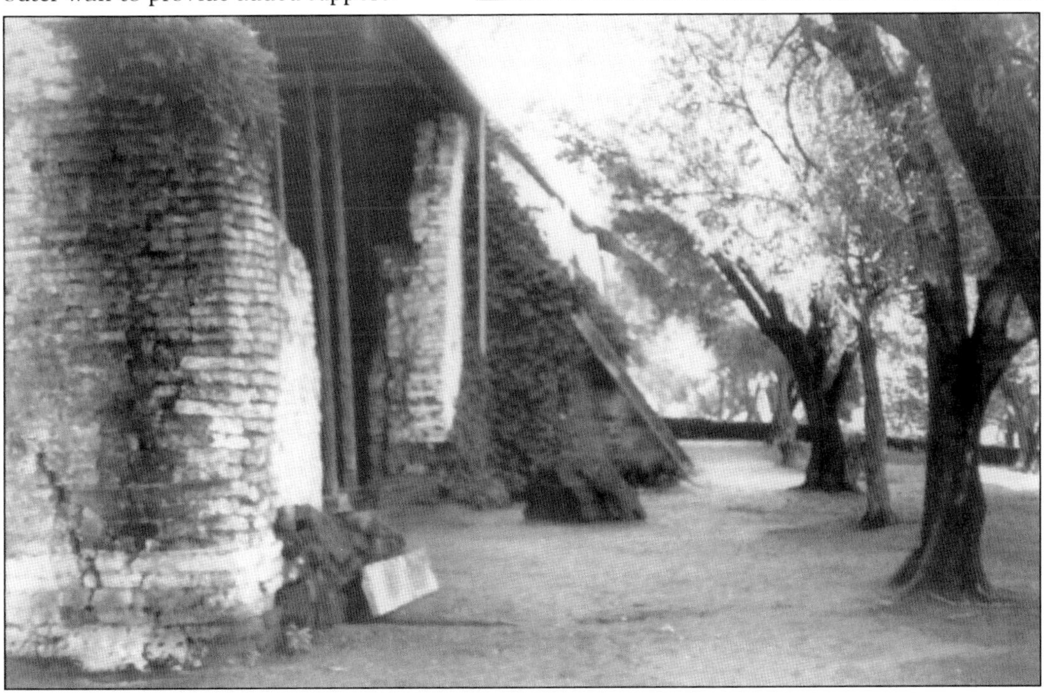

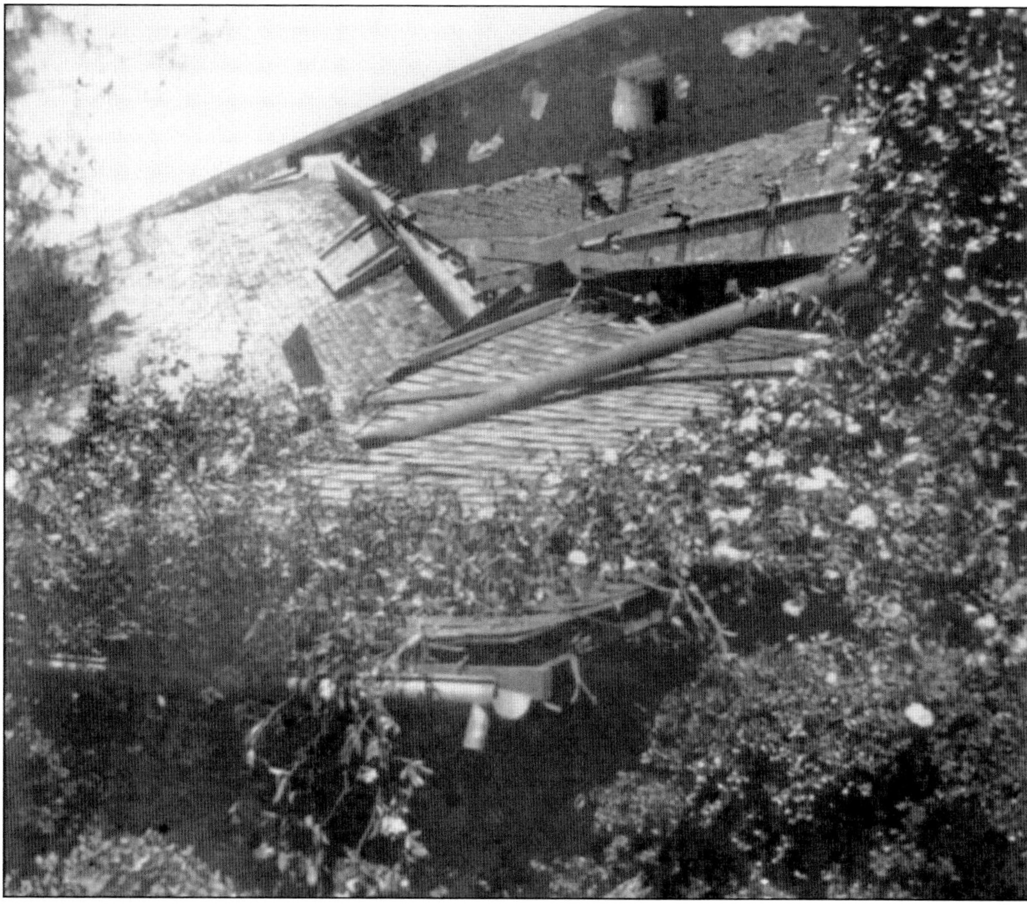

On April 18, 1906, a great earthquake occurred on the San Andreas Fault. It was felt throughout central California. Known as the San Francisco Earthquake, it caused tremendous damage to the mission buildings. This photograph, taken shortly after the quake, shows the harm to the adobe walls and the roof. The walls buckled and the adobe tiles slid off the roof, leaving a pile of rubble.

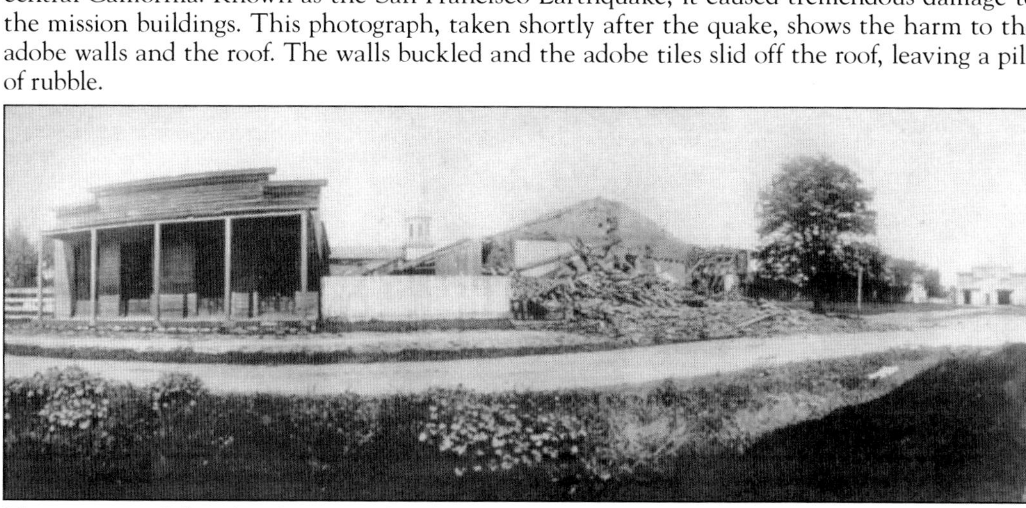

The interior of the church received only minor damage, although the inner arches had to be filled in with adobe bricks to prevent the total collapse of the entire roof. This image depicts the collapsed south end of the convento wing on Second Street.

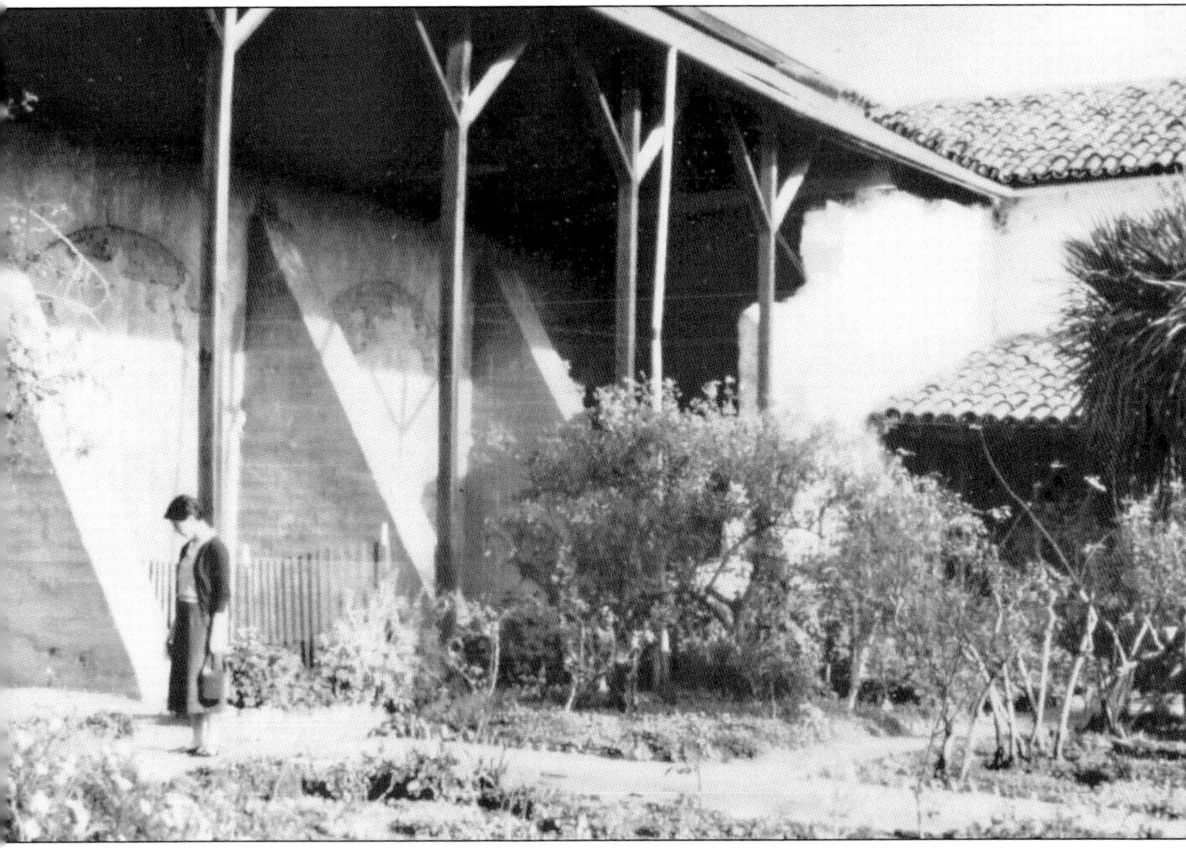

The church was not used for services for many years after the quake of 1906. In the 1920s, engineers decided to build concrete buttresses, as shown in this 1950s photograph. Once these buttresses were in place, the church could again hold services.

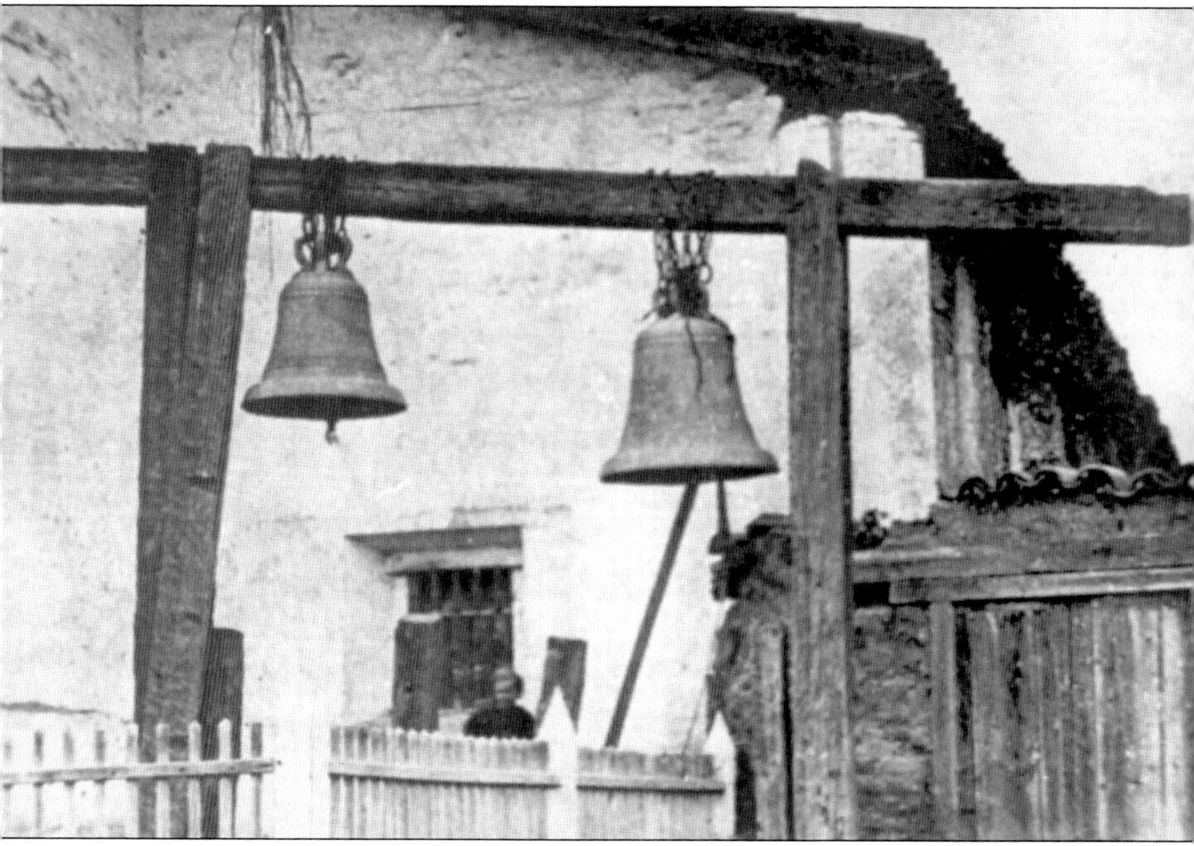

Mission San Juan Bautista originally had no bell tower; instead, nine bells of varying sizes were hung on oak posts and crossbeams in front of the church. Some had been taken from other missions and some had been cast in Mexico for San Juan Bautista. By 1987, only two bells remained. It is not known what happened to the other seven.

A severe windstorm blew the spire off the steeple in 1897. This resulted in the abandonment of the living quarters in the tower. From then on, priests lived next to the church in the convento wing.

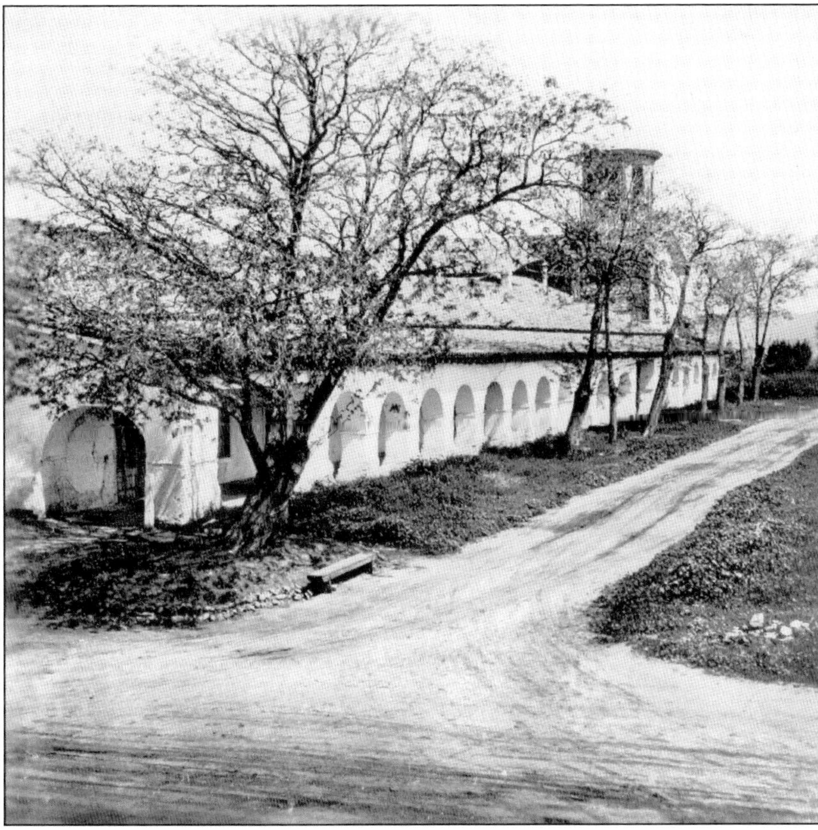

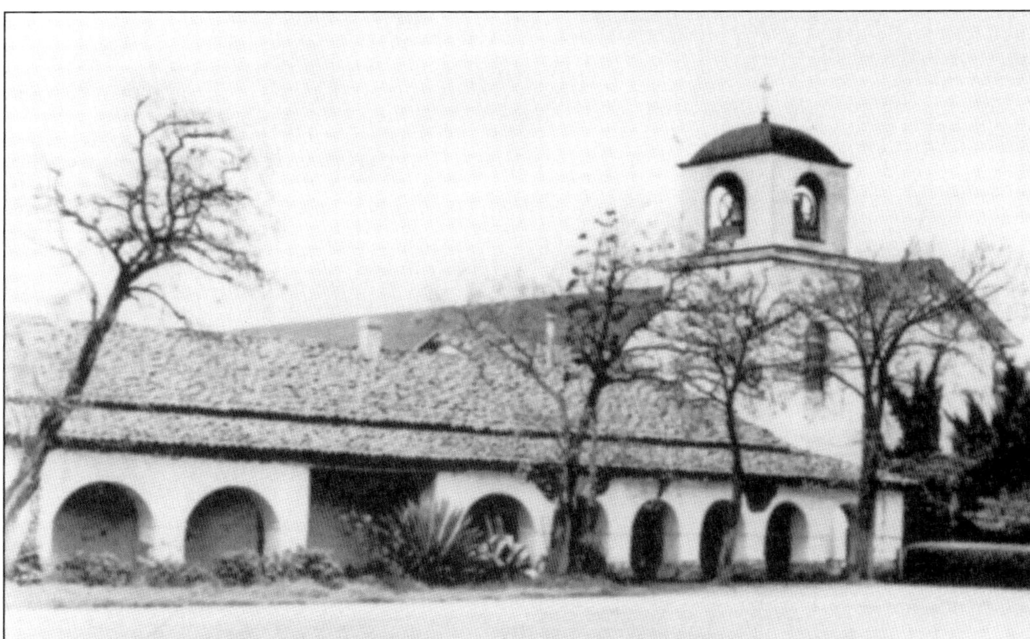

In the early 1920s, the old wooden tower was remodeled in a pseudo–Spanish mission style. The exterior was plastered and the domed top covered with tiles.

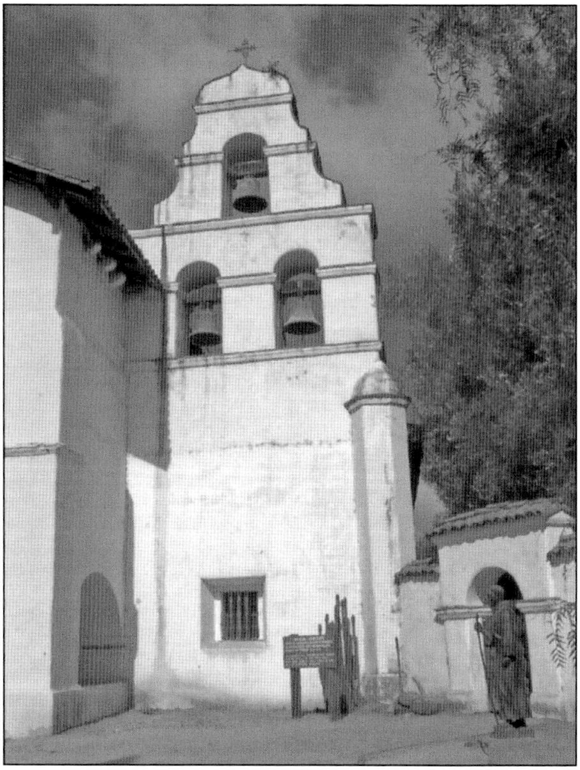

The present tower, built in 1976, has spaces for three bells. The top bell was a gift from the citizens of Vitoria, Spain, in honor of the founding padre, Fermin Lasuen. The bell on the lower left is original, while the one on the lower right was recast from broken mission bells in 1874.

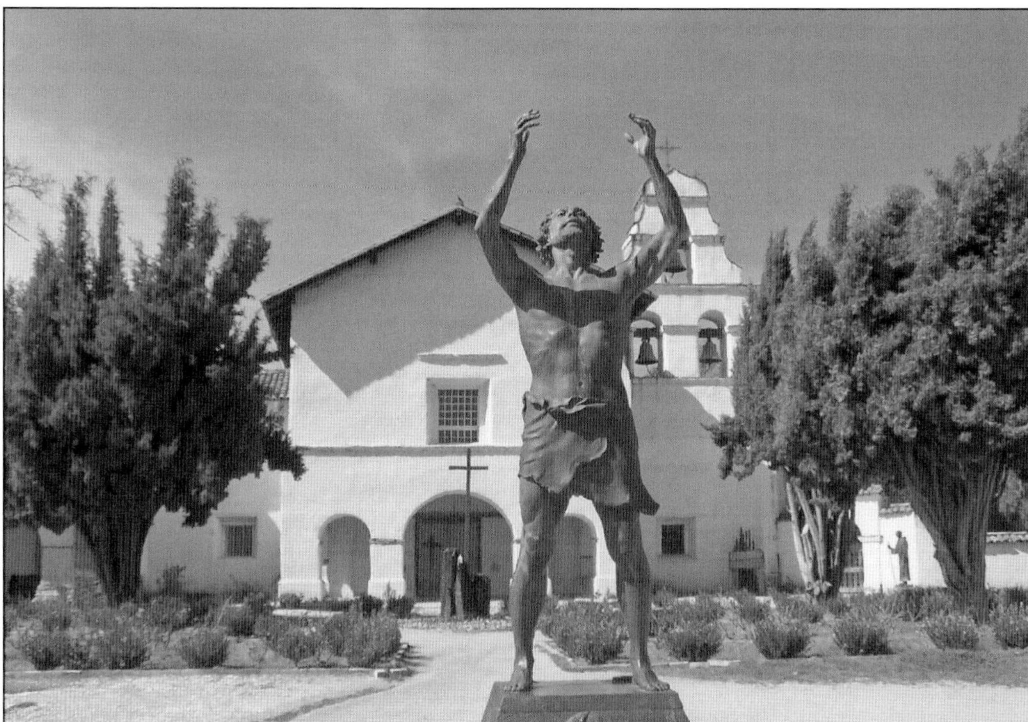

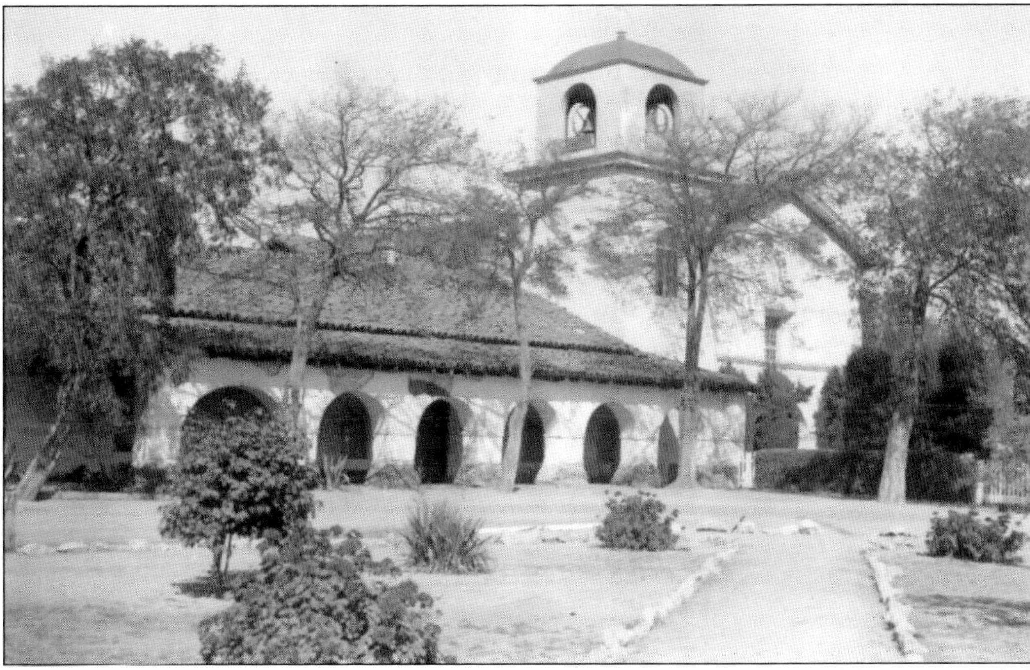

Alfred Hitchcock's *Vertigo* was filmed throughout California, but the suspenseful scene in the bell tower was to be filmed specifically at San Juan Bautista. Hitchcock was disappointed when he came to the mission in the early 1950s to find the tower gone. He had visited the mission many years earlier and remembered the tower. It had been removed in 1949 because of the danger of collapse. Exterior scenes were filmed at the mission but interior shots of the tower were filmed in Hollywood in a re-created set piece.

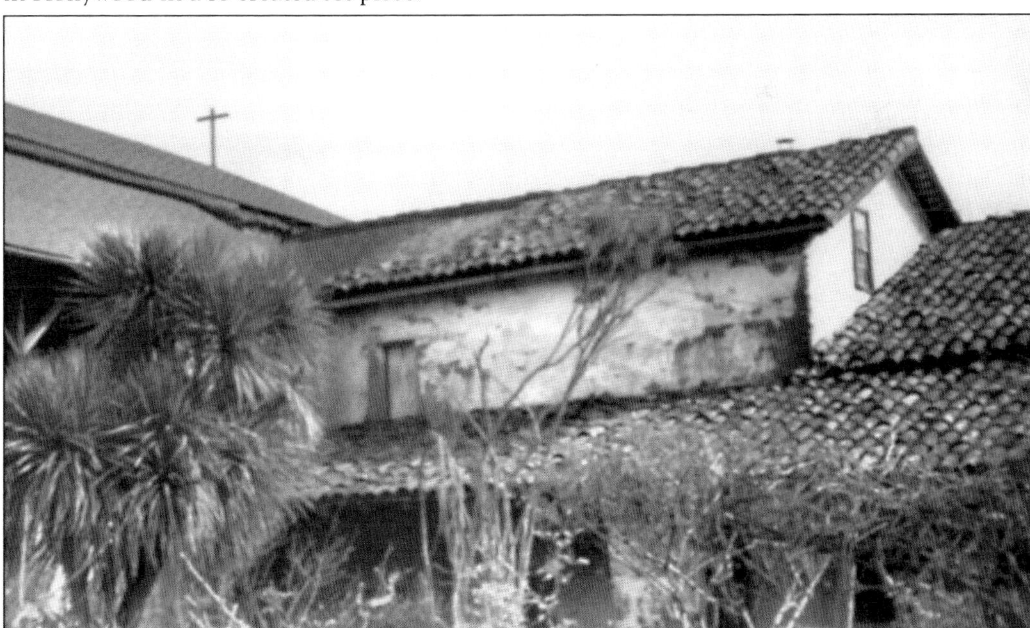

Taken in the early 1950s, this photograph shows the damage over time to the plaster coating on the adobe walls.

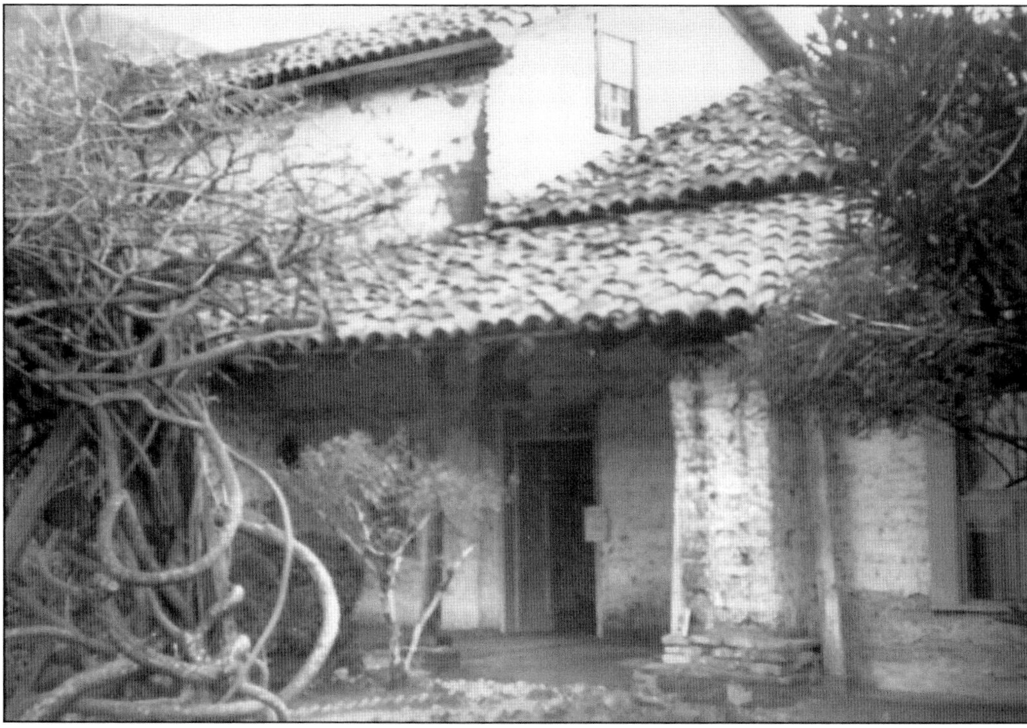

This 1950s view of the courtyard also reveals the need for repairs. The walls were made of adobe bricks, which were nothing more than dried mud. During the mission period, a crew of men worked year round to maintain the walls and the plaster coating. This was necessary to prevent damage leading to the walls' collapse.

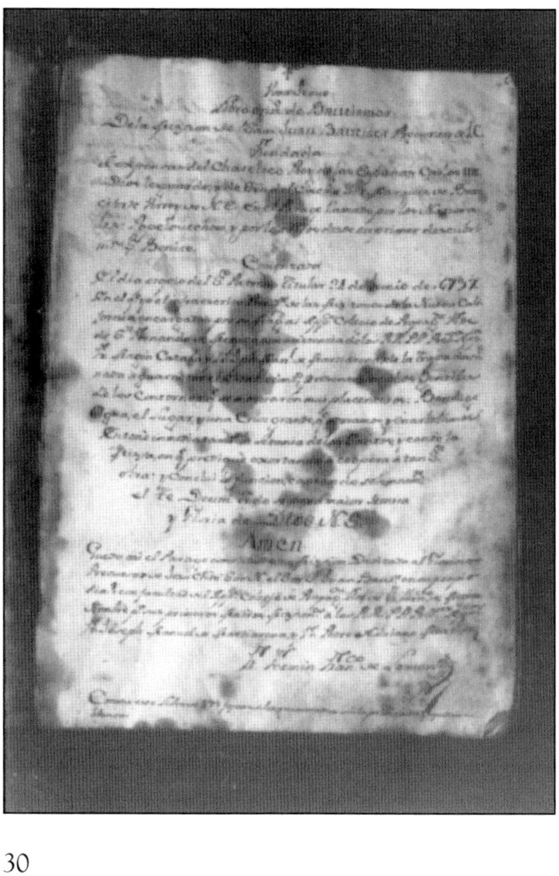

This letter was written by Padre Fermin Lasuen, president of the California missions and chief architect and founder of San Juan Bautista. Born in Vitoria, Spain, in 1736, he arrived in Alta California, in 1774. He served at various missions until 1785, when he was appointed president of the missions following the death of Padre Junipero Serra. He served in California until his death in 1803. During his presidency, Lasuen founded nine missions. He is buried next to Junipero Serra in Mission San Carlos.

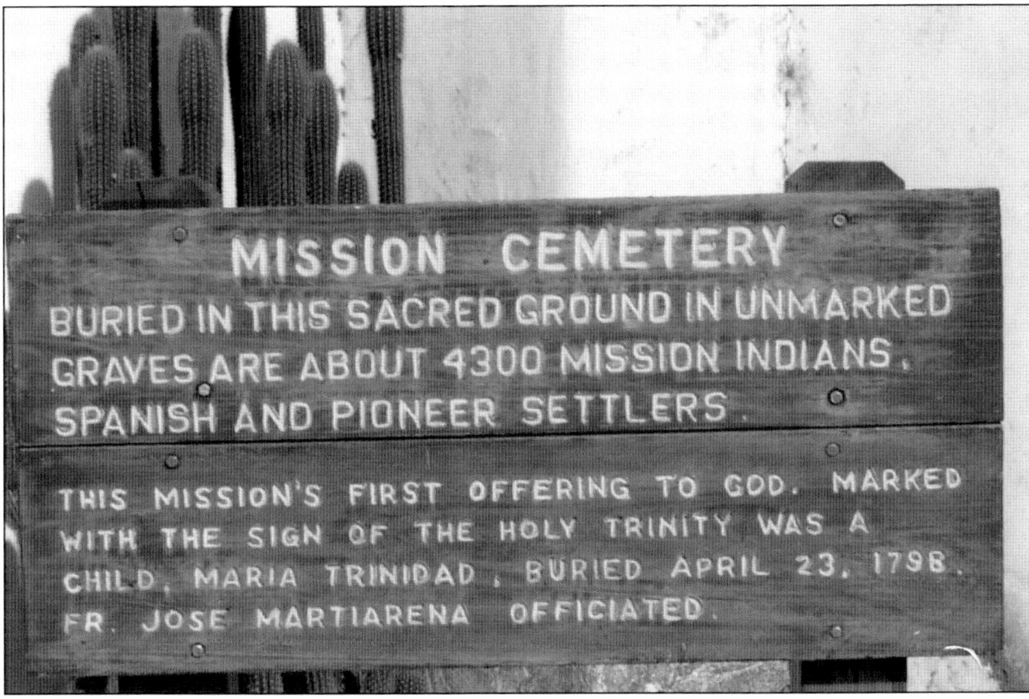

Over 4,000 Mutsun Indians were baptized at the mission, and most are buried in this cemetery next to the church. As the number of burials increased, the wall was raised and a layer of dirt was added so the newly deceased could be placed above the earlier graves.

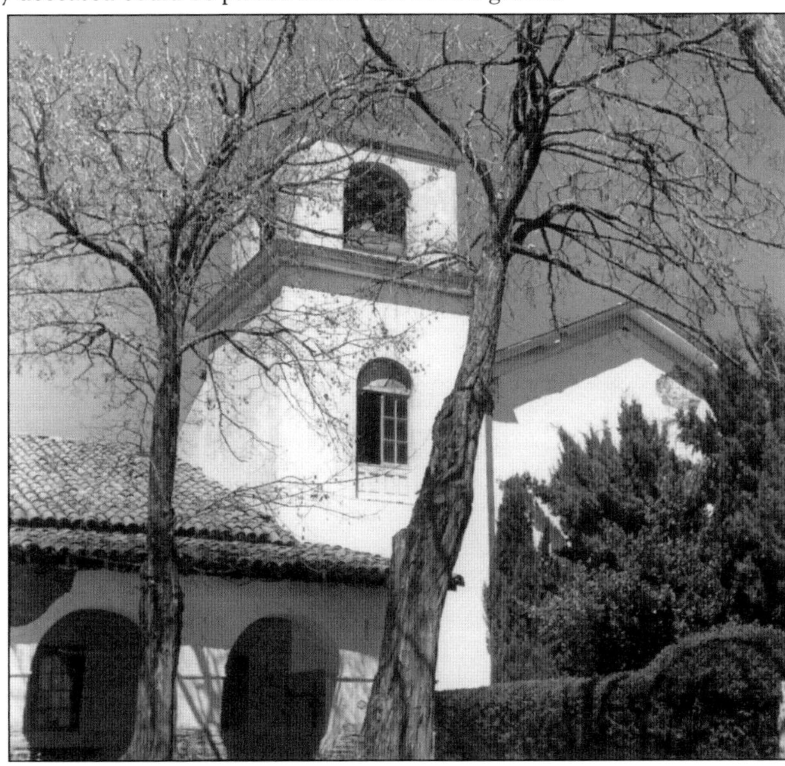

In 1949–1952, Harry Downie, chief restorer of Carmel Mission, performed an extensive study of the church. This study uncovered the original wall decorations as well as the ceiling paintings. Radiant heating was installed under the original floor tiles. Among other projects undertaken was the removal of the 1920s bell tower.

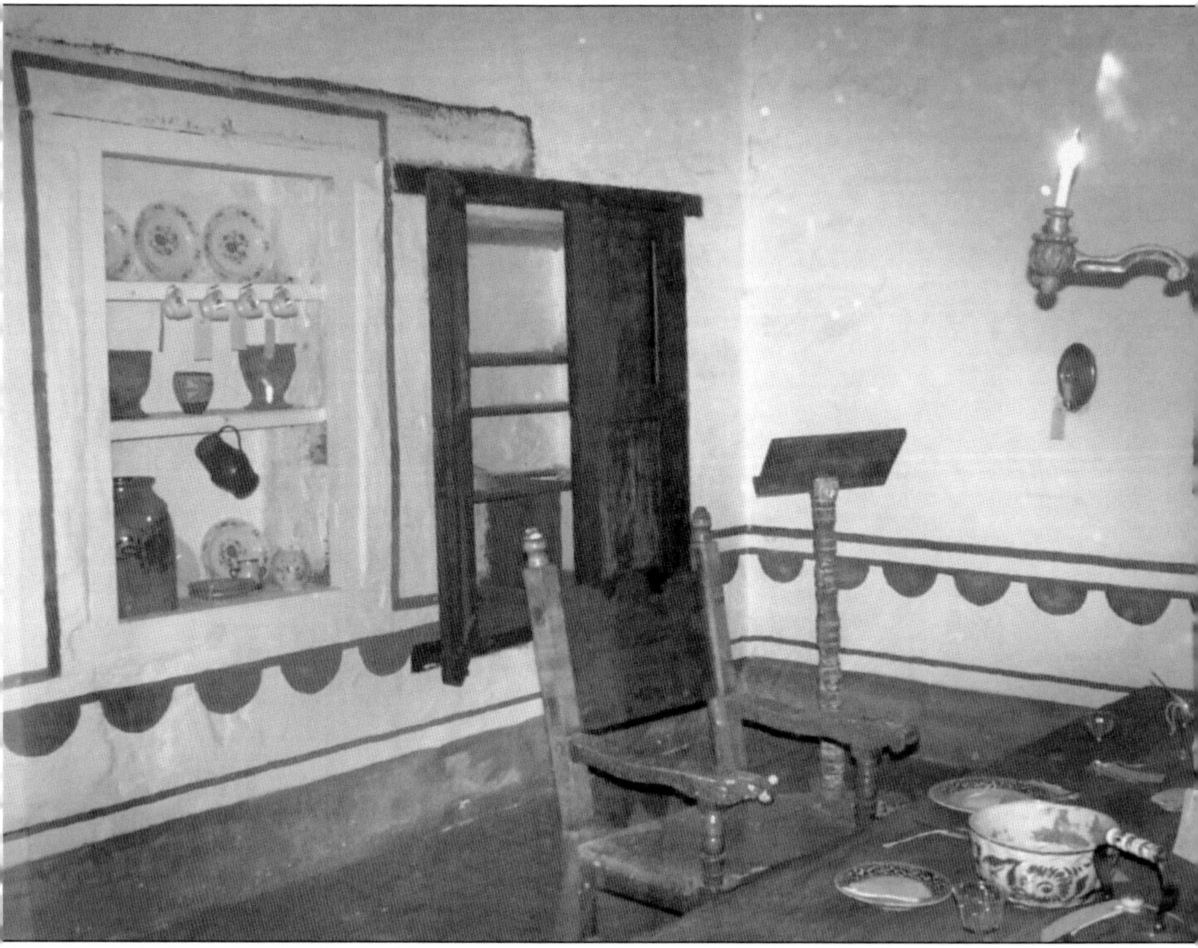

The padres ate in this refectory, adjacent to the kitchen. Access to the kitchen was provided through an opening in the wall, and a turntable between the rooms allowed food to be delivered to the padres. Doors on either side of this turntable gave privacy and prevented smoke from entering the dining room.

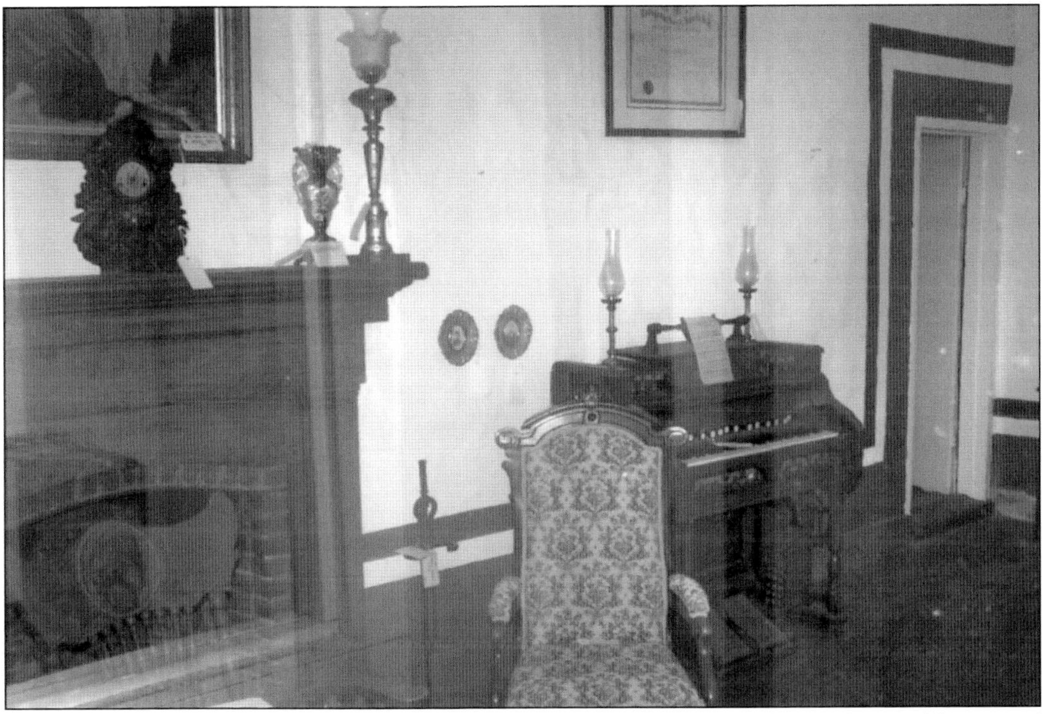

This Victorian-style parlor is typical of the decorations added by Father Rubio and later used by Father Closa.

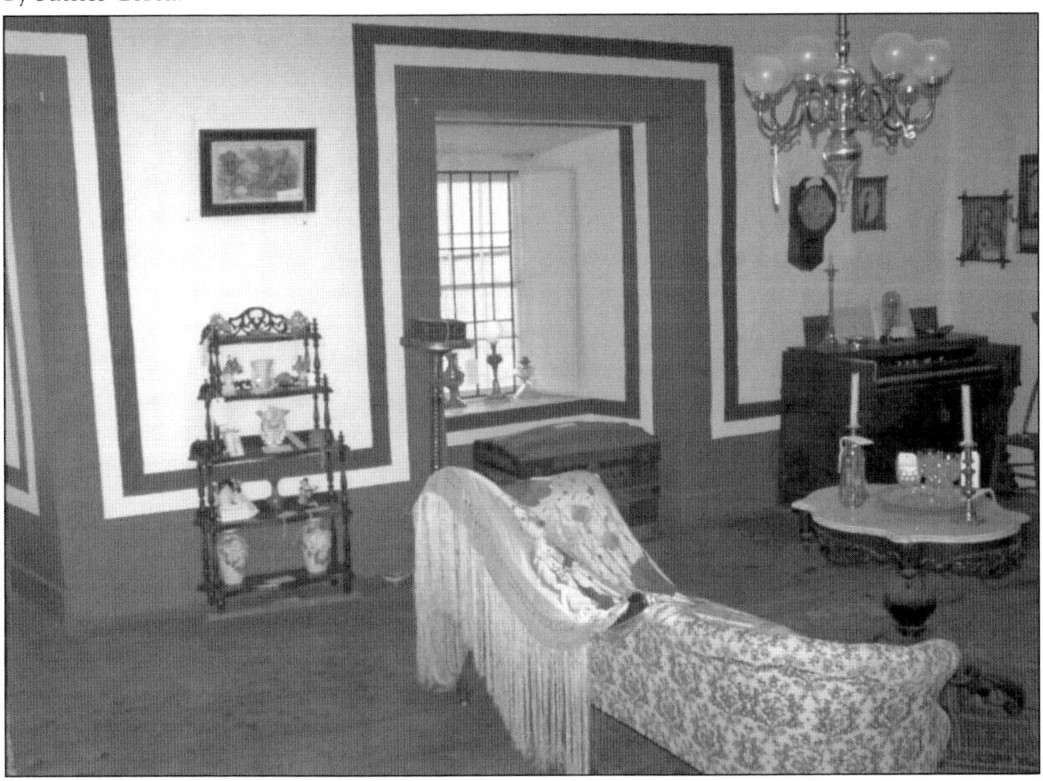

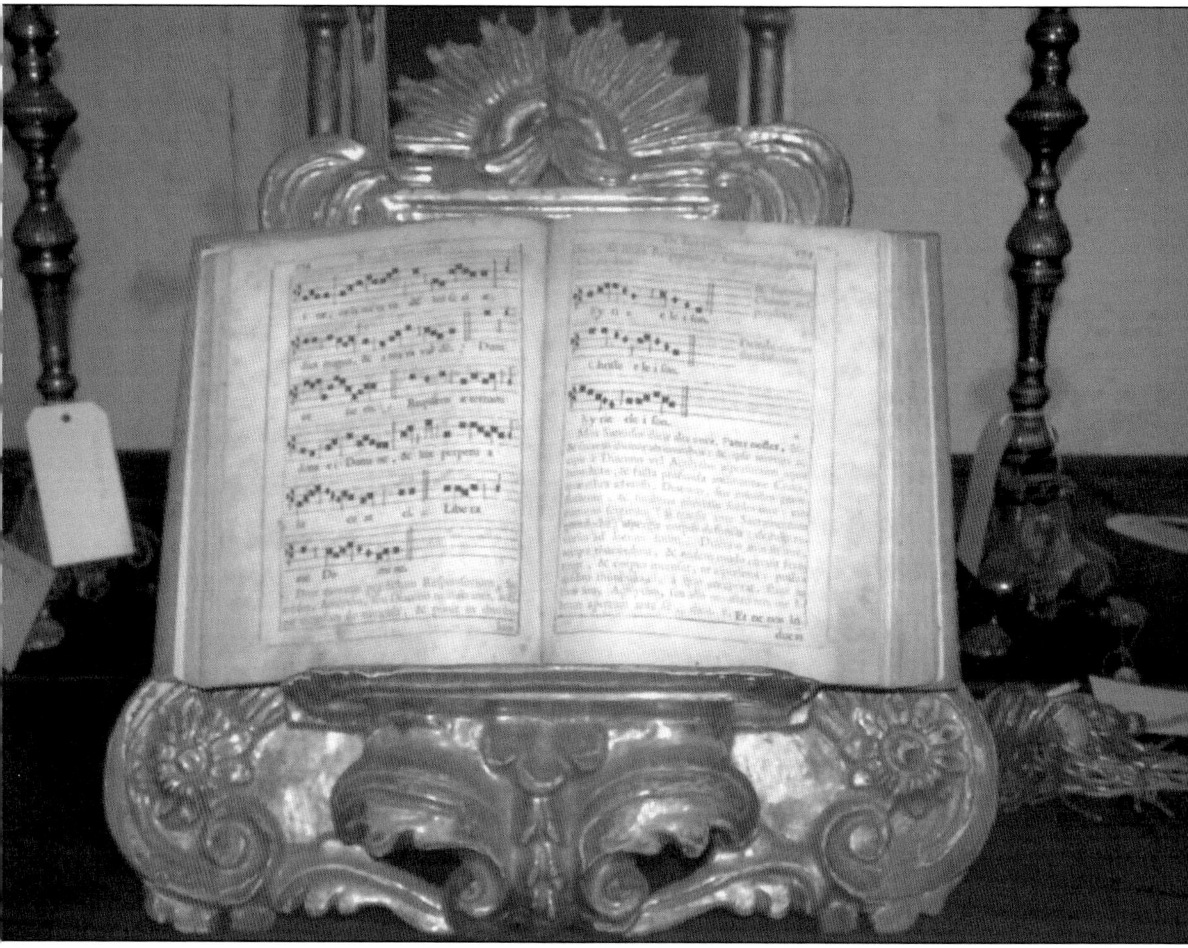

This book, an 18th-century missal used in Mass, is one of many early books used by the padres for church services.

Three

THE MEXICAN PERIOD

After the overthrow of Spain, the new Mexican government seemed to consider California an unwelcome stepchild. In addition to a general lack of economic aid, the incompetent governors sent from Mexico often caused great hardship to all in the area. Most of the non-native inhabitants of early California were second- and third-generation descendants of the original military and civilian families who settled there as early as 1769. These people often considered themselves as Californios and gave their allegiance more to California than Mexico.

On August 17, 1833, the Mexican government ordered the secularization of all the missions and the removal of all padres who favored the Spanish king. Local administrators were appointed to oversee the transfer of mission lands and properties. Tiburcio Castro oversaw the administration of Mission San Juan Bautista. The pastor, Padre Anzar, was to select only what rooms and property the church needed for his residence and worship services, while all other buildings and properties were doled out as land grants to the Californio settlers and sold.

As land grants multiplied in the late 1830s, rancho owners began complaining about the lack of military protection in the region, especially the ranchos east of the Pueblo of San Juan. Marauding bands of American Indians from the Central Valley were wreaking havoc on the landowners by attacking the ranchos, killing the herdsmen, and driving off the horses. By the time military authorities in Monterey could be notified, the culprits were gone. The response from the military was to create a detachment in San Juan under the leadership of Gen. Jose Castro.

In 1844, some of the Californios planned to overthrow Mexico and make California independent. The rebels selected General Castro to be the governor. This bloodless rebellion was short lived, and in nine months the California revolt ended. Neither Castro nor his coconspirators were given more than a reprimand.

In 1846, the United States declared war on Mexico, and soon the American and Californian governments would become the newest occupants of San Juan Bautista.

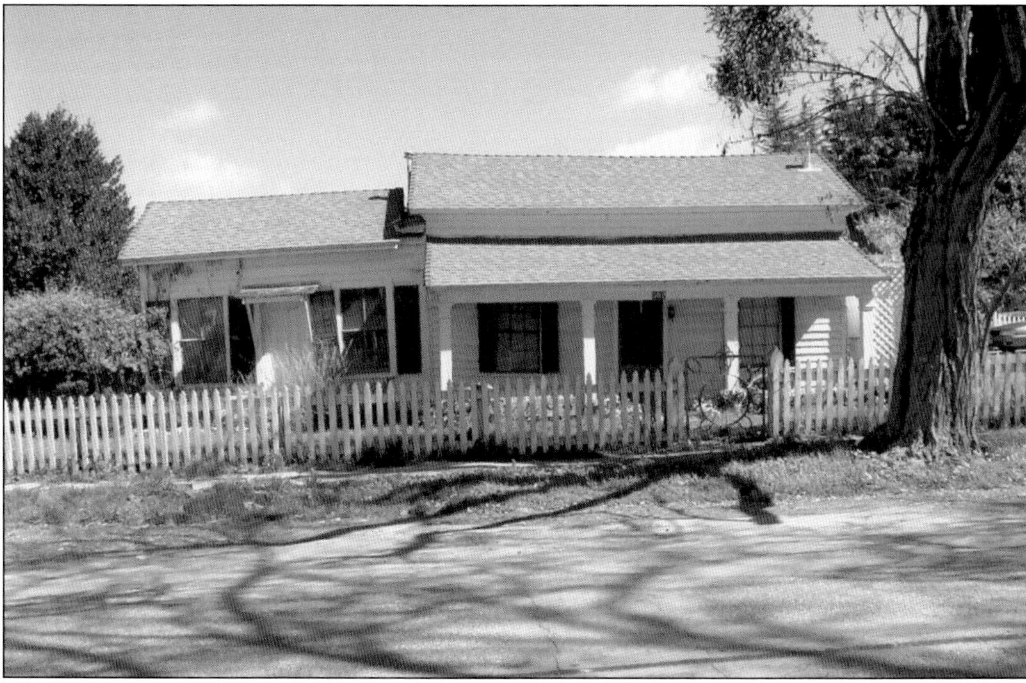

The Kemp House, built in 1860 and purchased by Frederick Kemp in 1864, was the scene of many social events in San Juan. Fred Kemp was the owner of the Boladeoro Saloon when the election for the incorporation of San Juan was held in 1869.

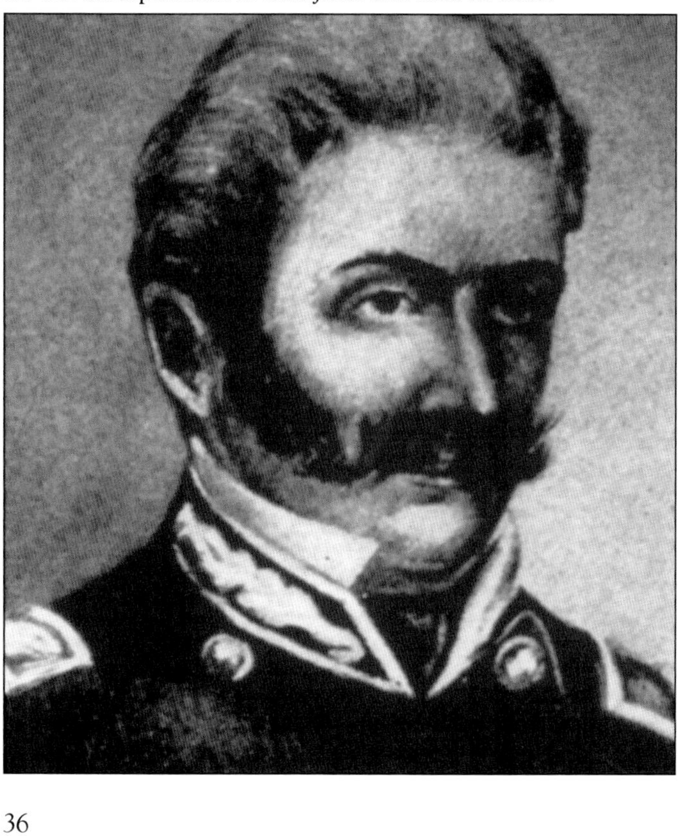

The son of a soldier, Jose Maria Castro was born in Monterey in 1813. He became a soldier and rose through the ranks to become a general. In 1839, he moved his headquarters from Monterey to San Juan Bautista, where he served as the administrator for the sale of the mission properties. He moved into the Castro Adobe, which became his residence as well as his headquarters. He and his friends Mariano Vallejo and Juan Alvarado planned to overthrow the Mexican government and make California an independent country but failed. When the Americans won the Mexican-American War in 1848, Castro fled California for Mexico. His wife sold the house to the Breen family and moved to Monterey.

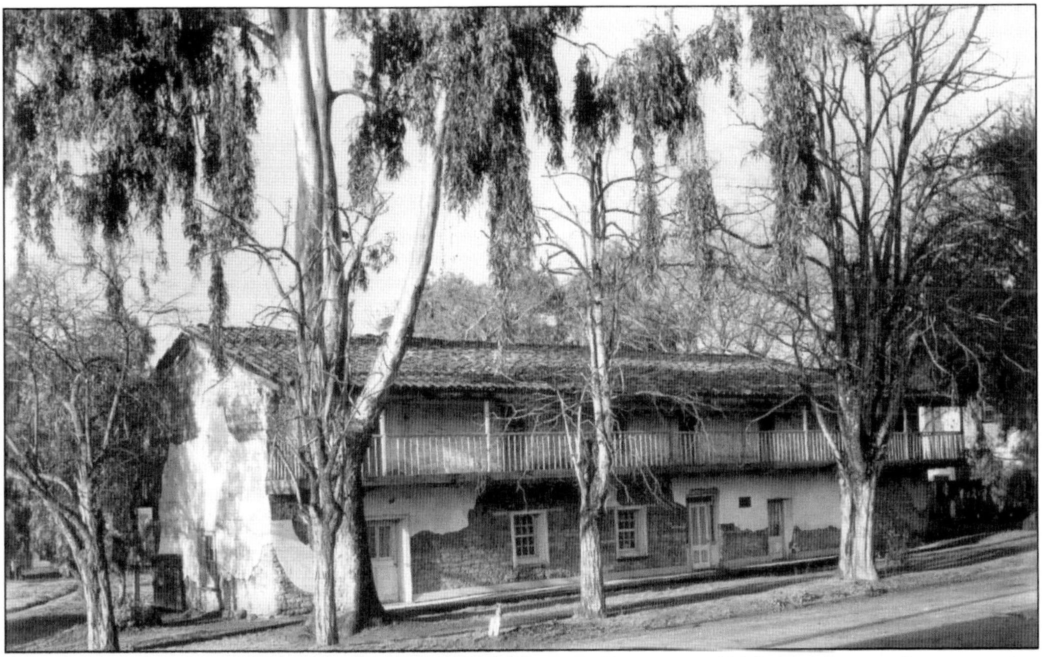

The Castro Adobe was built by Jose's father, Tiburcio Castro, in 1839. Constructed on a native sandstone foundation, it originally had three rooms upstairs for living quarters and three downstairs for administrative offices. A balcony on the second floor faced the plaza. The rafters were hand tied with rawhide to the main roof beam, one long piece of redwood. The roof was then covered with tile.

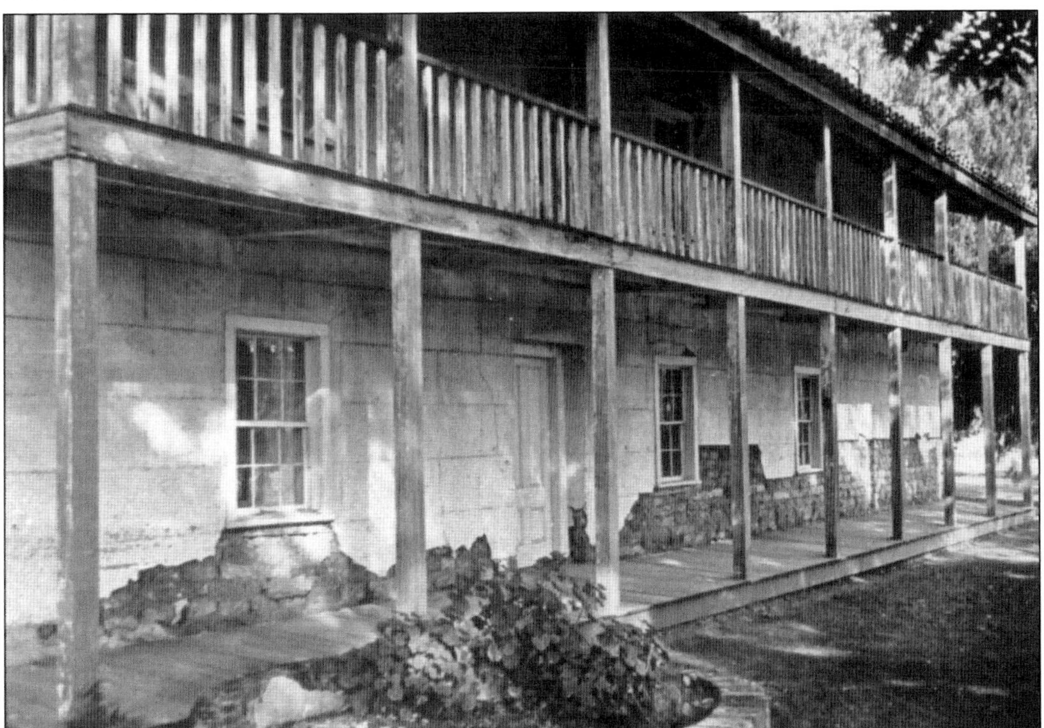

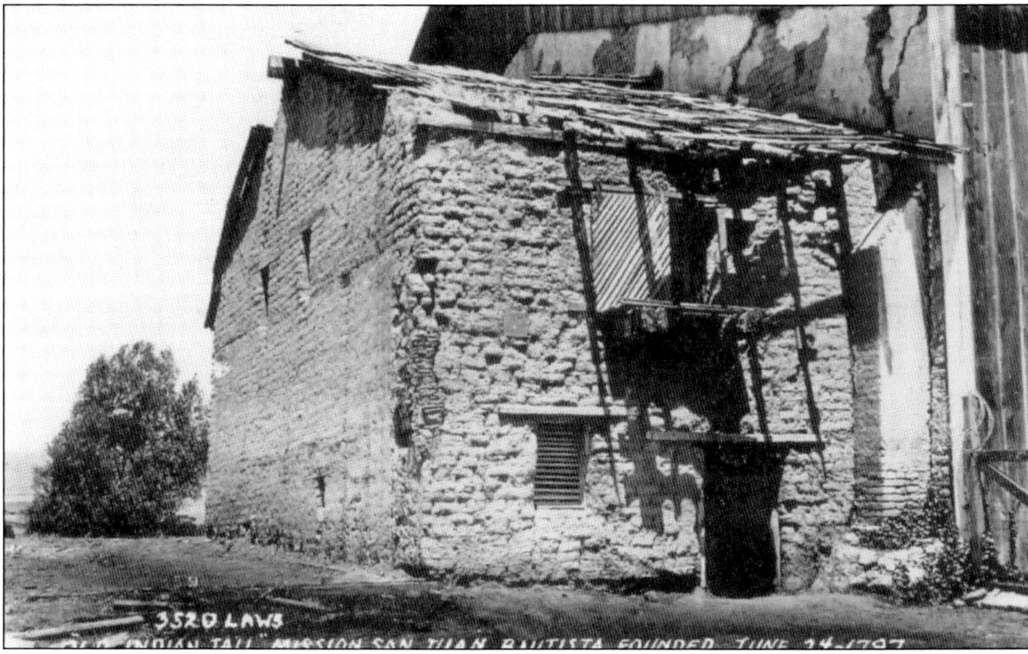

This building behind the church was called the "jail" by locals. The Native American choir members were very proud to sing every Sunday in church. Afraid of being tempted to get drunk on Saturday night, they presented themselves to the padre and asked to be locked up so they would be available to sing on Sunday. The first floor is now used for a tool room, and the second floor is the priest's residence.

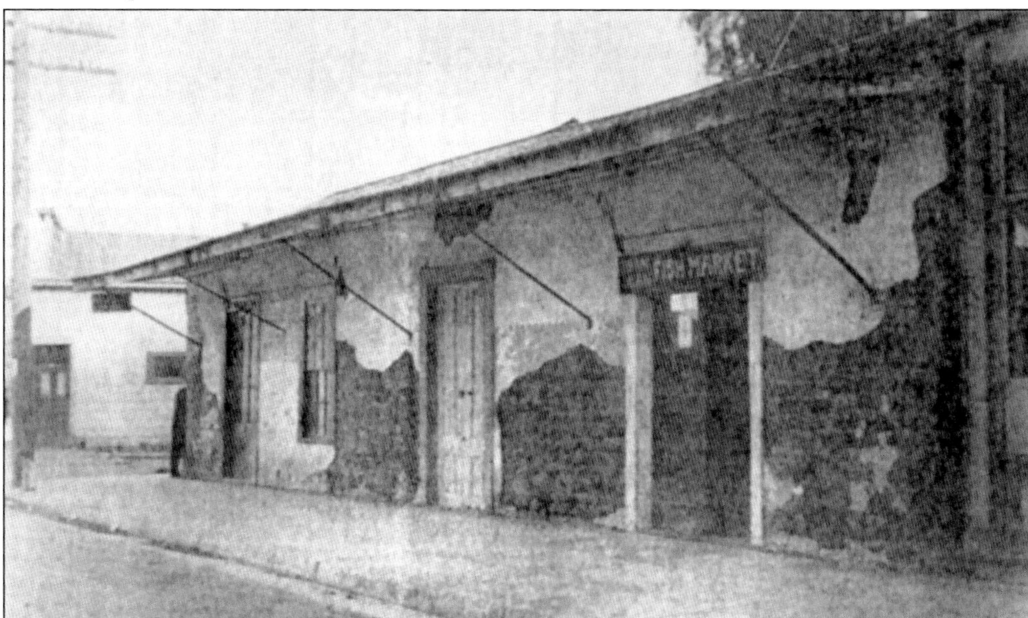

The Vasquez Adobe is located at Third and Mariposa Streets. It has been suggested that the room at the far end of the building was the location of a tomale parlor operated by the mother of the bandit Tiburcio Vasquez.

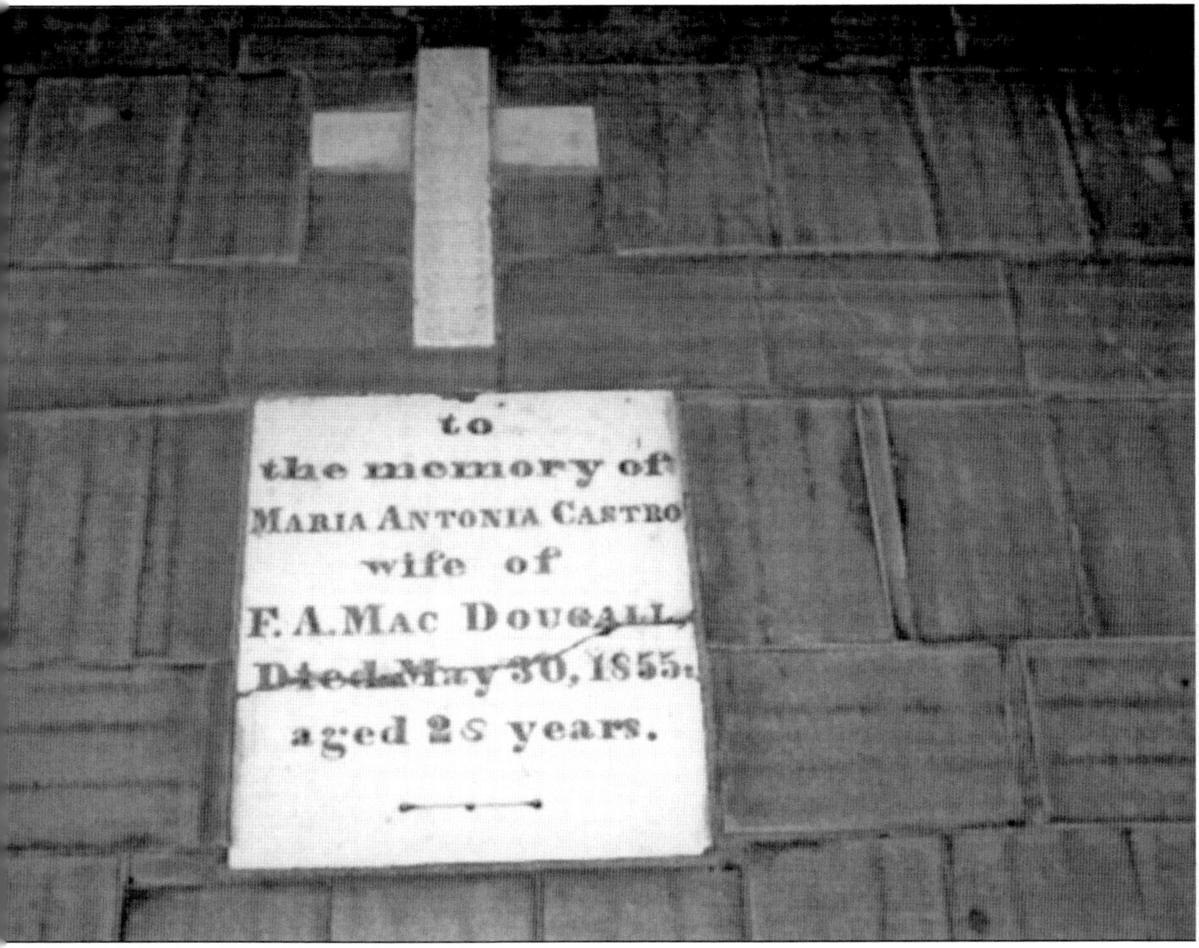

The niece of Gen. Jose Castro, Maria Antonio Castro, married Juan Anzar and had three sons: Juan, Anatol, and P. E. G. "Lupe" Anzar. When her husband died, she married Dr. Frederick McDougall. Maria died in 1855 as a result of a riding accident and was buried in the floor of the mission.

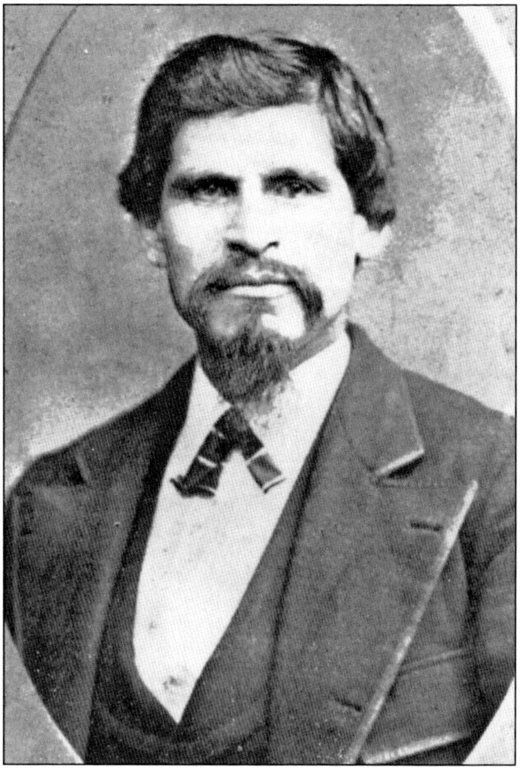

Tiburcio Vasquez was born in Monterey in 1839. At the age of 15, while attending a fandango, a fight started which resulted in the death of a constable. Thus began Vasquez's life of crime. He joined a gang of horse thieves and was sent to San Quentin in 1857. After his release, he returned to his criminal life, robbing stages and stores and kidnapping wealthy men. Largely ignored by local authorities, he frequently visited his mother in San Juan Bautista. He was eventually captured in Los Angeles and returned to San Jose, where he was tried and hanged in 1875.

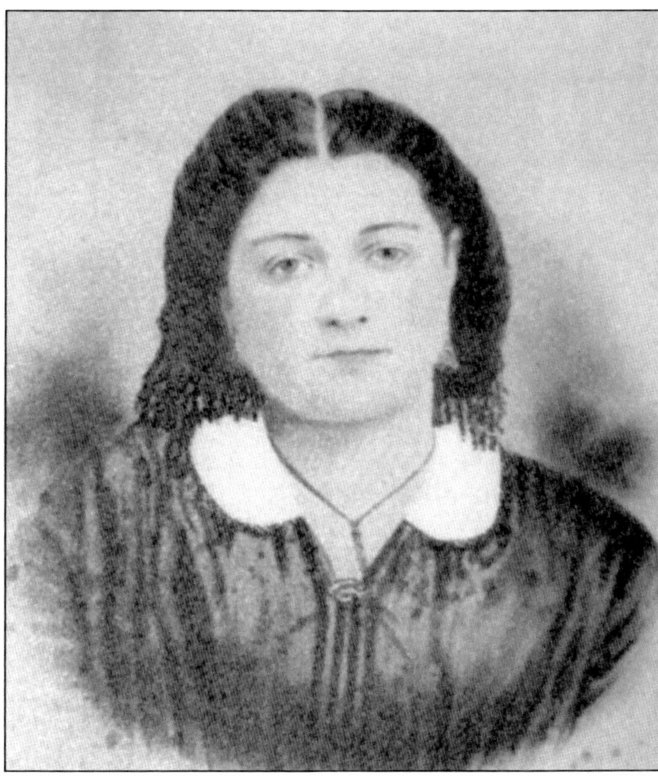

Modestita Castro, the daughter of General Castro, was born in San Juan Bautista on July 23, 1842. She married William C. Dana, the captain of a ship and a native Californio, in 1861. He was the cousin of Richard Henry Dana, the celebrated author of *Two Years before the Mast*.

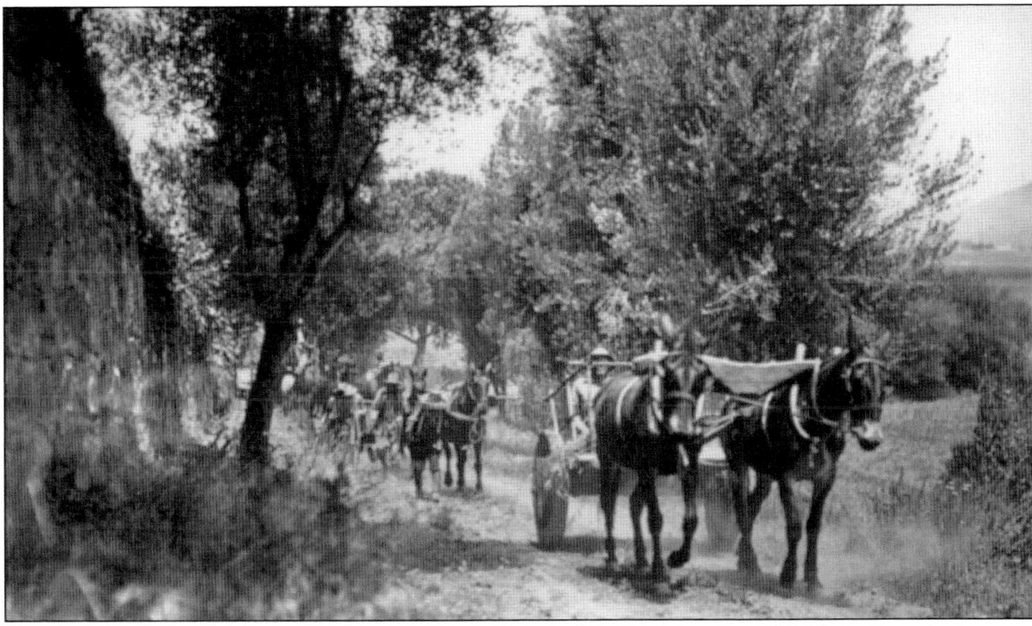

This scene from an early-20th-century fiesta depicts life on the original El Camino. As one can see, bullocks and carts were present during the early mission days.

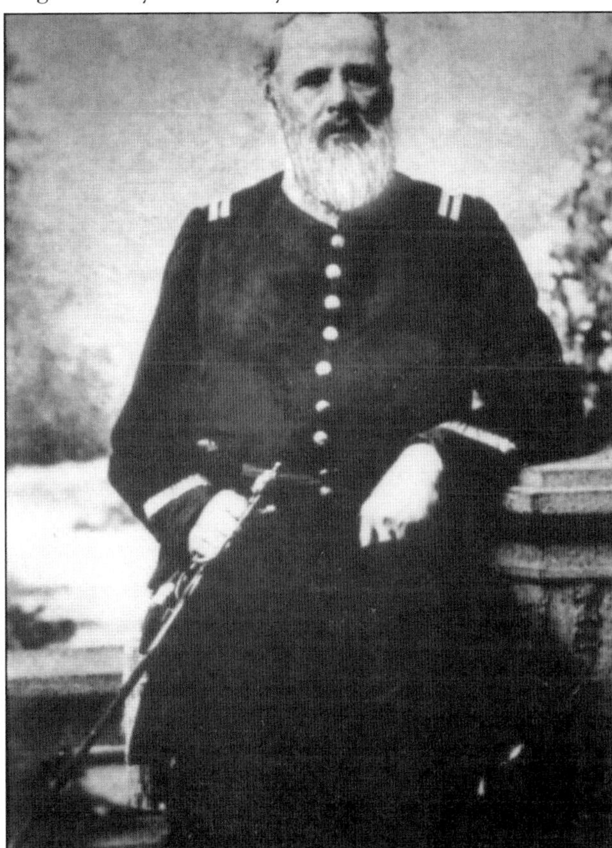

At the behest of President Polk, John C. Fremont led five expeditions from Washington to the West between 1842 and 1853. He angered General Castro for refusing to leave the area and the two men exchanged threats. Fremont and his men climbed a nearby hill and set up camp. Finally realizing they were outnumbered, he and his men abandoned the peak and headed for the interior valley of California, narrowly avoiding a war with the Mexicans. He gained great prestige during his campaigns in California and was given the rank of major by Commodore Stockton. Fremont organized the California battalion meant to defeat Castro and, while not in Sonoma for the Bear Flag Revolt, certainly encouraged the endeavor. This photograph shows him in his later years, when he ran unsuccessfully for president.

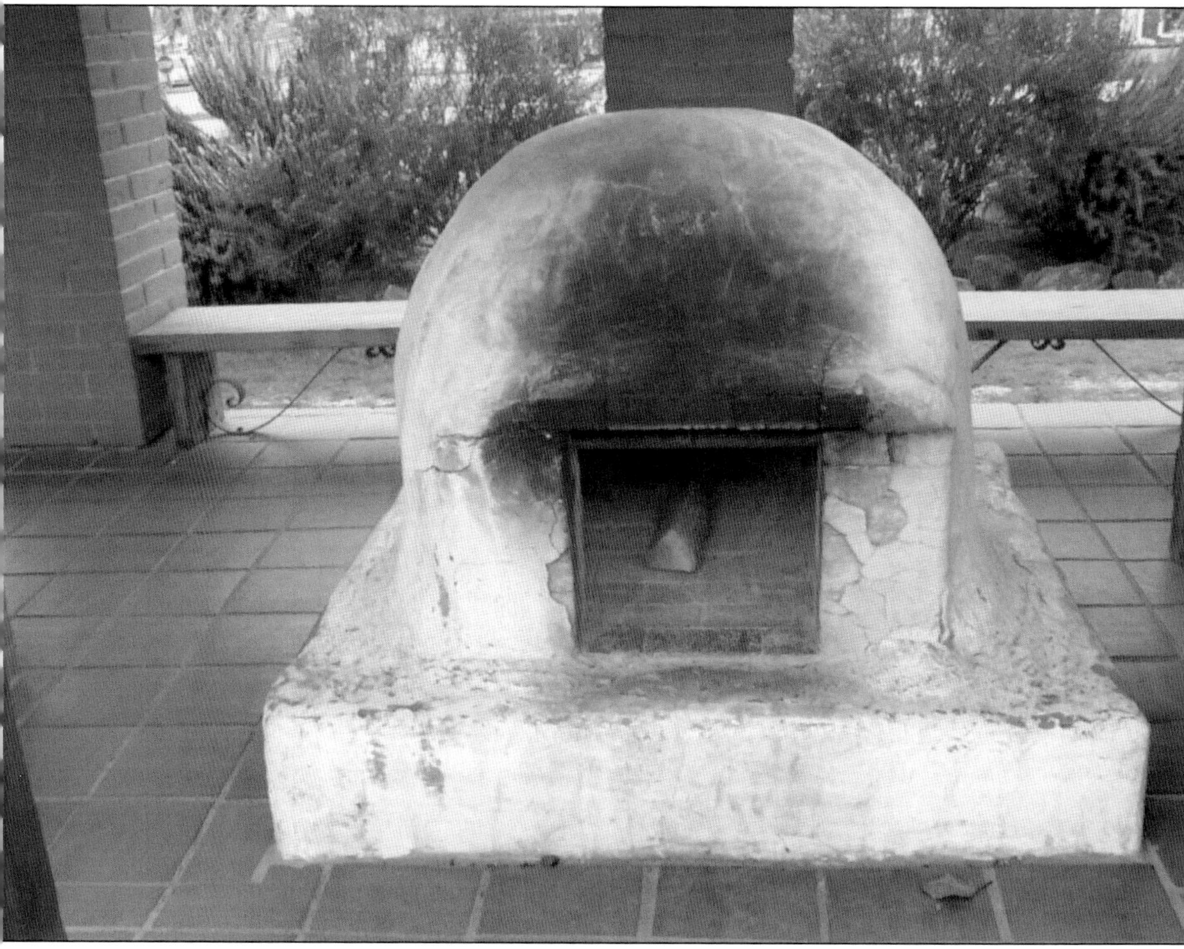

There were no interior kitchens in most Californio homes due to the absence of stoves. Cooking was done behind the house in a covered shed called a *ramada*. The *hornito*, or oven, was used for baking. A fire was set in the oven; after it was hot enough, the coals were removed and the food placed inside.

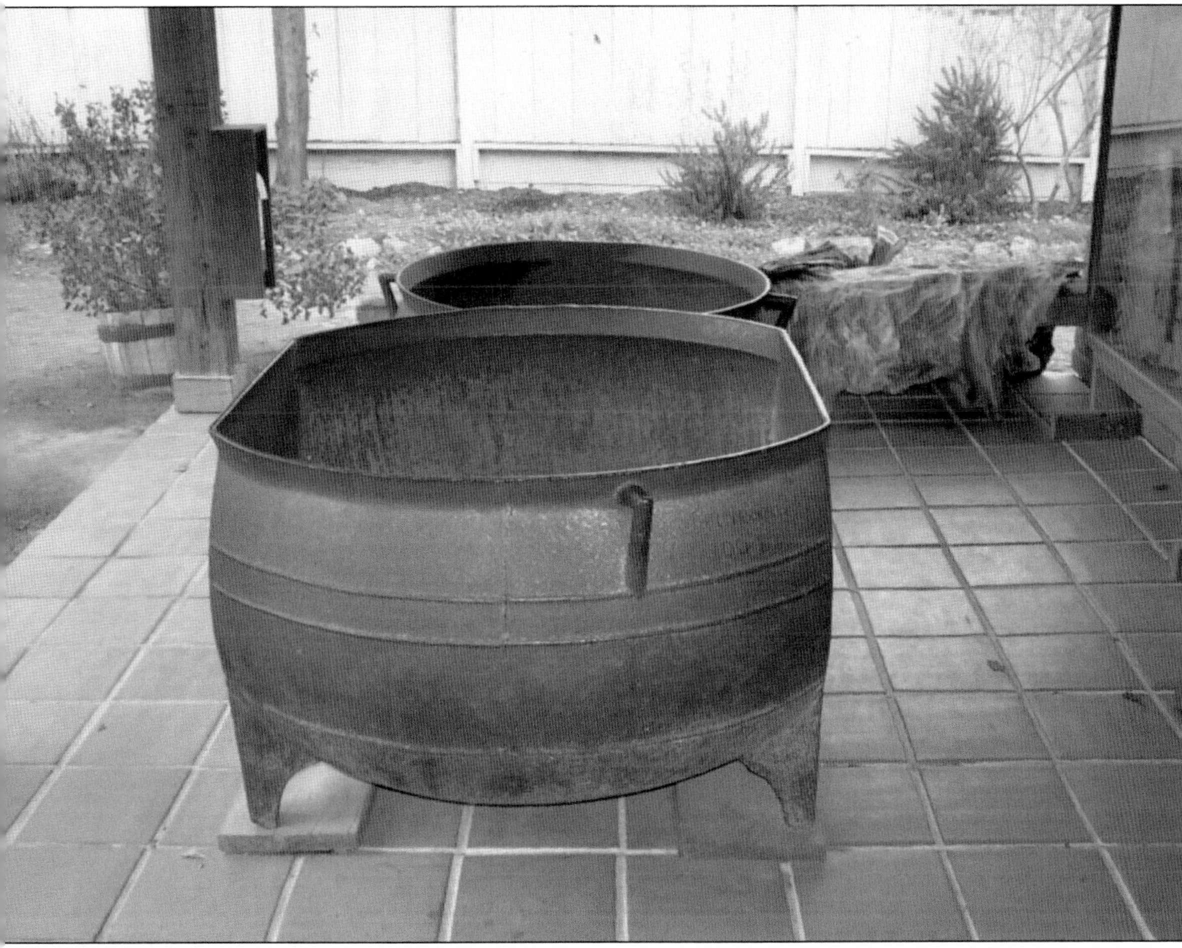

The hide and tallow business was first developed by the Spanish; however, the Californios would create a major industry from it. Tallow, or boiled animal fat, was cooked in these vats. It was later shipped by boat to Mexico, South America, or the United States for money or traded for supplies.

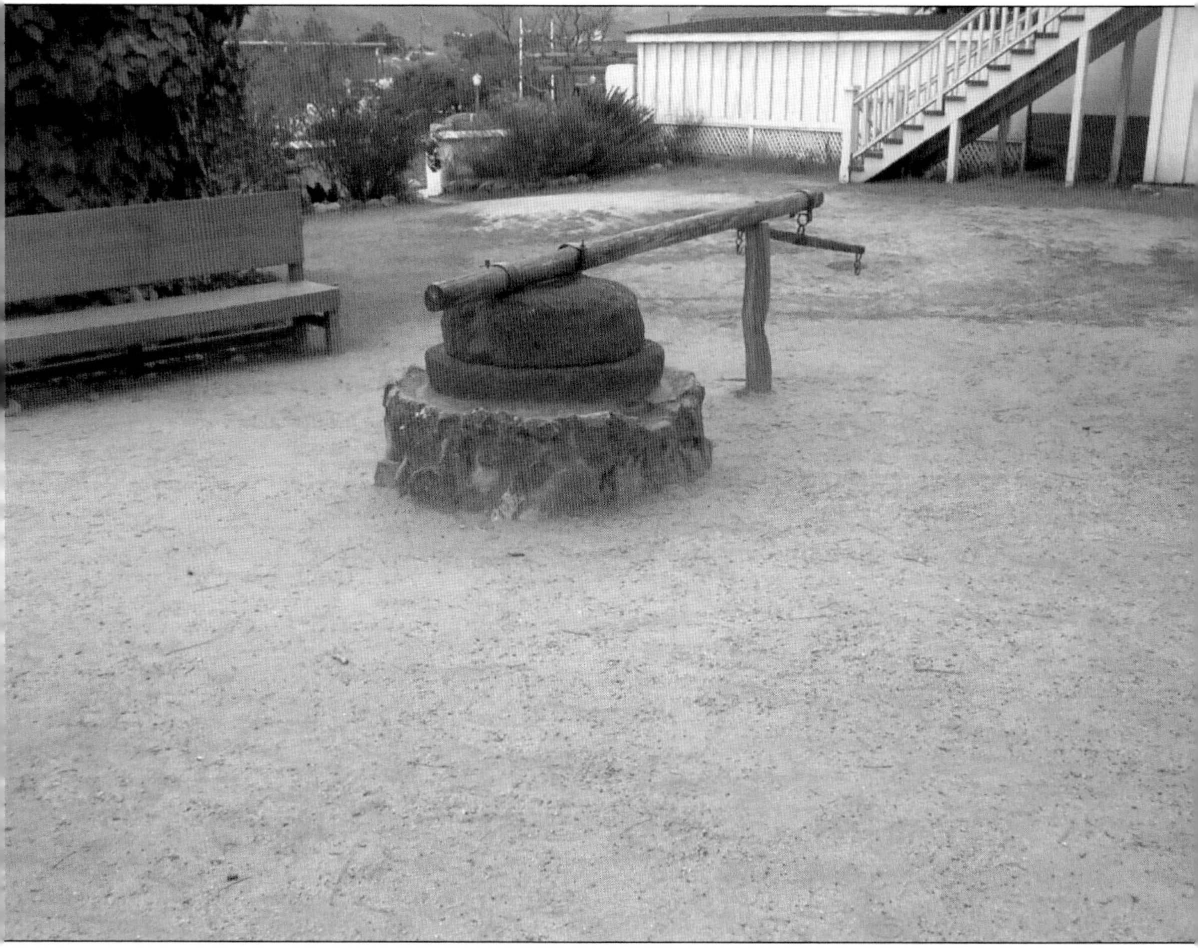

These grinding stones were used to mill grain and dried corn. The grain or corn was poured into a hole in the stone. As the stone revolved, the finished product was worked through grooves out to the edge. A burro was harnessed to the pole and walked in a circle to move the stone.

Four

Statehood and the American Period

When gold was discovered in California in January 1848, the Breens, destitute survivors of the famous Donner Party, had already come to San Juan Bautista. When word reached the settlement, their oldest son, John, went off to the hills in search of the metal. He returned a few months later with approximately $10,000 in gold. This enabled the family to purchase the Castro Adobe and 400 acres of land in the San Juan Valley.

The Breen family was not the only English-speaking family in San Juan. By 1849, other settlers had arrived, and soon stores were opened to provide supplies for the men on their way to the goldfields. The rancheros prospered from the sale of horses and burros, and as the population of the gold seekers grew, many of the rancho owners drove herds of cattle to the hills to provide meat and hides to the mines.

By the 1850s, San Juan Bautista had become the crossroads for travel in central California and shortly thereafter the center of commerce, with the opening of the New Idria quicksilver mines 70 miles south of town. All supplies destined for the mine and for the goldfields passed through San Juan. Many farms began to grow hay, grain, horses, and cattle for shipment to San Francisco, and soon San Juan Bautista became the largest town in central California.

Seven stage lines had permanent facilities, with the largest being the Coast Line State Company, which ran stages between San Francisco and the cities of Southern California. Many independent freight companies hauled supplies to and from New Idria and Alviso at the southern tip of San Francisco Bay, where the ore was smelted.

During the 1860s, officials discussed San Juan becoming the seat for the new county of San Benito. This never materialized, because a fire destroyed several blocks of the business district in 1867. Many shop owners never rebuilt and then moved to the new town of Hollister when the railroad bypassed San Juan in the early 1870s. Soon more businesses followed this move to Hollister, and by the 1880s, the once-booming town and commercial center had faded into history. By the end of the 19th century, it was almost a ghost town. San Juan would not recover from this blow until well into the 20th century.

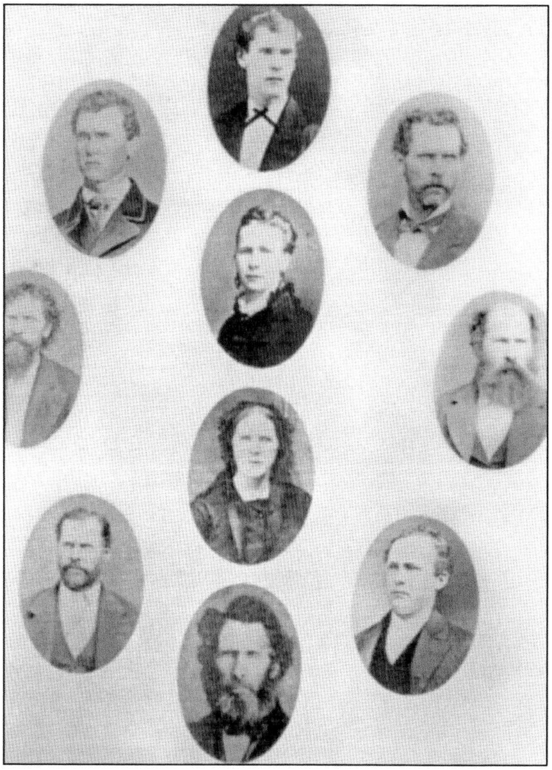

Patrick Breen was born in Ireland in 1795. He immigrated to Canada and then to the United States with his wife, Margaret, and two children, eventually settling to farm in Keokuk, Iowa, in 1834. He became a citizen of the United States in 1845, and in 1846, the family joined the Donner Party heading for California. After surviving the winter of 1846 in the Sierras, the family arrived in San Juan, where Patrick took up farming again. The Breens were the first Americans to settle in the community, and Patrick was to become a respected member of the town. He died in his adobe in 1868. In this composite photograph, he appears in the lower center. Margaret Bulger Breen was born in Ireland in 1810. Like her future husband, her family also immigrated to Canada. She married Patrick there and had two children before migrating to the United States. Eight more were born in this country; however, one died in Iowa. Margaret, known in San Juan for her hospitality to visitors, can be seen in the center of the image.

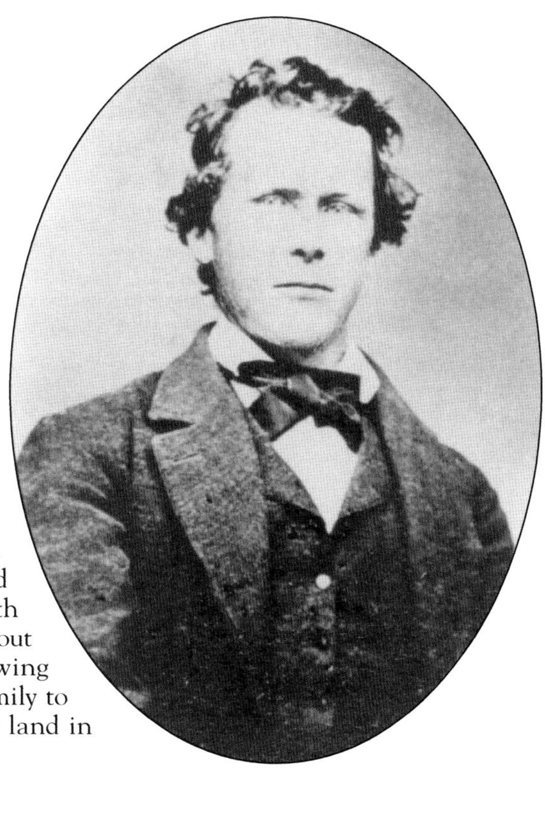

John Breen, born in Canada in 1832, was the eldest son of Patrick and Margaret. He and his brother Edward played an important role in the family's survival during the winter of 1846 because they took responsibility for food gathering when their father became incapacitated. In early 1848, a man from Sutter's Fort in the Sacramento Valley stayed with the Breen family and impressed John with samples of gold. In June of that year, John set out to make his fortune and returned the following March with $10,000 in gold, enabling the family to purchase the adobe and 400 acres of prime land in the San Juan Valley.

Edward Breen, born in Canada in 1833, also helped the family during the period of his father's illness in 1846. He eventually owned vast ranch land in San Benito, Monterey, and Humboldt Counties in California. His largest ranch, the El Topo near King City, spanned 24,000 acres. Edward's son Harry became the family historian, gathering documents including the famous diary of Patrick Breen, written during the time when the family was snowbound.

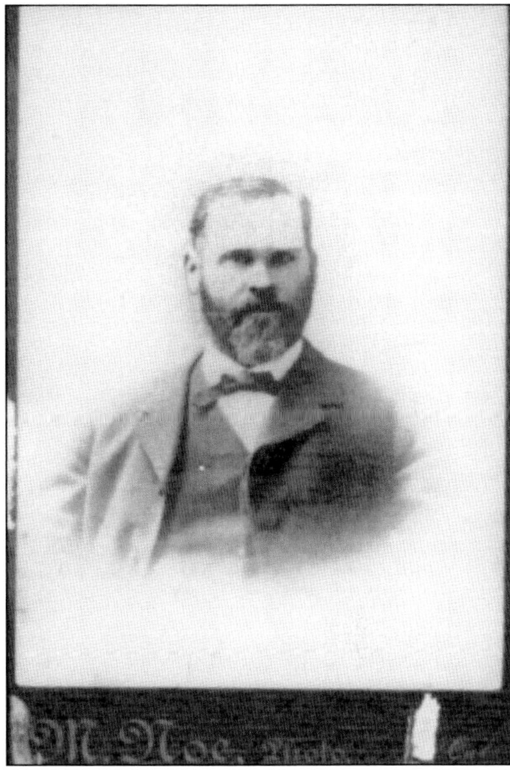

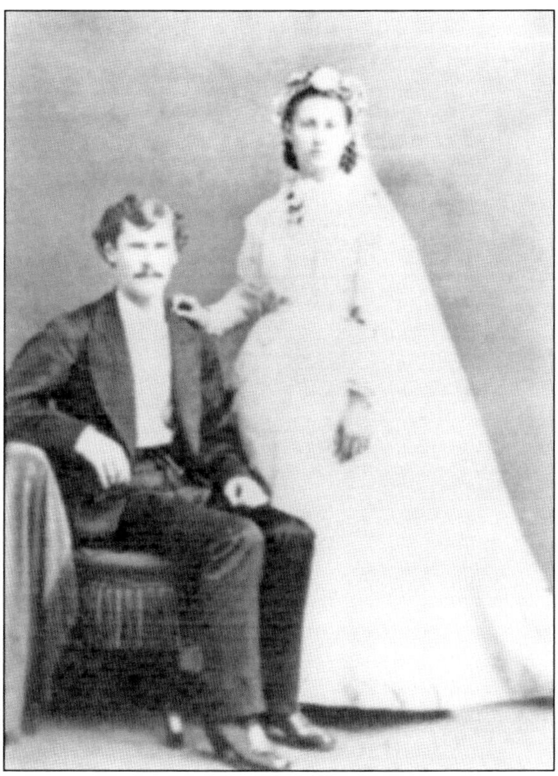

William was the only Breen child born in San Juan Bautista. Born in 1849, he knew nothing of the family's struggles during the snowbound winter. He married Mariquita Zanetta, the daughter of Angelo Zanetta. William died at the age of 25, leaving his wife and daughter, Mary.

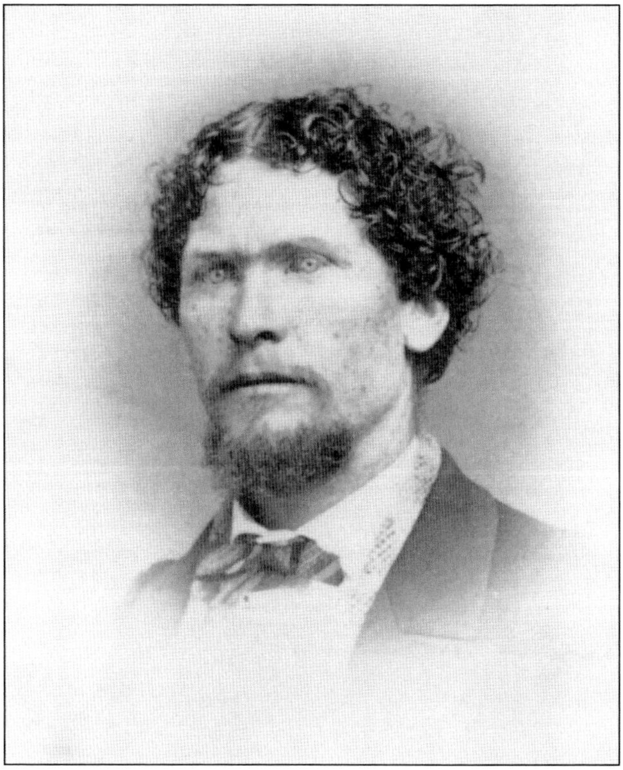

Simon Breen (1839–1899), born in Iowa, was not as interested in acquiring land as his brothers and was known for enjoying a good time. Like his father, Simon loved music and was an accomplished violinist. He was well known for his horsemanship and could outride most men. He had red, curly hair and, when angry, would use some very colorful language. He married Constance Pedancet and had two daughters.

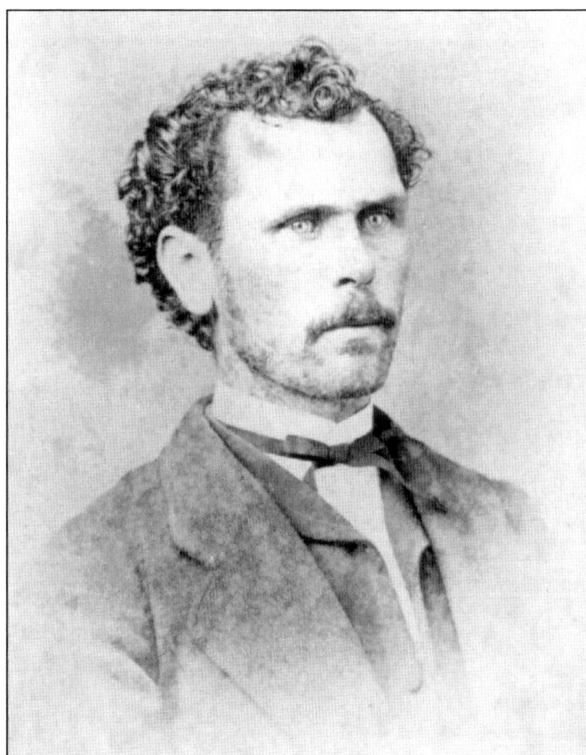

Patrick Breen Jr. was born in 1837 and would become a successful sheep and cattle rancher in the San Juan area. At present, 1,400 acres remain with his descendants, who share jointly in the income. Many descendants of Patrick Jr. still live in the San Juan Bautista area.

James Frederick Breen was born in Iowa in 1842. He attended Santa Clara College and became an attorney practicing in San Francisco before he settled in San Juan. In 1871, he was elected Monterey County judge and was later appointed judge for the district court in the newly formed San Benito County from 1874 to 1875.

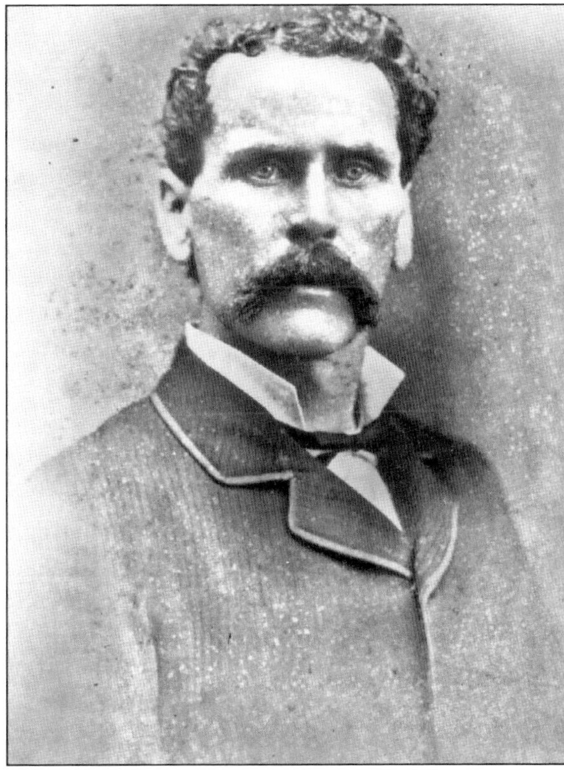

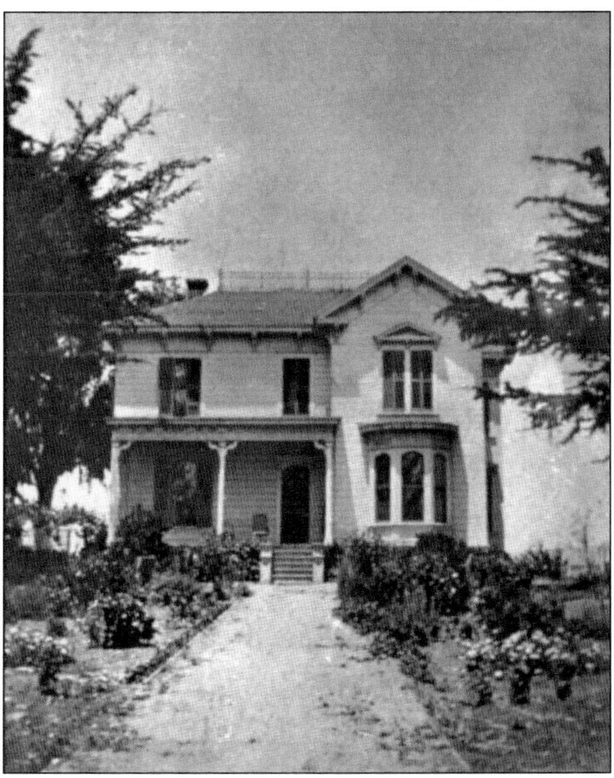

In 1876, the San Juan City Council appointed James Frederick Breen to the position of city attorney. He became superior court judge for San Benito County in September 1879. James married Catherine McMahon and moved into this house on First Street, pictured in 1900.

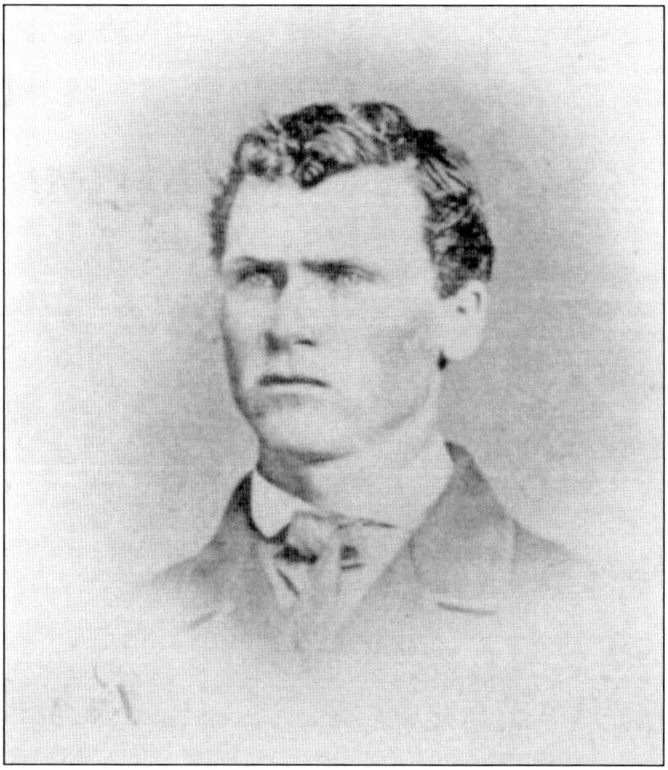

Peter Breen, born in Iowa in 1843, was just a small child when the family was snowbound during the winter of 1846. He was killed on his 27th birthday in a riding accident when his horse stumbled crossing the Pajaro River west of town. He was thrown from his horse, knocked unconscious, and drowned.

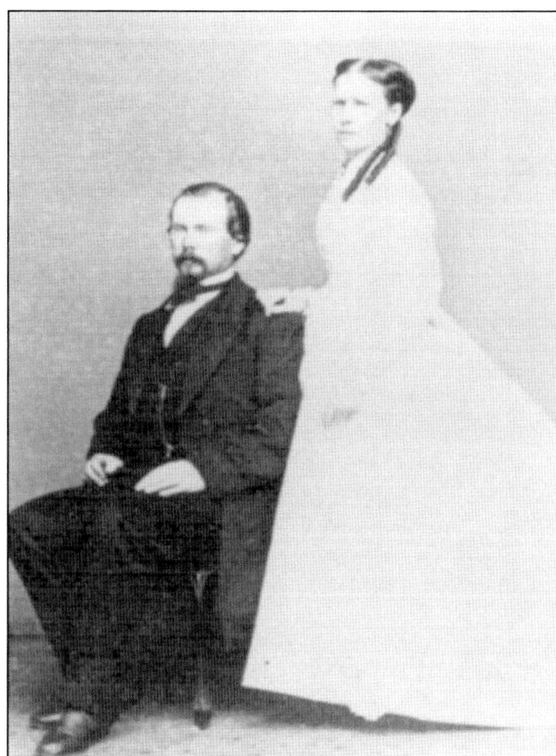

Born in Iowa in 1845, Margaret Isabella Breen was known by all as "Bella" and received the finest education of the day at a young ladies' academy. She married Thomas Morgan McMahon in 1869 and settled in Hollister, where she lived until her death in 1935.

Margaret Isabella Breen's wedding dress is on display in the state park in San Juan Bautista.

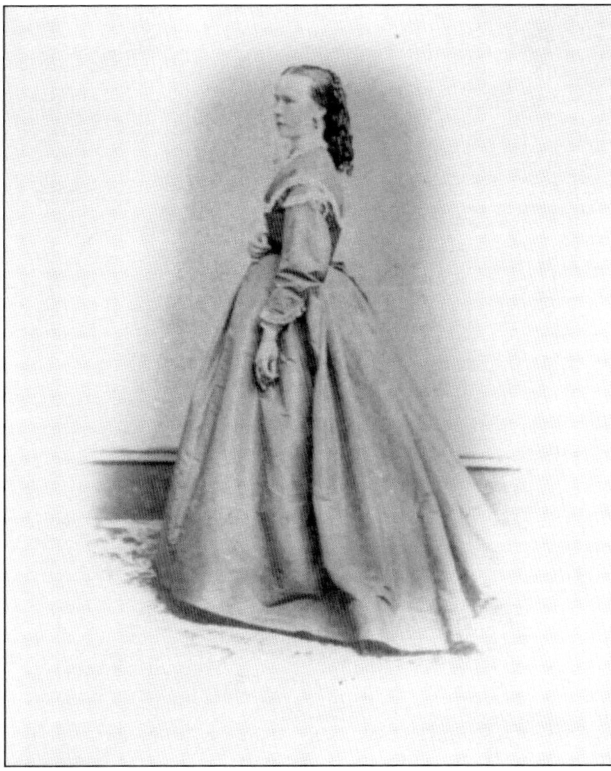

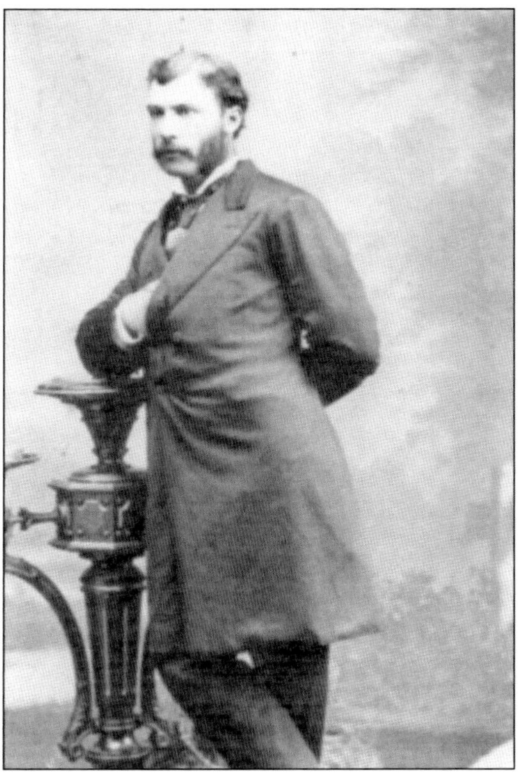

Polocronio Escolastico Guadalupe Anzar, known as P. E. G. or "Lupe," was the son of Juan Anzar and Maria Antonio Castro. He was born in 1851 in the old Spanish-Mexican barracks owned by his father. The building, later sold to Angelo Zanetta, eventually became the Plaza Hotel. In 1877, P. E. G. married Mariquita Zanetta Breen, the widow of William Breen.

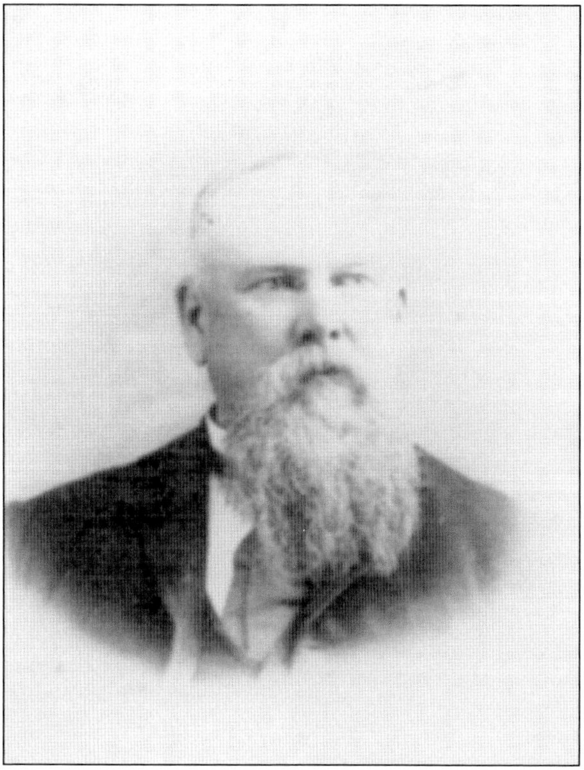

Thomas Morgan McMahon, the son of James McMahon Sr., came to San Juan Bautista from his native Ireland in 1849. His father opened a mercantile store in San Juan and became a successful businessman. Inheriting the store, Thomas moved it to Hollister in 1872 when the railroad bypassed San Juan. He also was a successful rancher and hotelier in Hollister. Thomas married Isabella Breen in 1869.

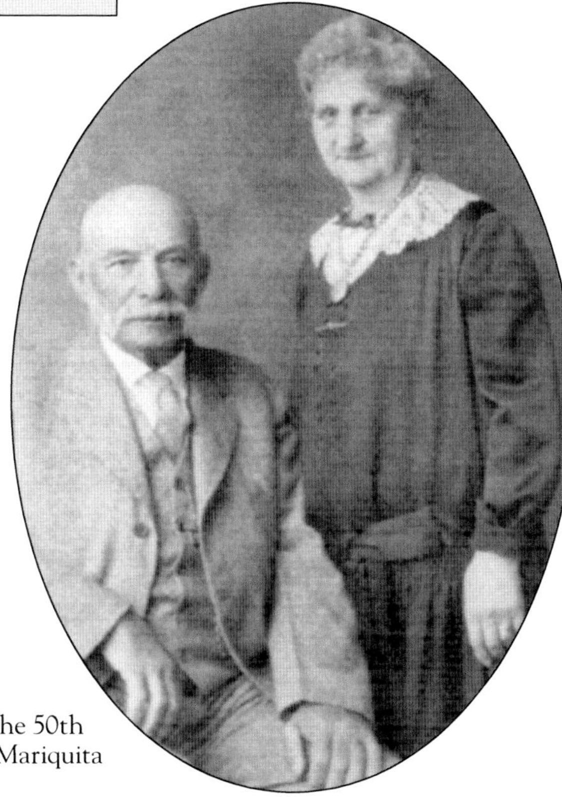

This photograph was taken at the time of the 50th wedding anniversary of P. E. G. Anzar and Mariquita "Mary" Zanetta Breen Anzar in 1927.

A native of England, John Comfort immigrated to San Juan in the 1850s. He became the partner of Angelo Zanetta, owner of the Plaza Hotel. Comfort, a genial host, oversaw the operation of the hotel and the barroom. He died at an early age and was mourned by all who knew him.

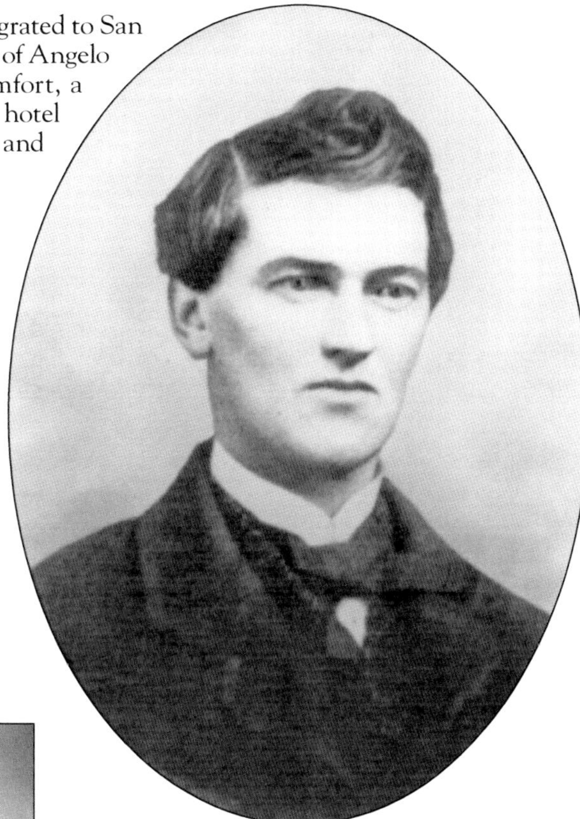

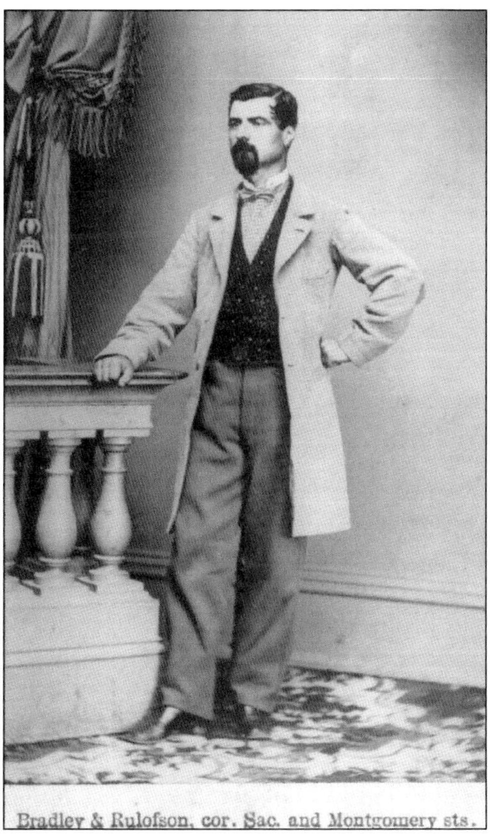

Angelo Zanetta was born in Northern Italy, the son of a hotelier. He came to America and ran a hotel in St. Louis before moving to California. After operating a hotel on Third Street, he built the Plaza Hotel on the ruins of the old Spanish soldiers' barracks. He and partner John Comfort built the Plaza Hall and the Plaza Stable, thereby owning three buildings in town. After a lengthy illness, Zanetta died and was buried in the town cemetery.

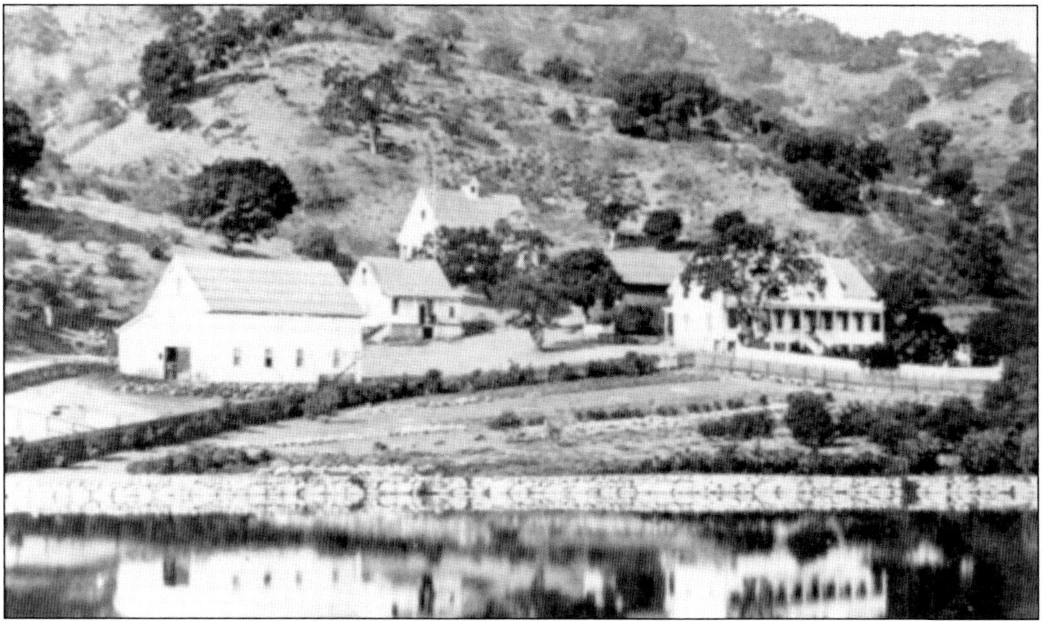

Dr. Thomas Flint was born in Maine is 1824 and came to California with his brother and cousin in 1851. He settled in San Juan Bautista in 1856 and purchased the 35,000-acre Rancho San Justo with his partner, Colonel Hollister. Later, Col. William Hollister split the partnership and selected the acreage where the city of Hollister was founded. Dr. Flint eventually owned the Coast Line Stage Company in San Juan and constructed the home seen in this early photograph of his ranch.

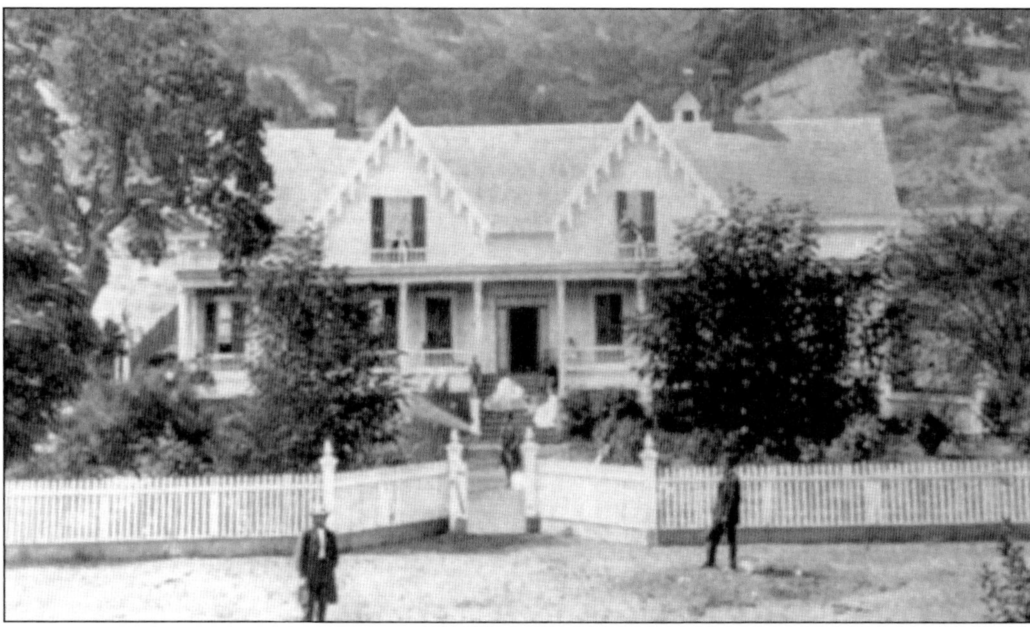

The Flint-Bixby House, built in 1864, was home to three families—that of Thomas Flint, Benjamin Flint, and their cousin Llewellyn Bixby. The home included a central kitchen and dining room, and the wives rotated the supervision of the cooking for the combined families. Each family had its own sleeping quarters, and the men shared a separate office. This photograph was taken in 1865.

Born in Vermont and educated at Dartmouth College in New Hampshire, Dr. Charles Cargill came to San Juan in 1872 and opened his medical office. In conjunction with his practice, he opened a store selling drugs, stationery, schoolbooks, and music instruments. Cargill also served as the Wells Fargo agent and postmaster. A school trustee and state assemblyman, he was elected justice of the peace in 1878, an office he held until his death in 1900.

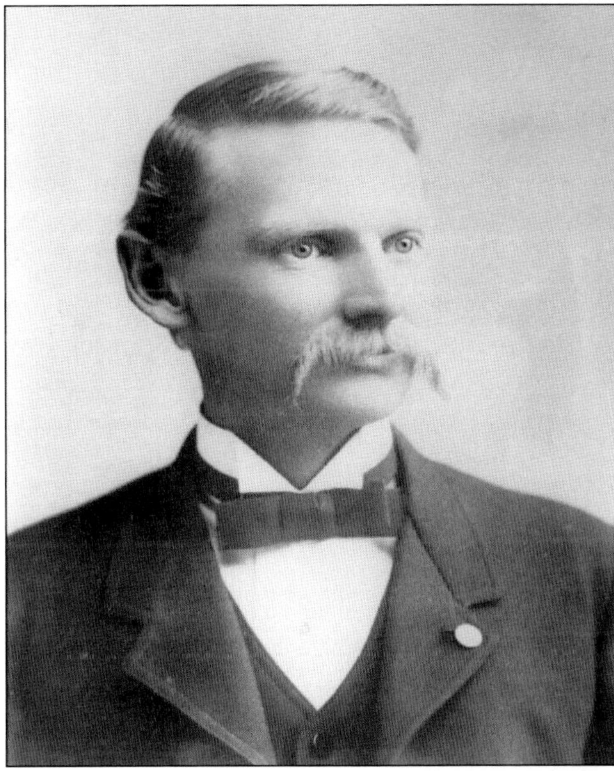

Dr. Cargill was the organizer and leader of the San Juan Bautista Cornet Band. These accomplished musicians played at all the civic and cultural functions.

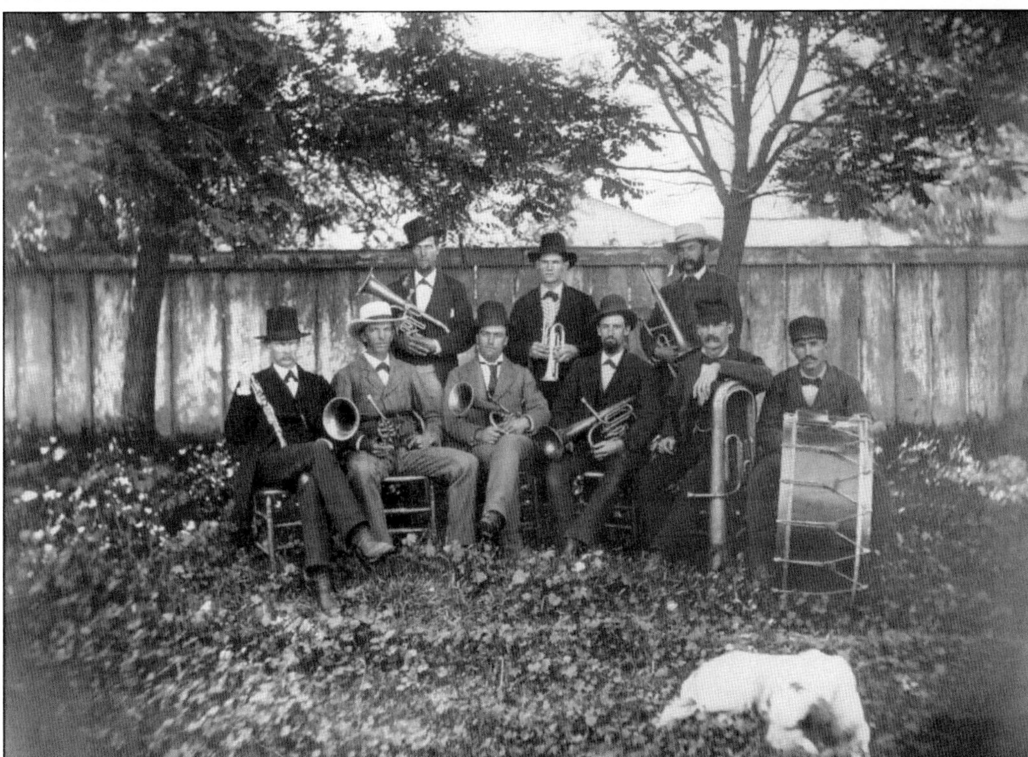

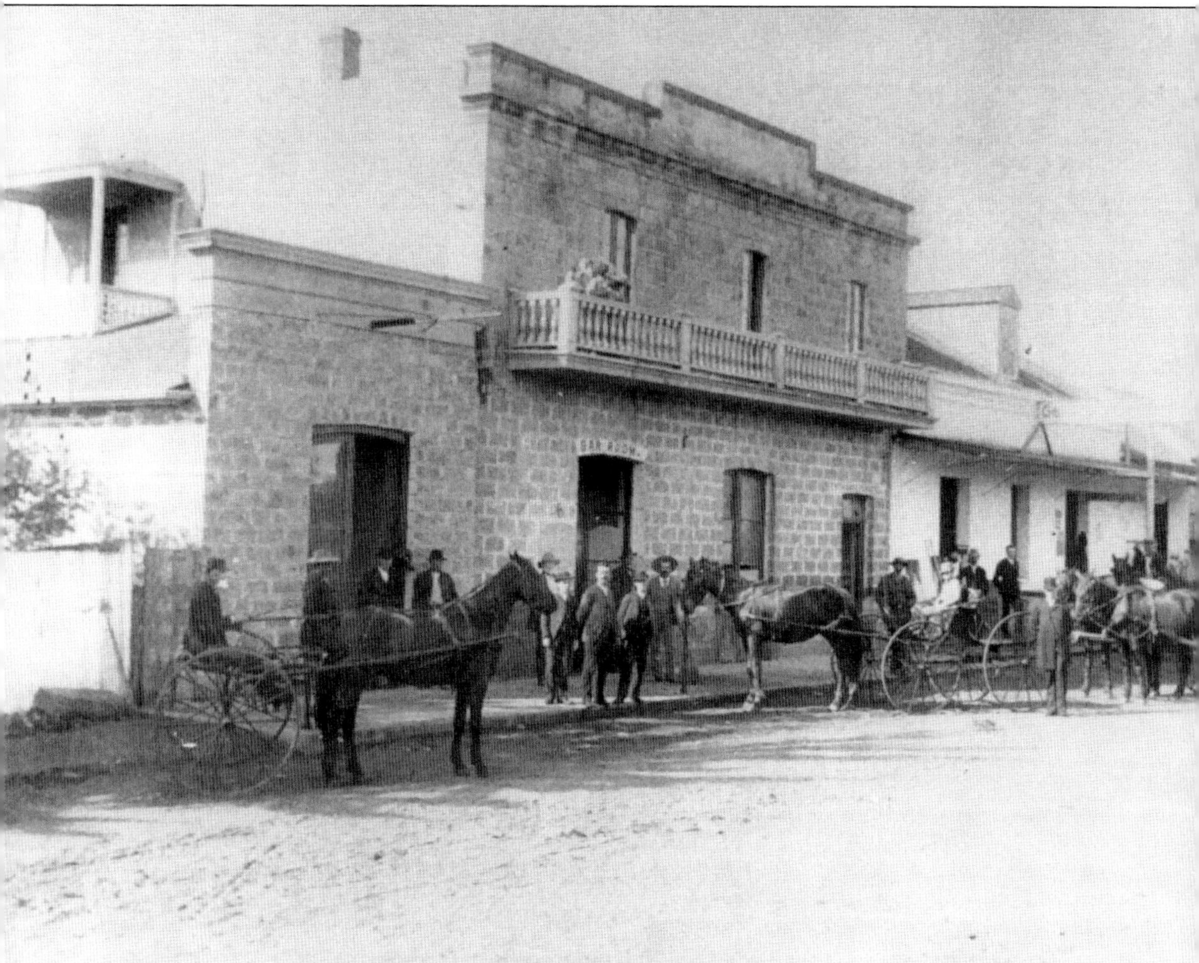

Antoine Taix was born in France in 1852. He left for San Francisco in 1871 and held many jobs there. Ill health brought him to Monterey County, where he worked on a sheep ranch. After becoming a citizen in 1879, he arrived in San Juan in 1883 and opened a butcher shop. He was one of the early mayors and was also a director of the local bank. Taix constructed this building, which he used as a general merchandise business.

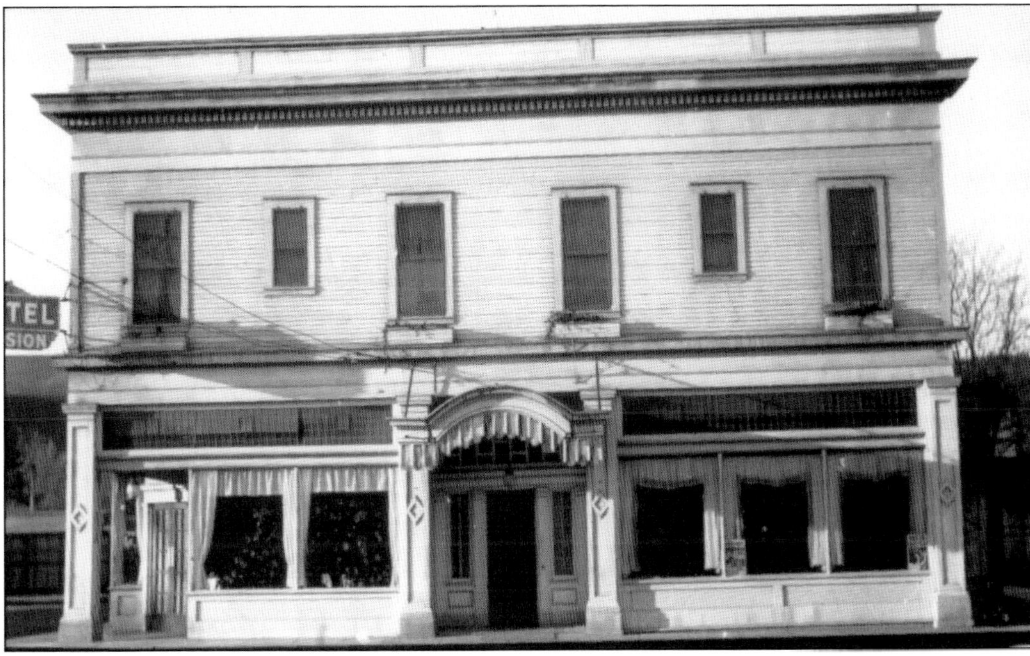

Known for its fine dining room, the Hotel Mission catered to visitors from all over the world. A typical lunch included soup, salad, choice of entrée and vegetable, dessert, and coffee, tea, or milk for 65¢. Dinner specials were 75¢. The state purchased the property in 1933 and demolished the building.

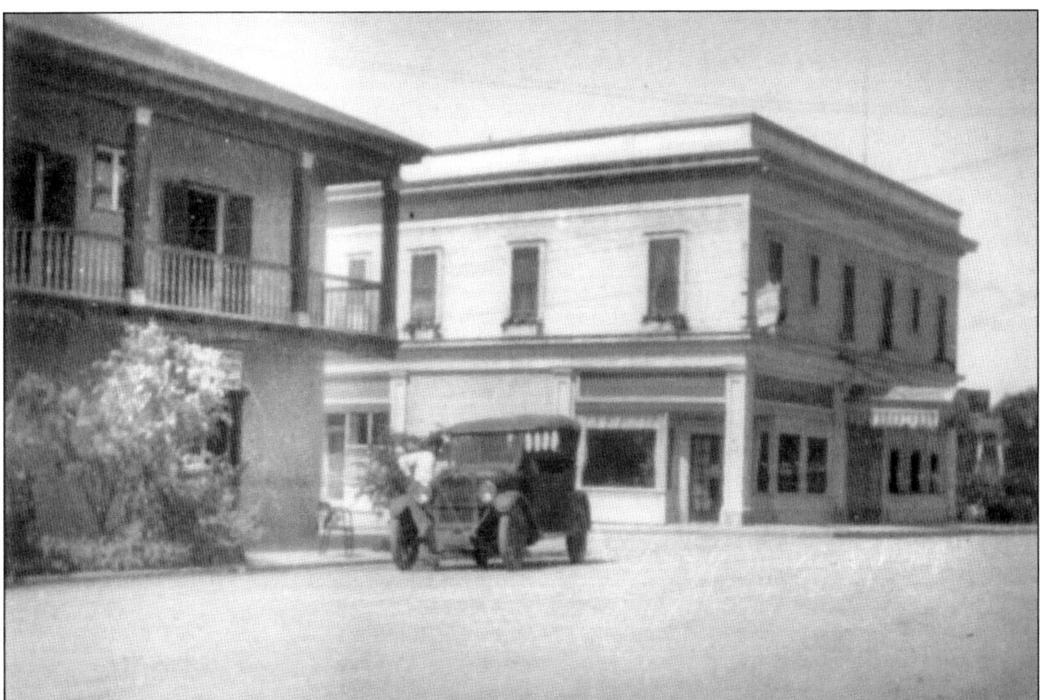

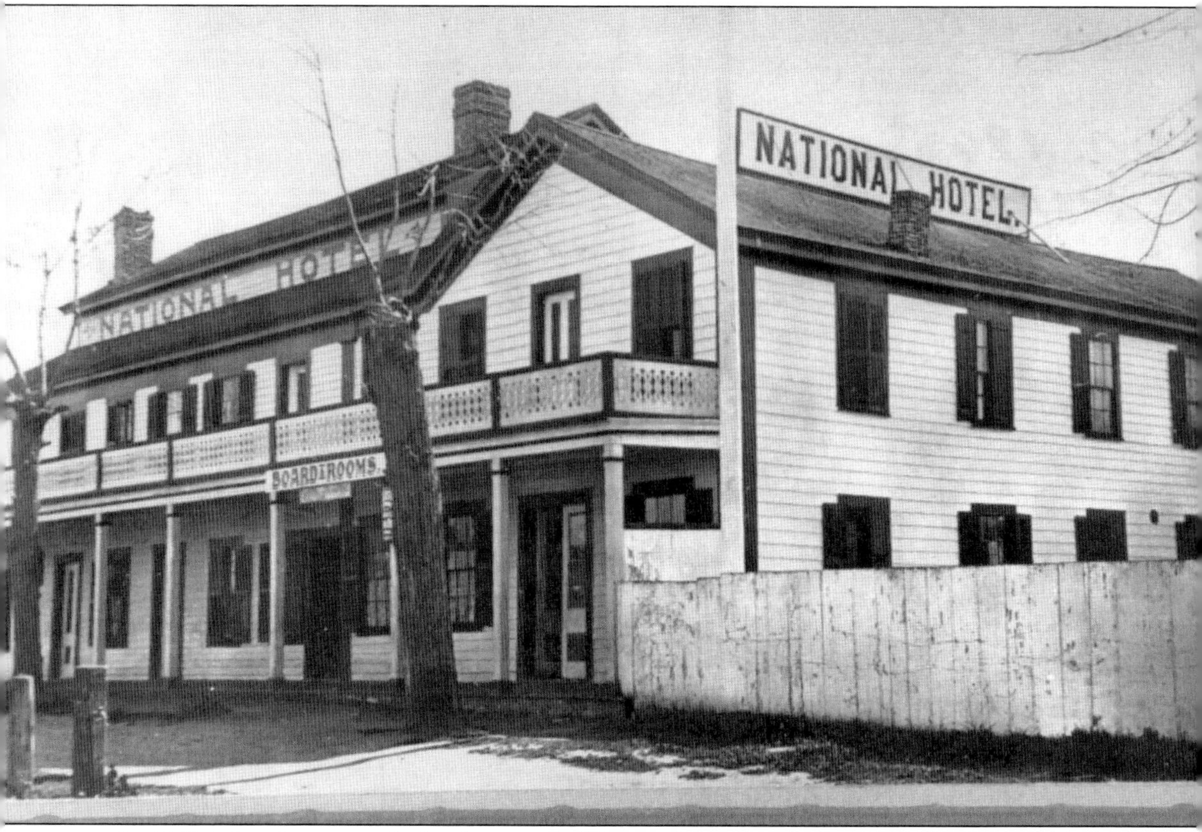

In 1858, John Geaster built the three-story National Hotel at the corner of Second and San Jose Streets. The first floor contained the bar, billiard room, dining room, and kitchen. The guest rooms were located on the second floor, and the third floor was used by the Texas Masonic Order for meetings. Geaster was a Mason and one of the group's charter members, yet he was blackballed from the lodge in 1865 when the 6th California Infantry Volunteers took over the building. It was to become the headquarters for Camp Lowe, whose duty was to prevent uprisings from the many Southern sympathizers.

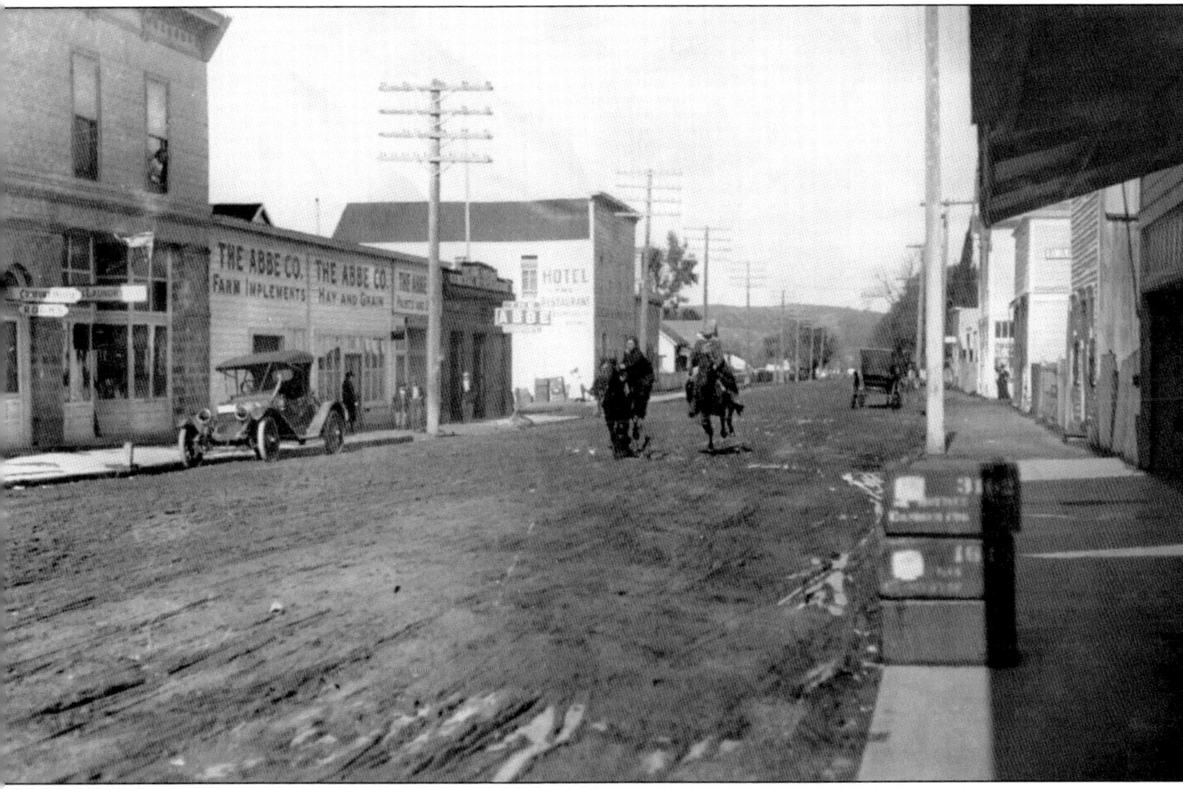

This early photograph of Third Street shows the business district between Polk and Mariposa Streets. The Carlitos Store, seen in the background, was one of the important buildings in town. The two-story structure in the far background is the American and Swiss Hotel.

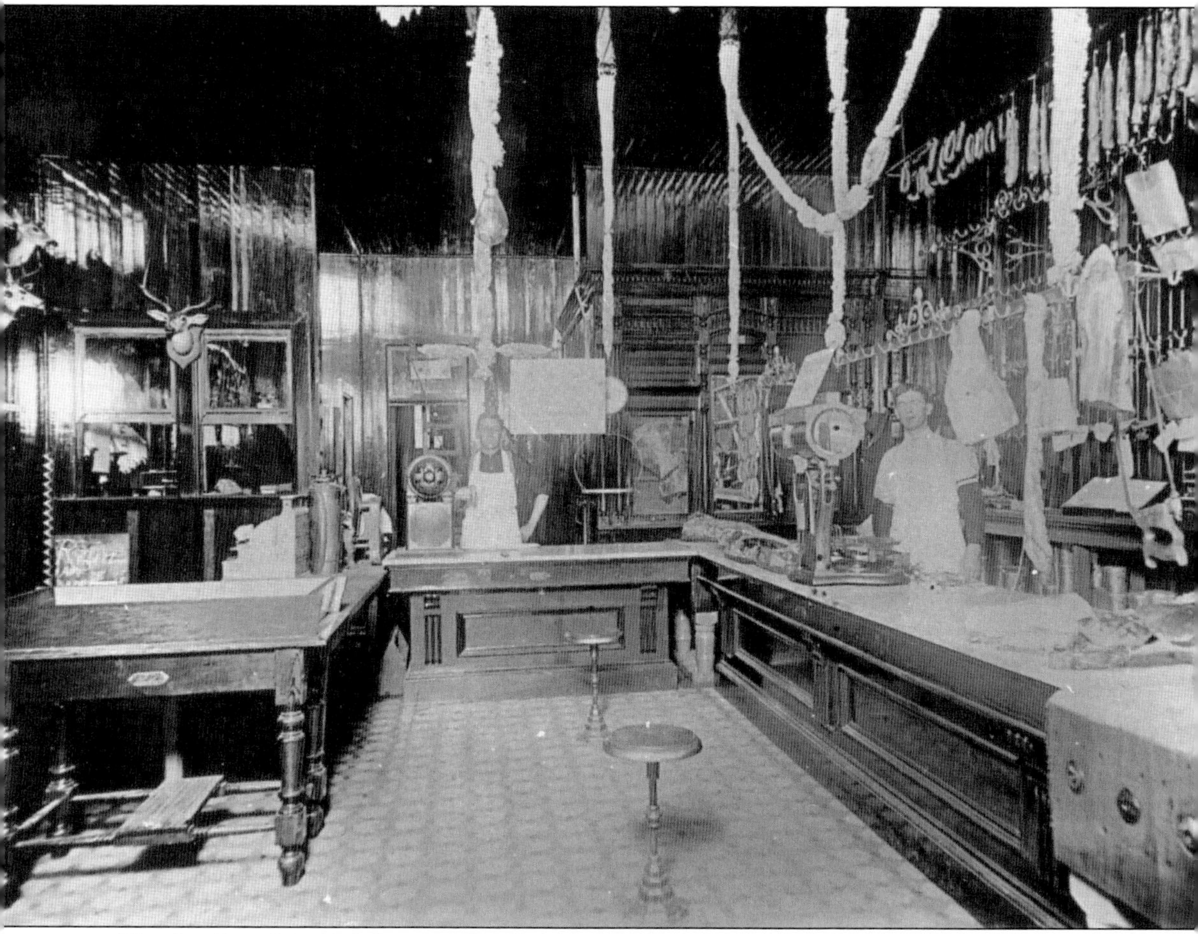

The San Juan Meat Market on Third Street was owned and operated by John Marentis and Jake Beautler. Meat was cut to order and weighed on the scales shown in the photograph. Fresh meat was rare since there was no refrigeration.

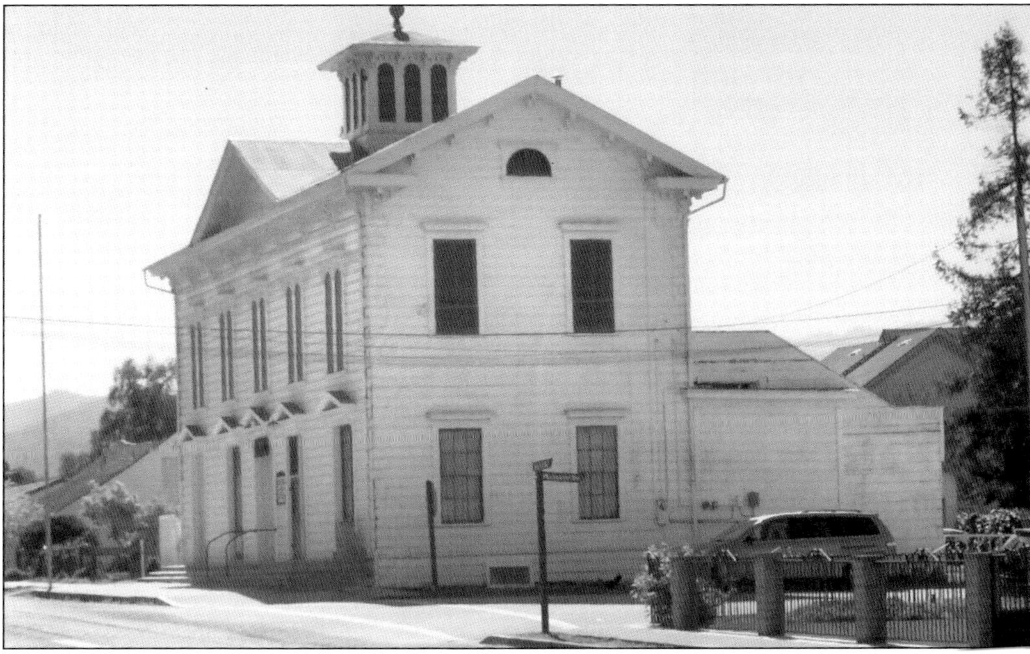

The Masonic Lodge No. 46, chartered on May 6, 1854, had for many years met in many buildings, including the National Hotel. When membership reached 100, the lodge decided to build its own facility. This building was constructed in 1868 at the corner of Second and Muckelemi Streets. The Texas Lodge was so named because most of the members came from Texas after the Civil War. The Masonic Lodge was an imposing building whose first floor was used as the city hall, post office, and library. The Masonic building is still used for lodge meetings today.

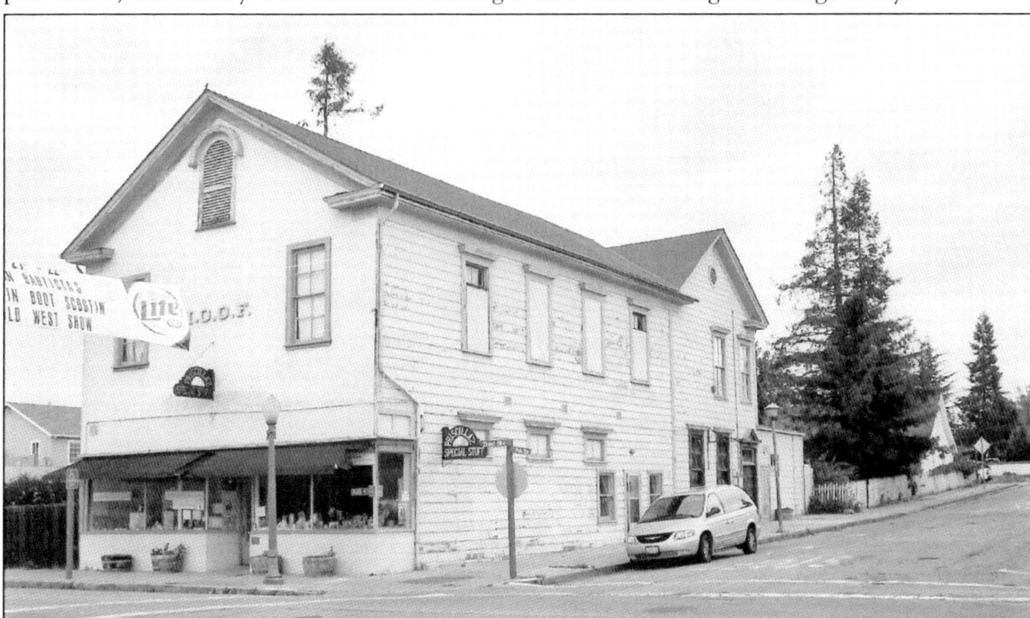

The Odd Fellows Lodge was built as a school in 1869. The lodge bought the building in 1907 and moved it to its present location at Third and Mariposa Streets.

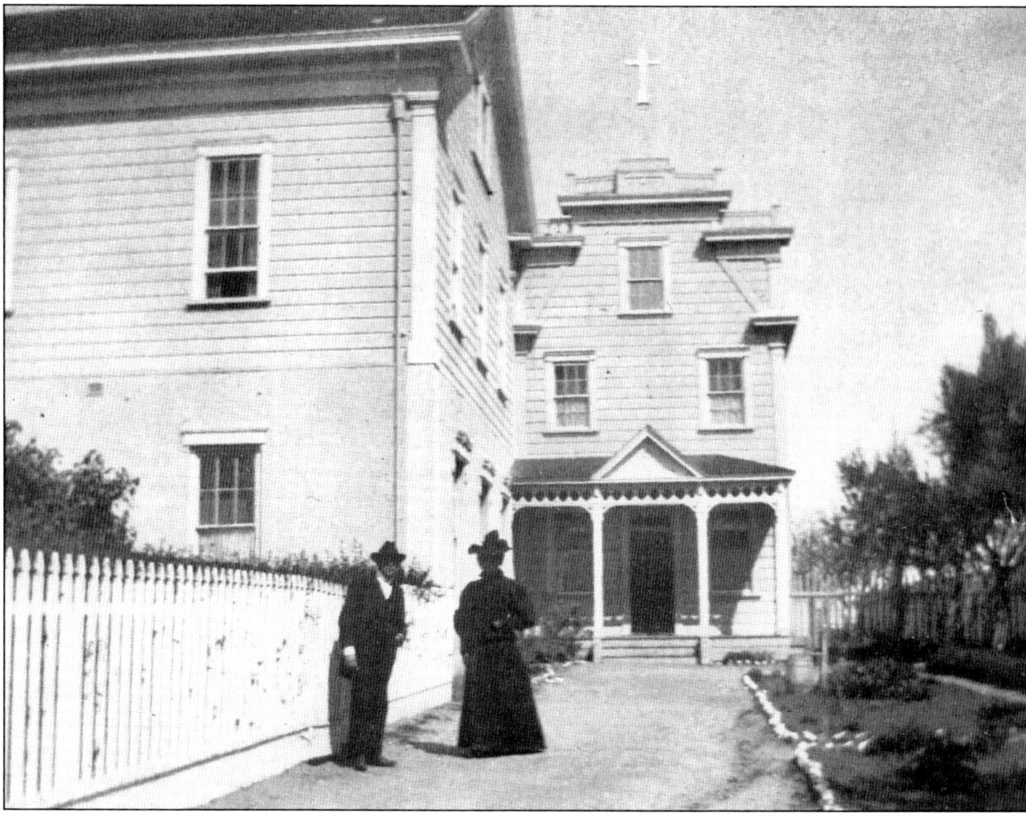

In 1861, the Sisters of Charity opened an orphanage and day school behind the mission. Over the years, it was operated by several orders of nuns. The site included a two-story dormitory as well as a convent for the sisters. The school was destroyed by earthquake on April 24, 1890. As a result, the children were sent to other schools and the building was subsequently torn down.

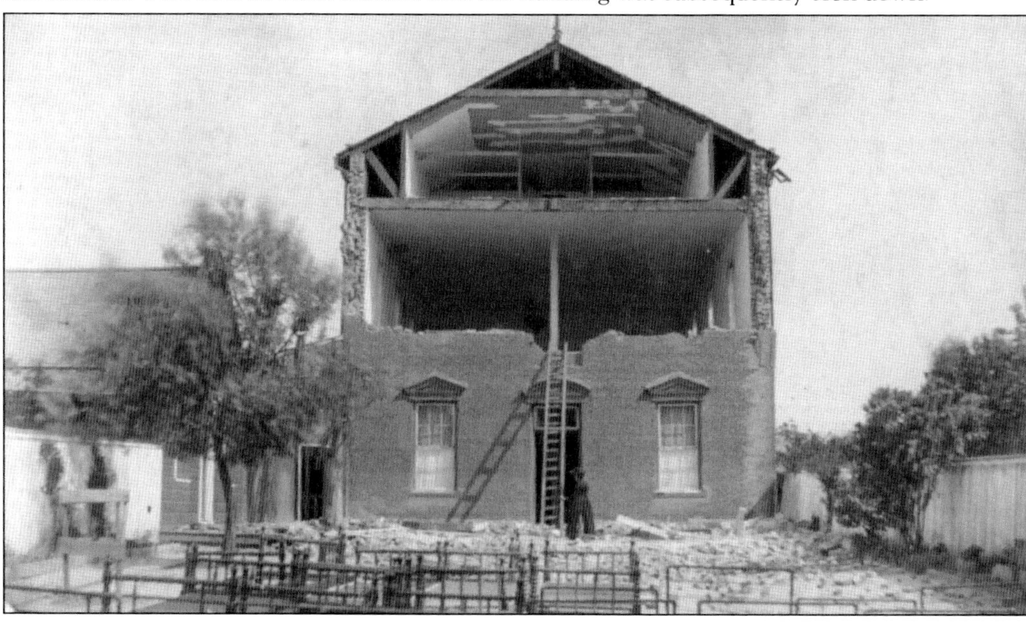

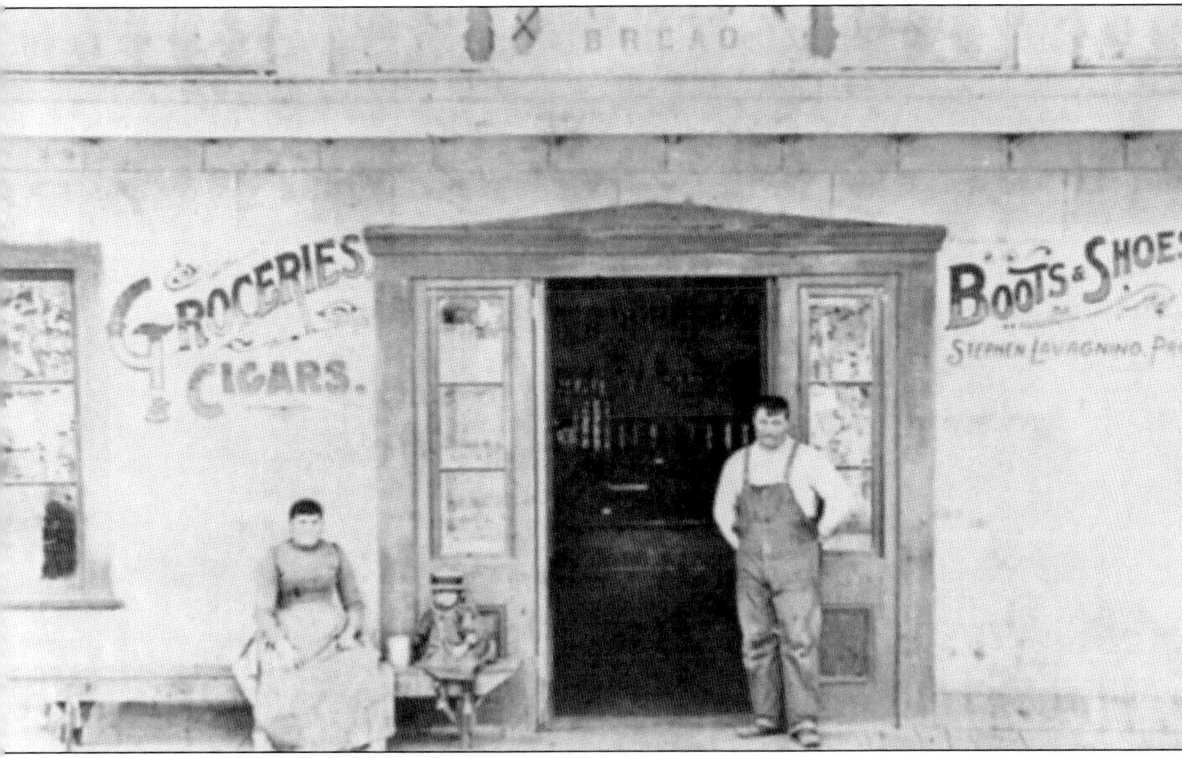

Stephen Lavanino and his wife and daughter pose in front of their general store on Third and Washington Streets. The family lived on the second floor. Lavanino refused to reside there after the 1906 earthquake, so a new home was built on Fourth and Washington Streets.

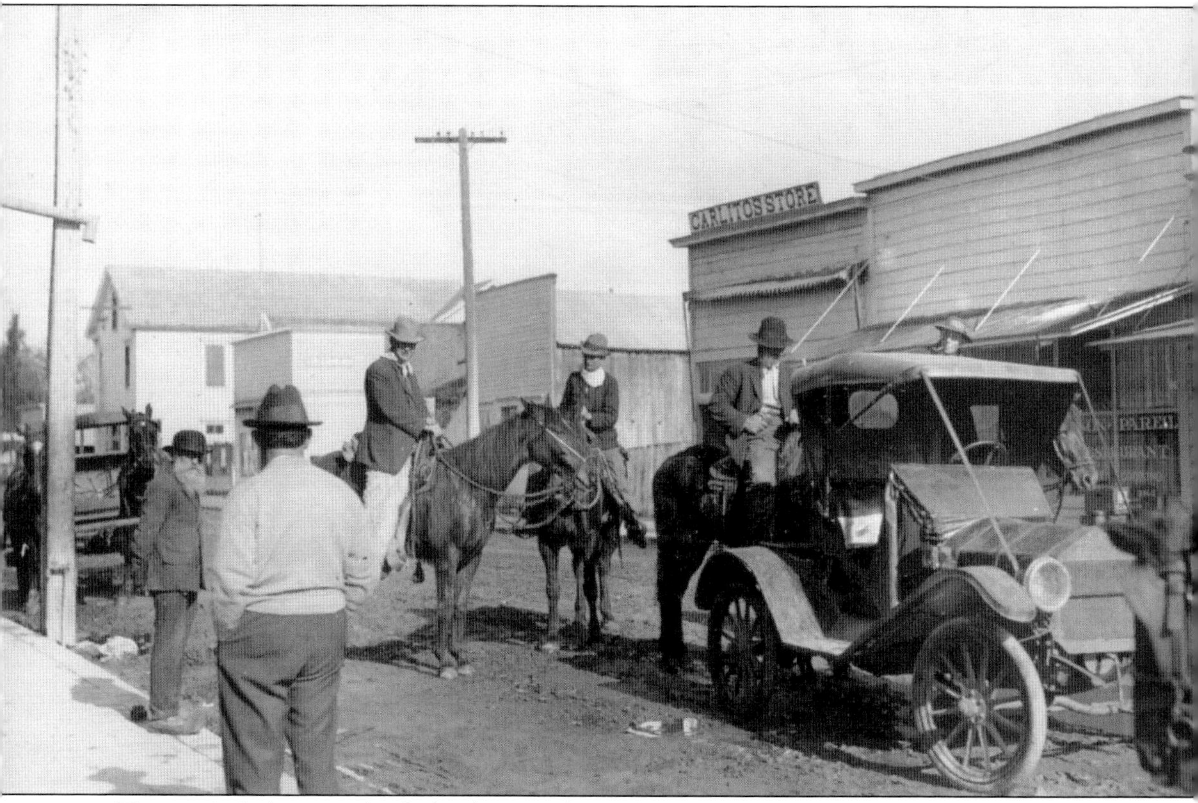

This *c.* 1915 photograph of Third Street shows the transition between horses and automobiles.

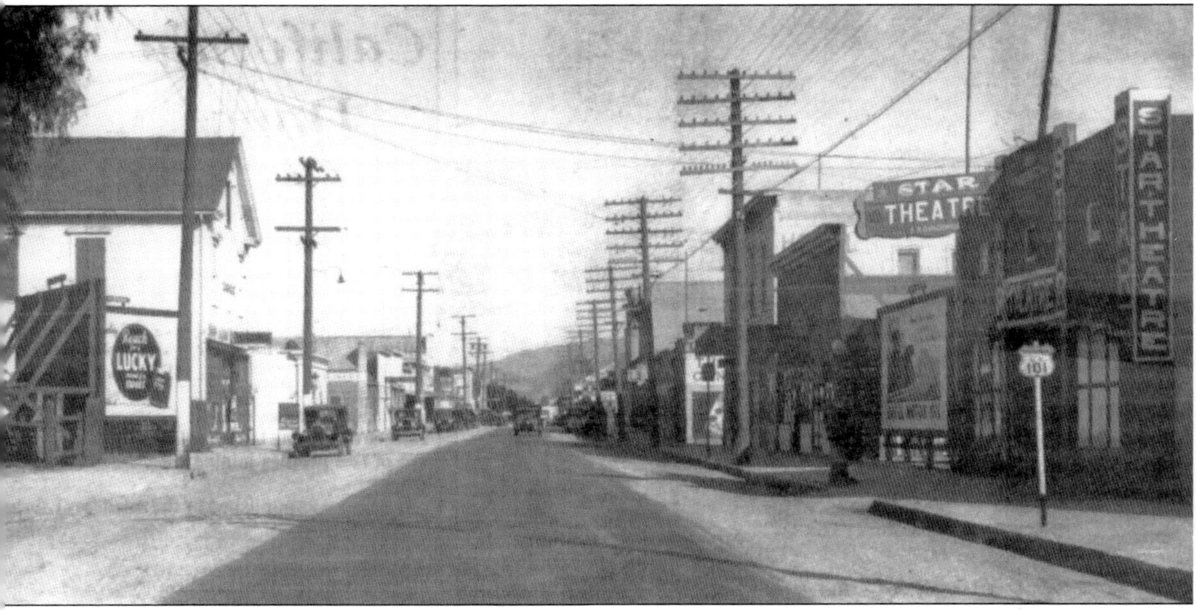

This photograph of Third Street was taken in the 1930s. At the time, many people still had barns behind their houses where they kept livestock and automobiles.

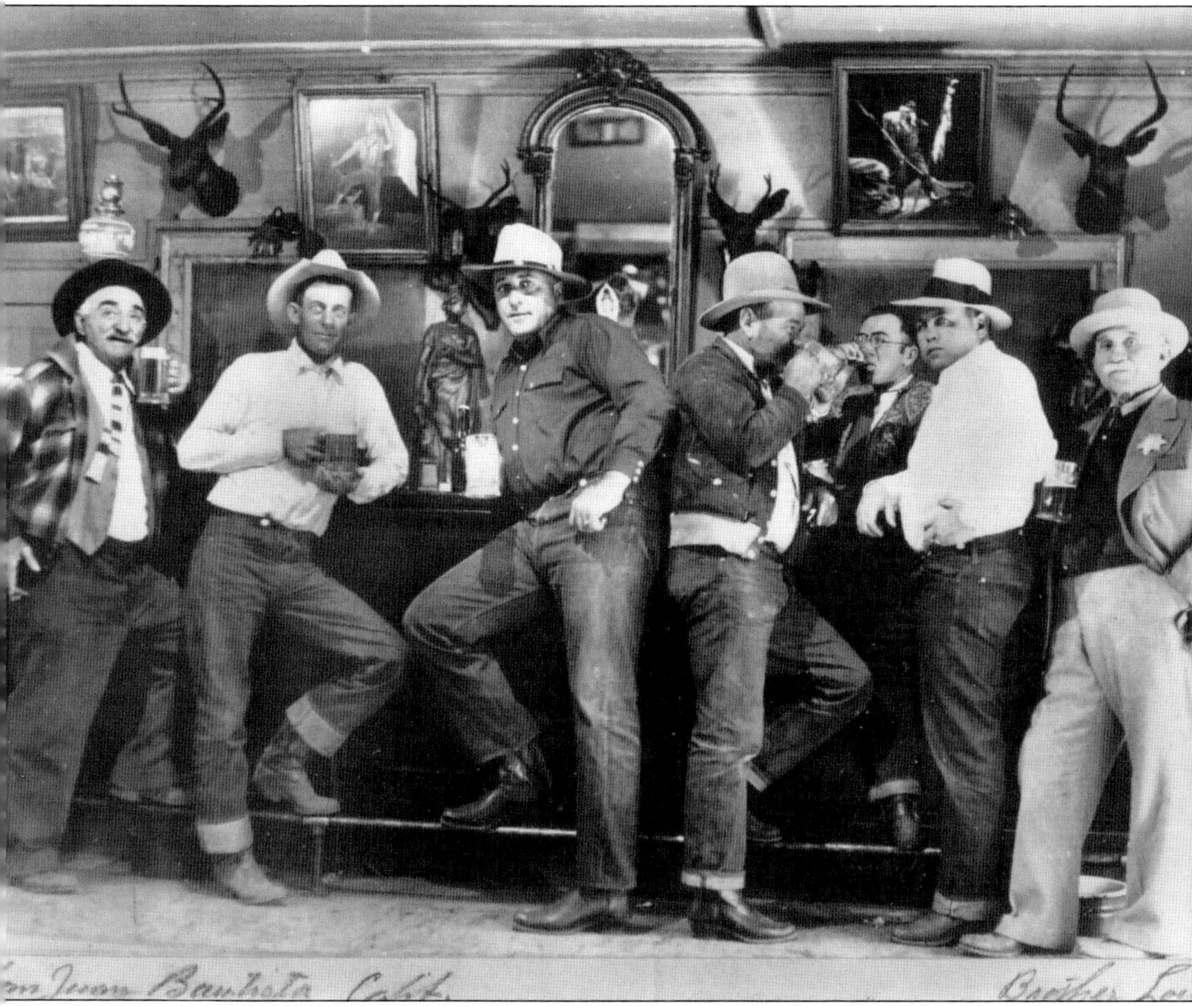

This scene depicts the Plaza Hotel barroom shortly after the end of Prohibition in 1933. "C. C." Zanetta (right), the son of the hotel builder, served as town constable for many years. Next to Zanetta is Edward Murphy, a superior court judge from San Francisco.

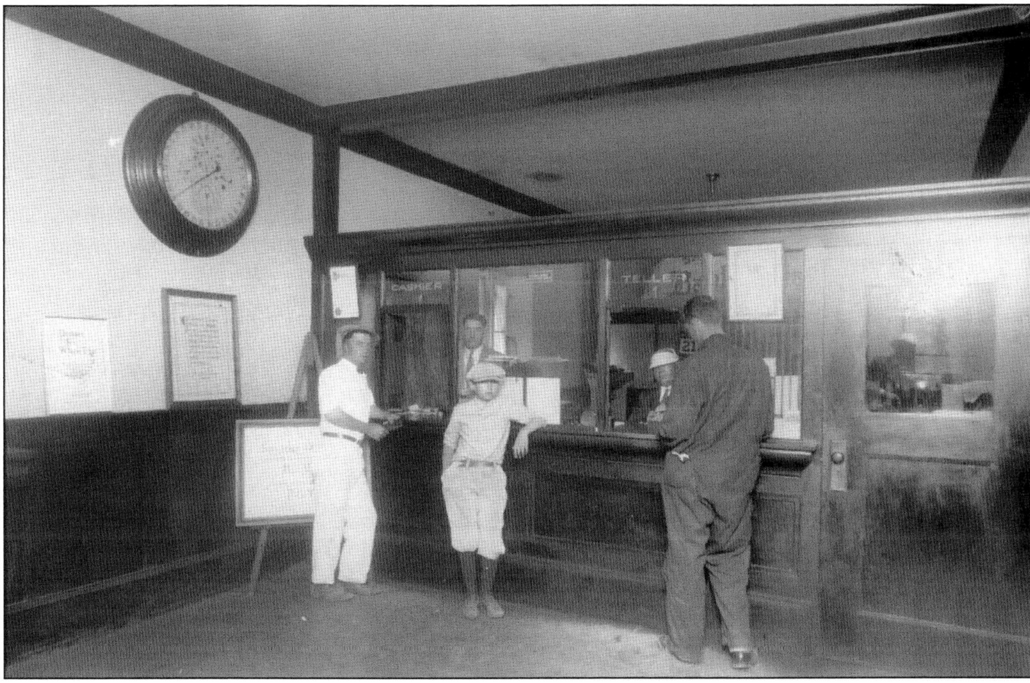

A. P. Gianini, founder of the Bank of Italy, opened a branch in San Juan. The bank, shown here in a 1920s interior photograph, later became the Bank of America.

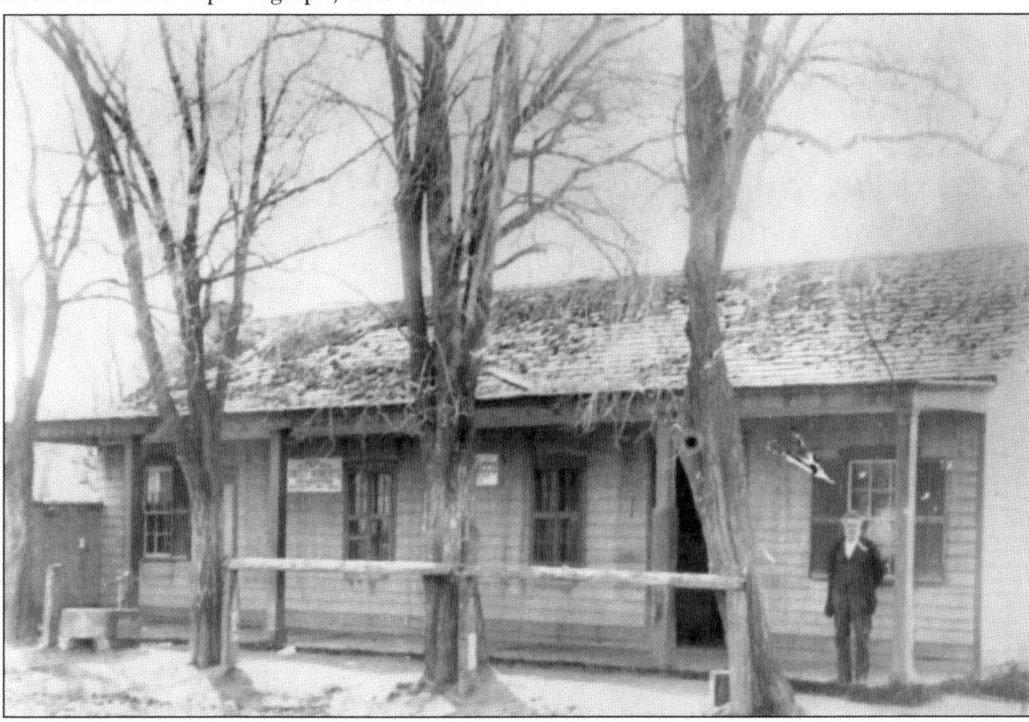

Ed Kemp, standing in front of his saloon, was known as a quiet and unassuming man. His establishment was more of a social club than a saloon, where businessmen and farmers would gather to discuss business and politics.

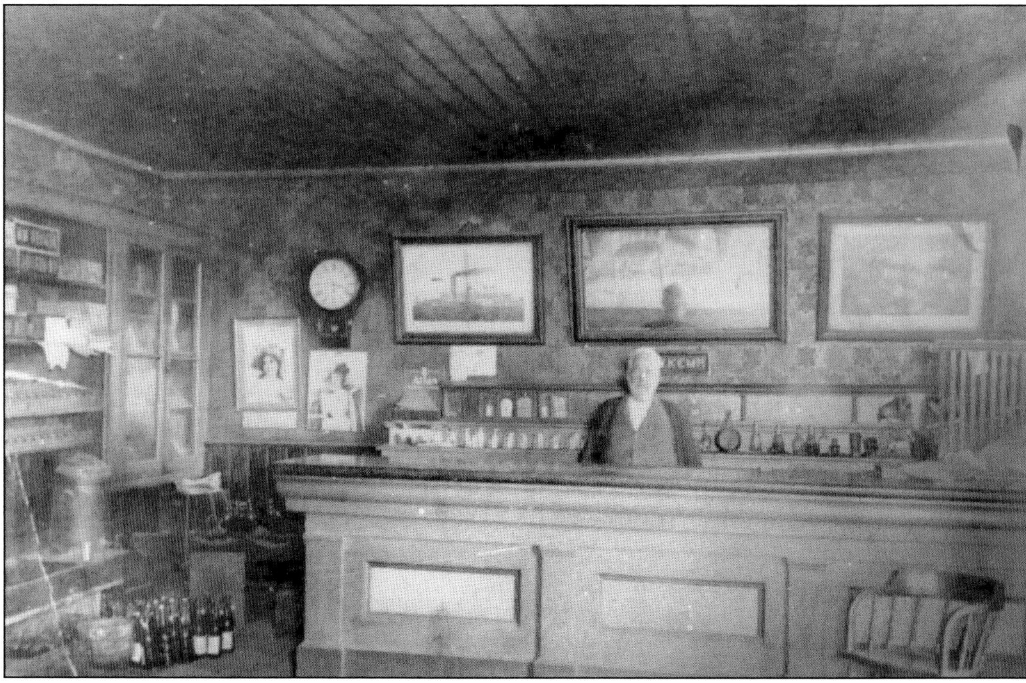

The Kemp Saloon on Second Street, pictured here with Mr. Kemp behind the bar, was the scene of a famous killing in town. Andrew Barker, always armed and known for his violent temper, accused Vic McGarvey of stealing $5,000 and swore he would kill him. McGarvey borrowed a shotgun, returned to the saloon, and killed Barker. McGarvey was tried but a jury acquitted him of murder.

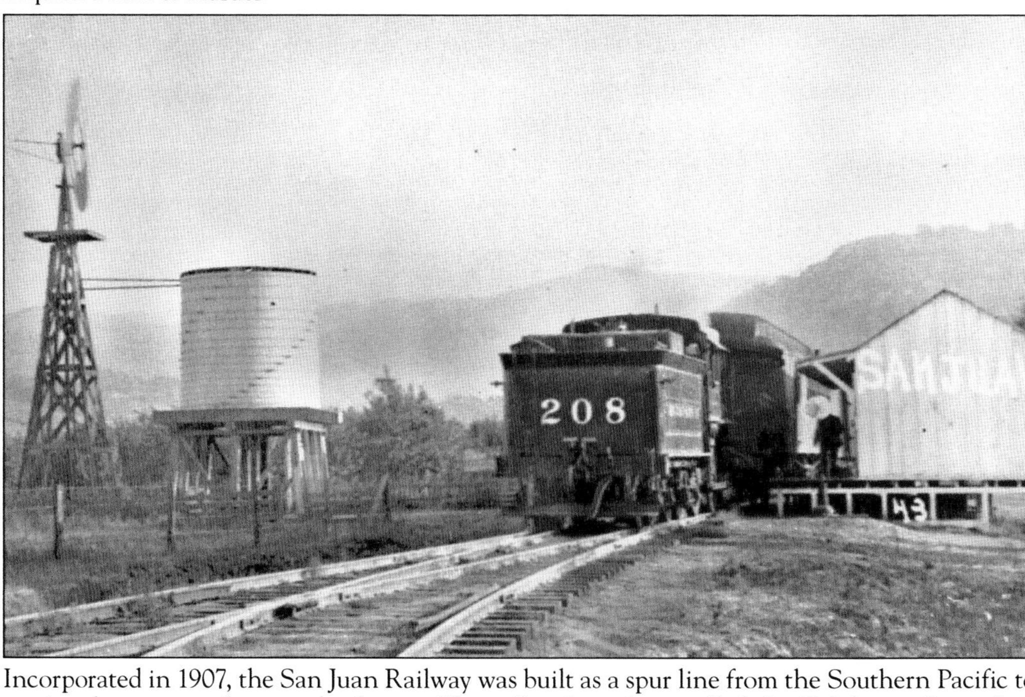

Incorporated in 1907, the San Juan Railway was built as a spur line from the Southern Pacific to service the cement plant south of town. The railroad was later called the California Central.

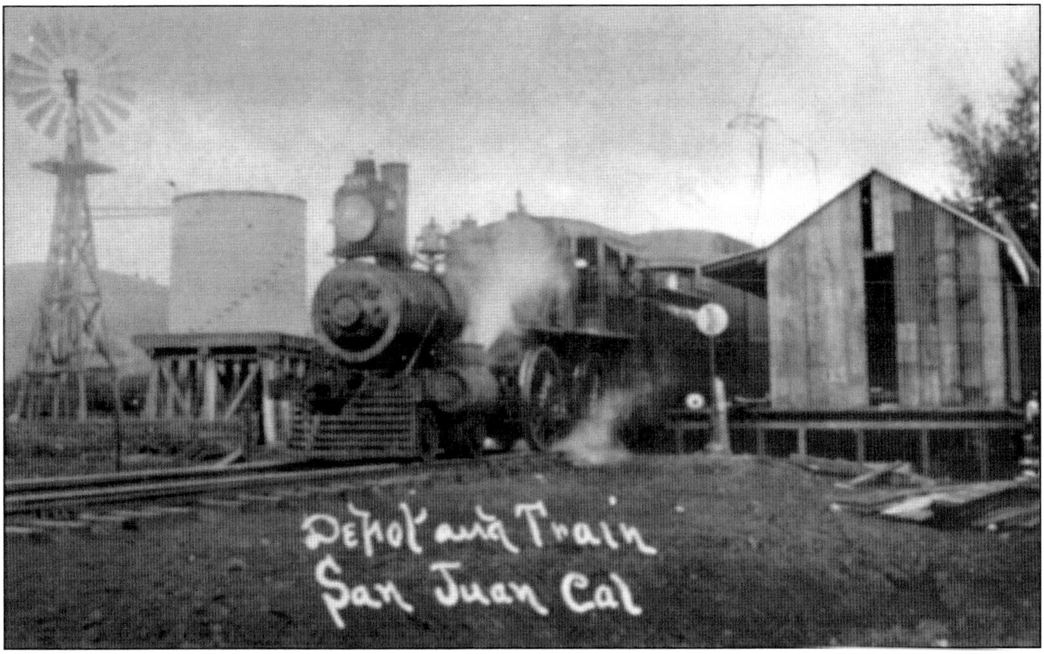

The California Central depot was located at the junction of Third and Alameda Streets. Supplies for the mines and local businesses were brought to town on this line, and cement and agricultural products were shipped out. The line was closed in the late 1940s.

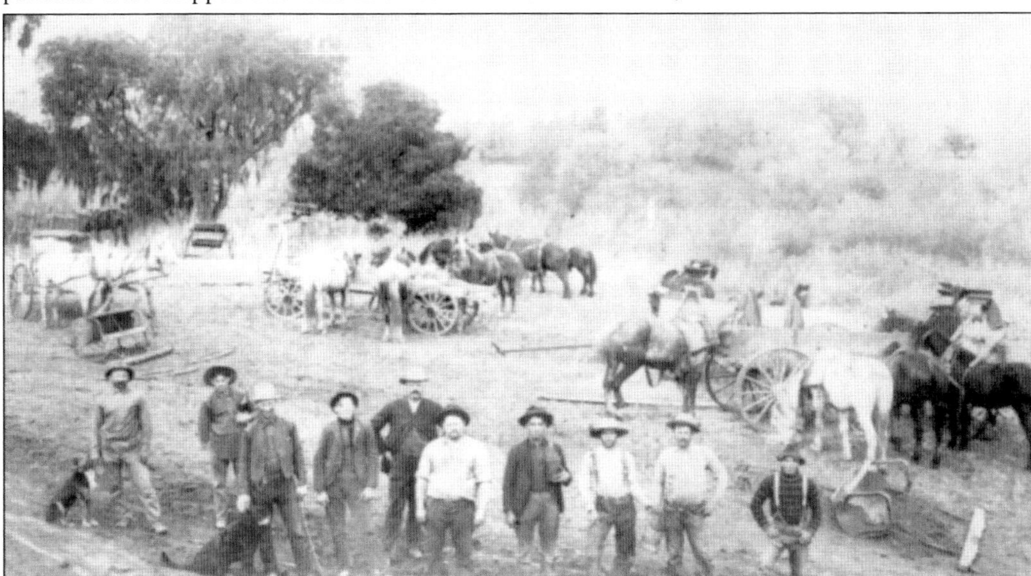

Each landowner in the area was charged a road tax of $2 a year for building and repairing roads. Owners of land could get out of the tax by agreeing to work on the roads. In the 1880s, road building was a labor-intensive job. Picks, shovels, Fresno scrapers (early road graders), and a lot of muscle were the only tools available. The scrapers were metal scoops drawn by a horse or mule as a man held down the scoop with a long metal handle. Frequently, the leading edge of the scraper would hit a rock and turn over. If the man did not let go soon enough, he would be injured or killed.

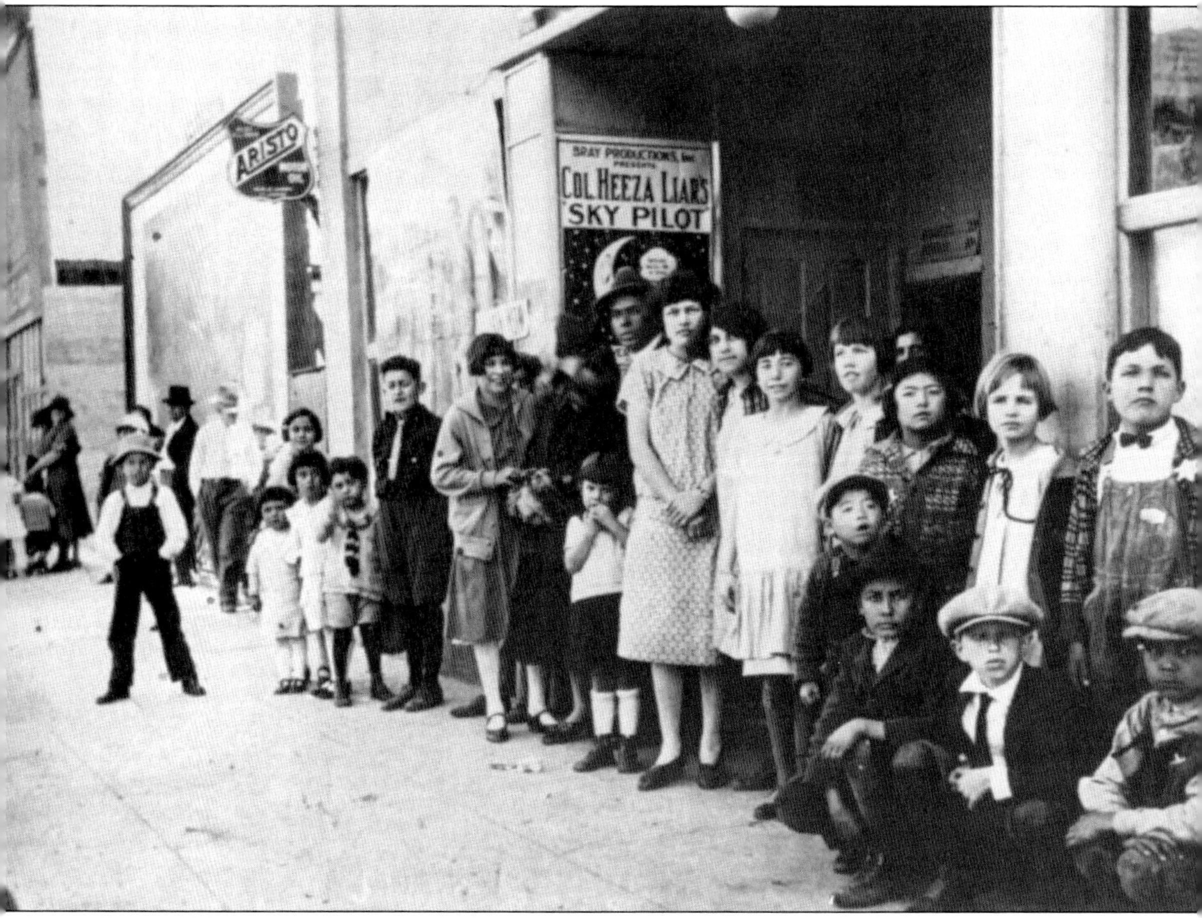

Saturday matinee at the Star Theater, the only theater in town, was very popular with the kids. The film being shown in this mid-1920s photograph is Cal Heeza Liar's *Sky Pilot*.

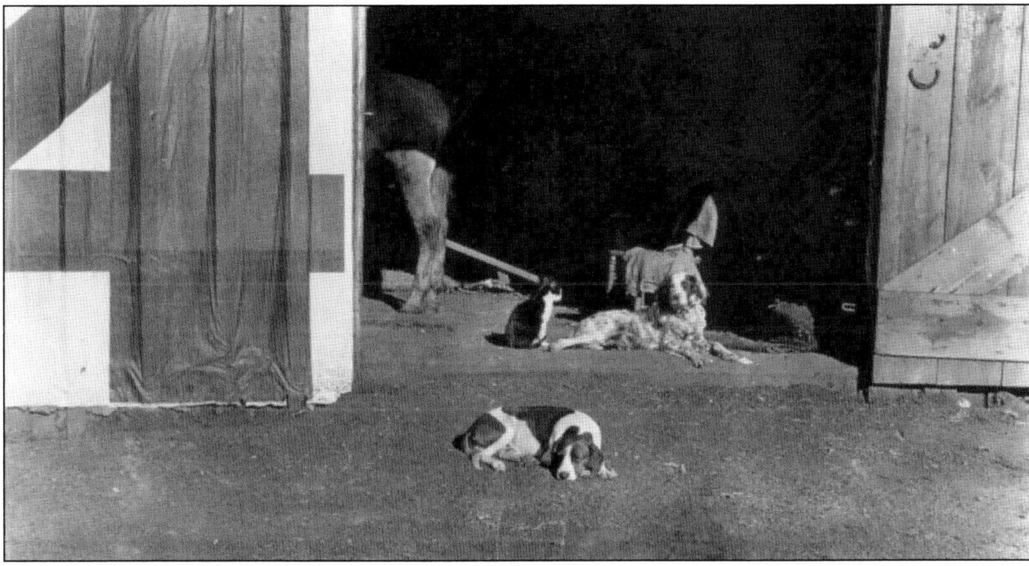

There were several successful blacksmiths in town because of the large number of freight wagons and carriages. A good blacksmith could repair anything made of metal and was always kept busy shoeing horses. A skilled harness maker was also perpetually in demand. This scene from the 1930s shows a quiet day at Sam Silk's blacksmith.

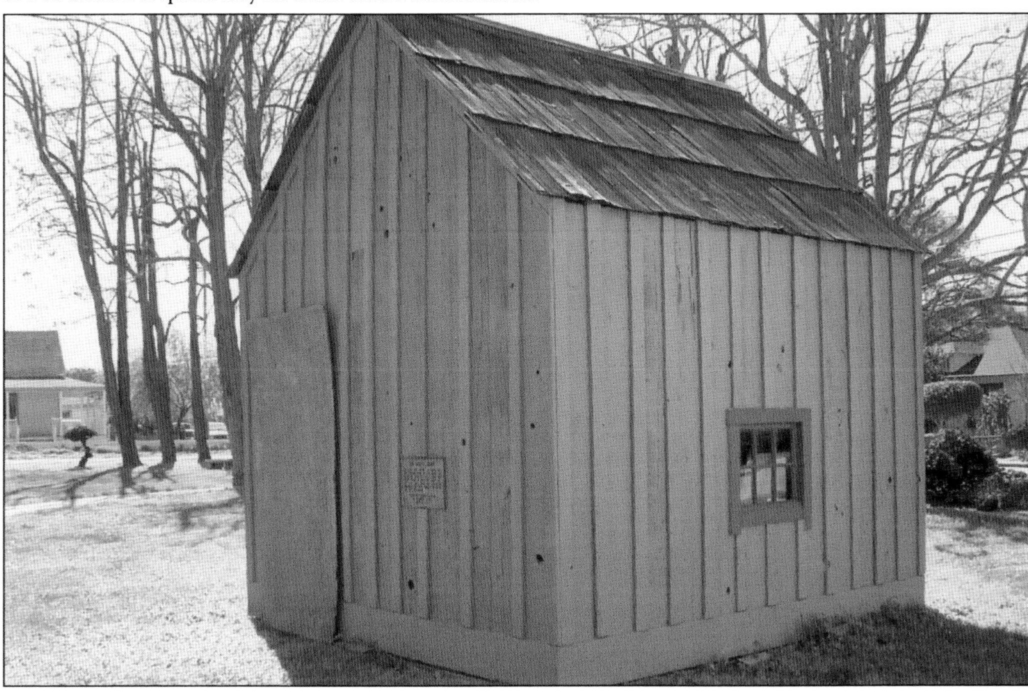

Jim Jack came to San Juan from China in the 1880s to work for the Flint ranch. He was initially hired to poison squirrels that ruined the grain crops, but his job soon changed to gathering the wild mustard that grew in the valley. This crop was sold to the French restaurants in San Francisco for a good profit. Jim Jack was greatly admired for his generosity to the poor and all missed him when he returned to China to die. In 2006, the San Juan Bautista Historical Society restored his one-room cabin and moved it to the site of the museum at Third and Monterey Streets.

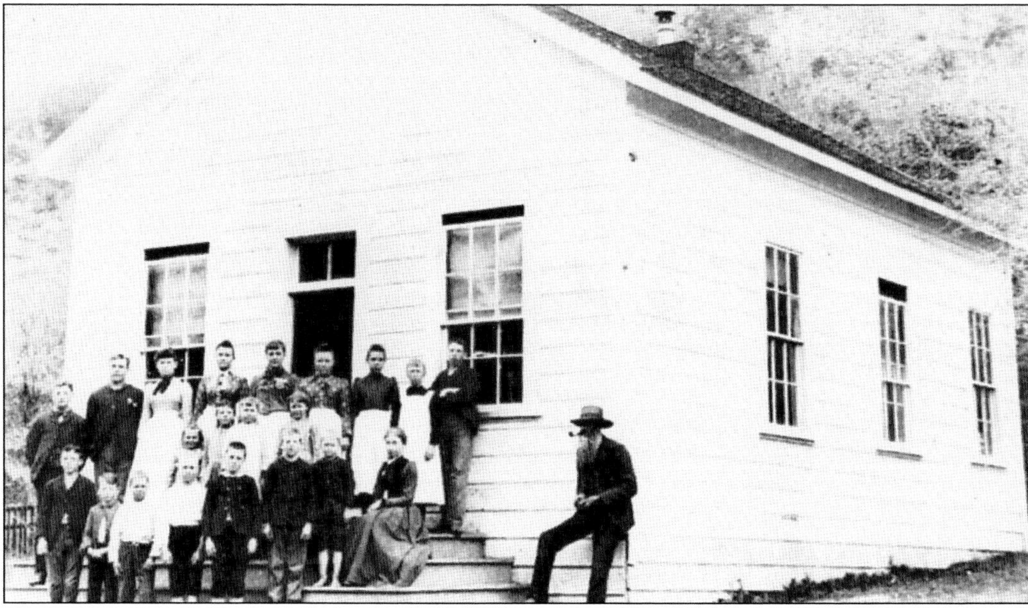

As the town grew, a school district was formed and property owners were charged a school tax of $2 per year. The first educational institution was built in 1859 near the city cemetery. The school shown here was constructed outside of town in San Juan Canyon. The one-room building housed students from all grades, who were taught by just one teacher.

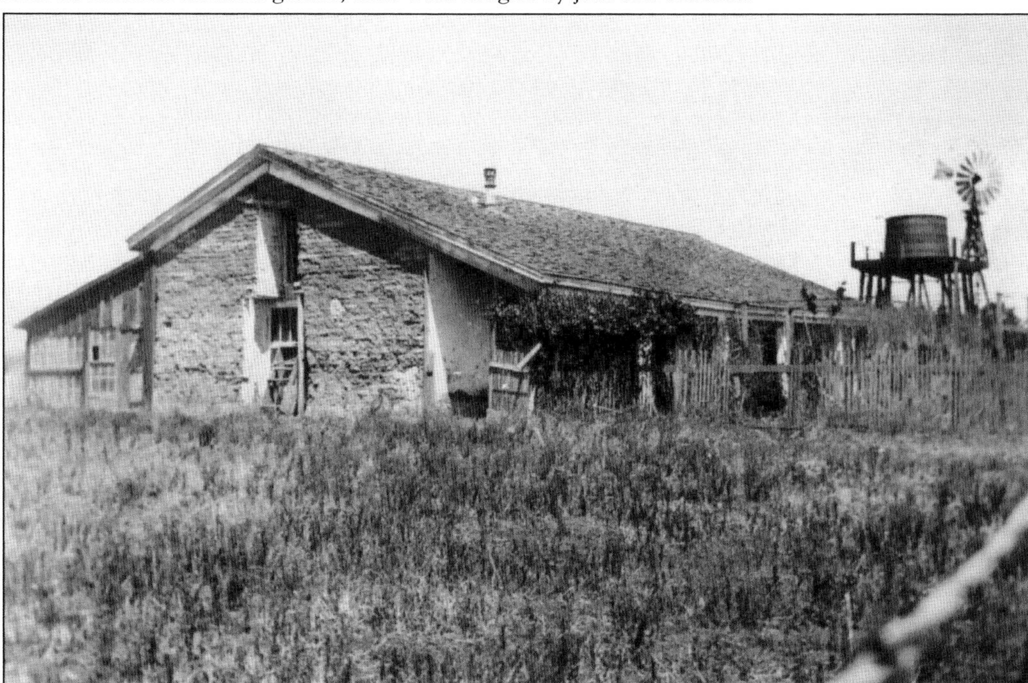

The old Mariano Castro Adobe was still standing, though in decay, in the 1930s. This home was located on Third Street southeast of the business district. In addition to this house, the Castro family owned Rancho de las Animas northeast of San Juan. Consisting of 28,000 acres, the site is the present city of Gilroy.

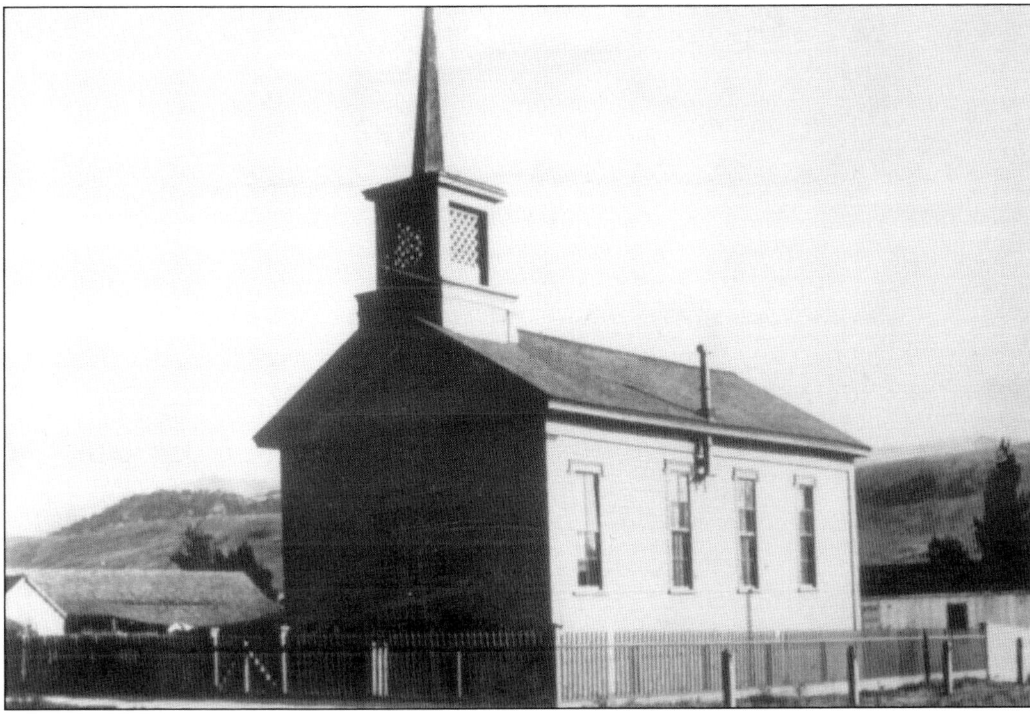

Built in 1863, this Baptist church was located near the cemetery. Many years later, it was moved to its present site at Third and Muckelemi Streets. It is now called the Glad Tidings Church.

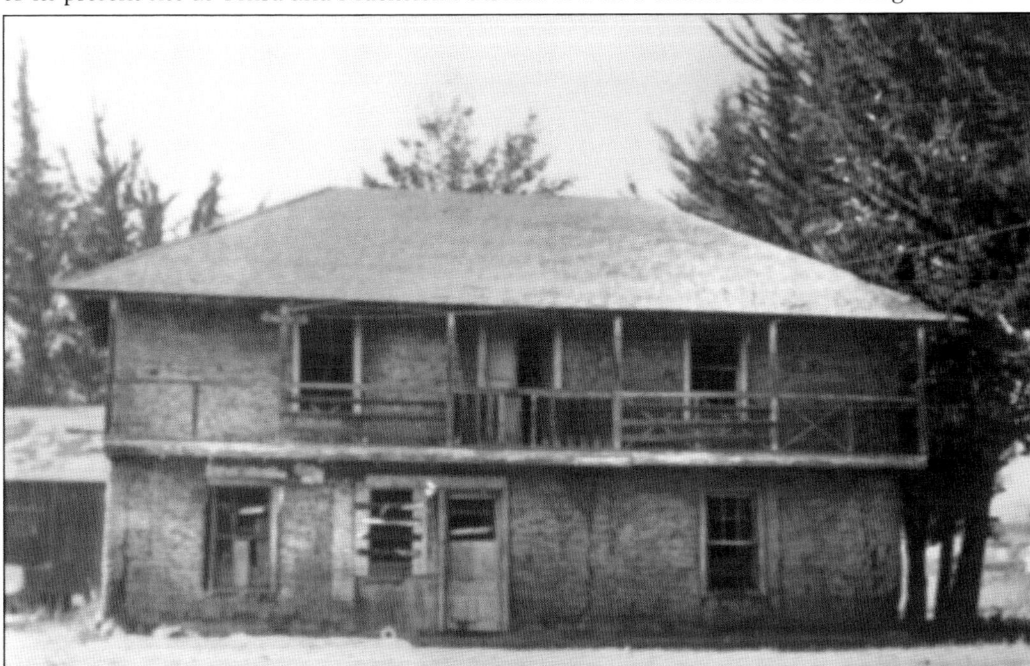

The old Pico Adobe was built in the mid-19th century. When this photograph was taken in the 1920s, the building was in a sad state of disrepair. It was purchased by the Native Daughters of the Golden West in 1935 and restored for use as a clubhouse.

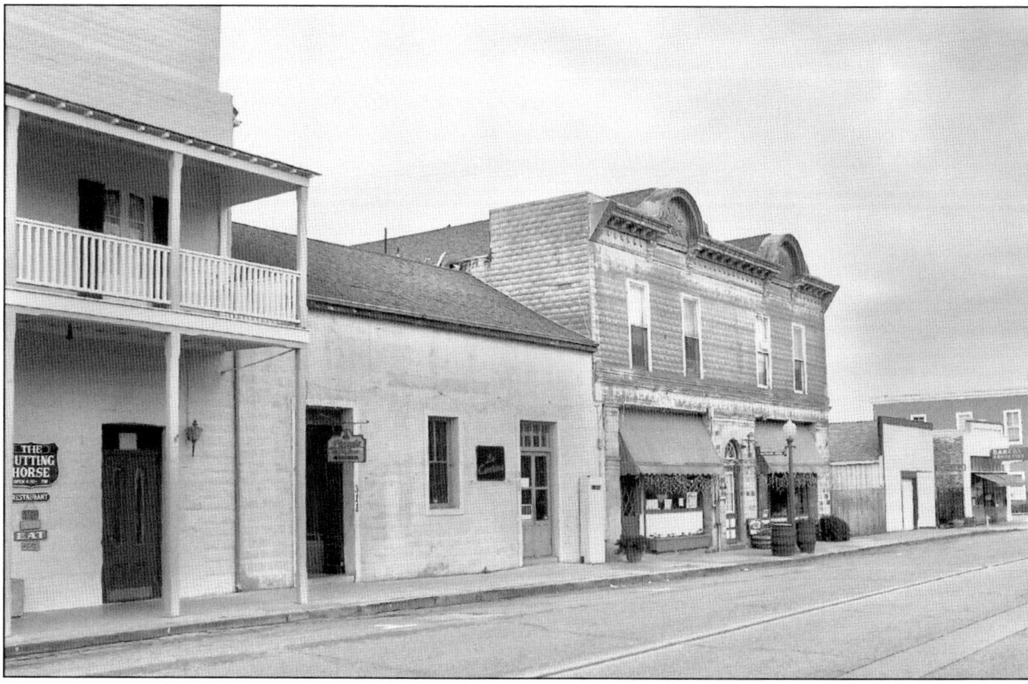

This view of Third Street shows many old buildings in San Juan. The large building on the left with the balcony is the Galacoma Building, built in 1870. It was a hotel and bar. Next to it is the first sandstone building in town, built in 1868. It housed a general store called Pearl of San Juan. Next is the large Taix Building of 1908. The second floor is zinc coated in case of fire.

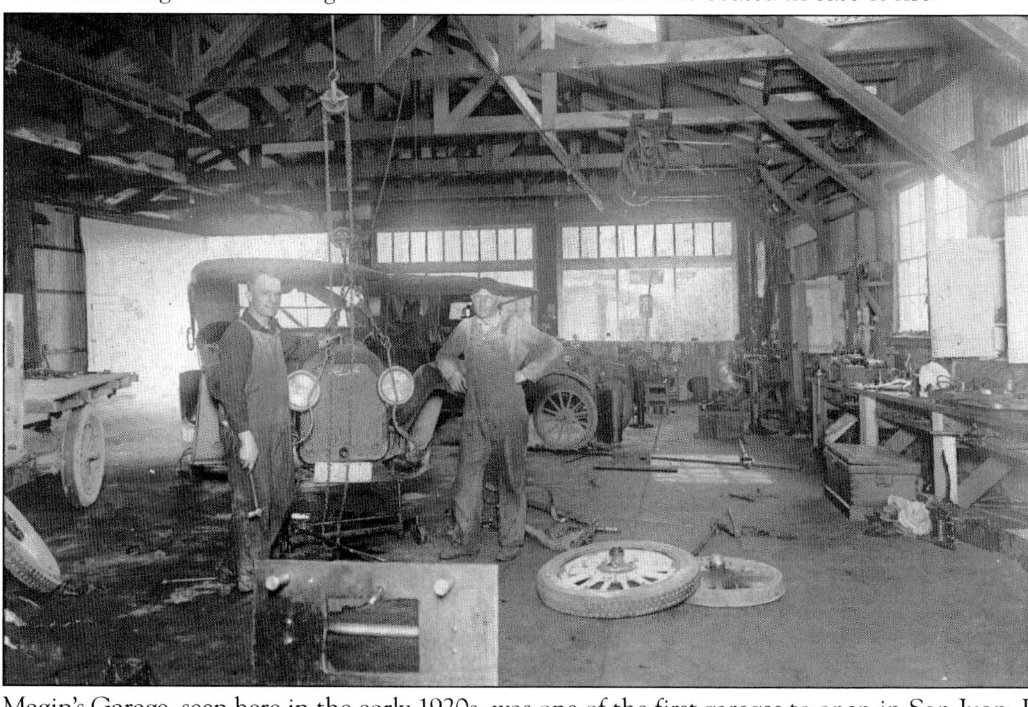

Magin's Garage, seen here in the early 1920s, was one of the first garages to open in San Juan. It was very successful because everyone wanted a new automobile.

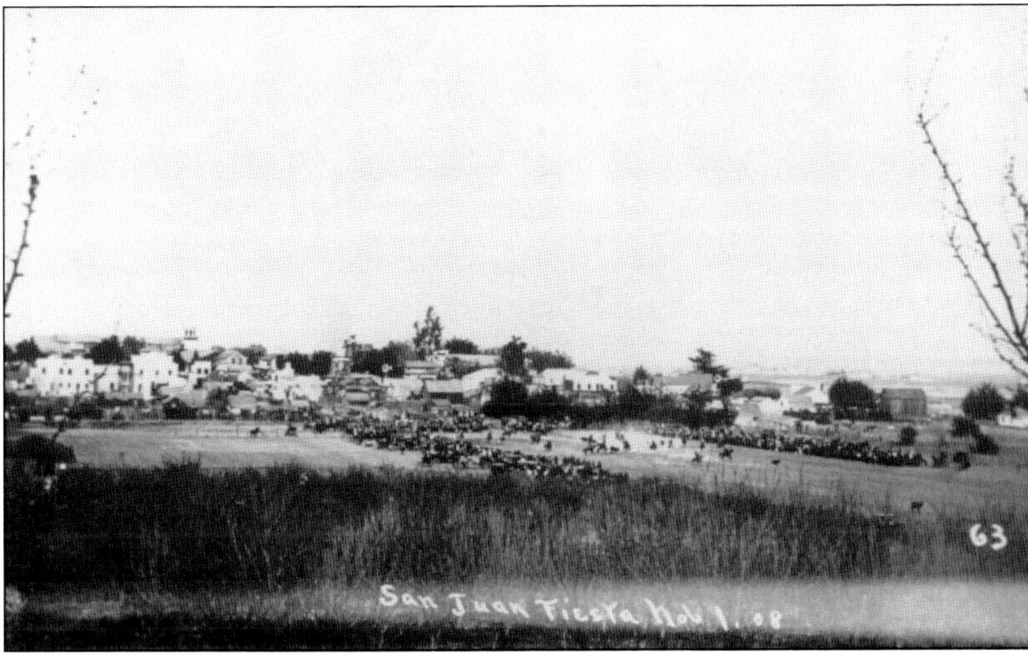

This panoramic photograph of San Juan was taken during the fiesta of November 1, 1908. The tower of the mission can be seen in the background.

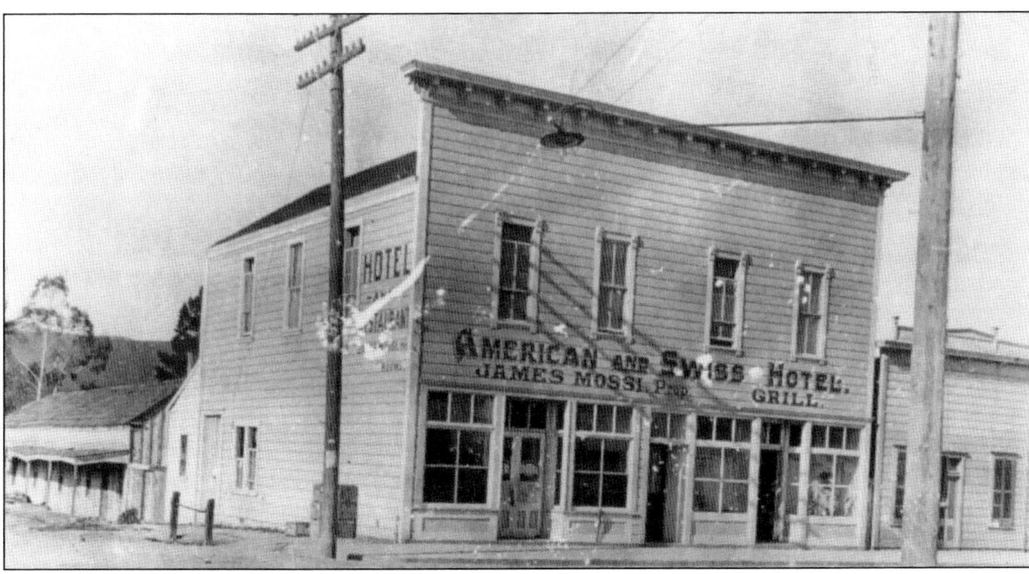

The American and Swiss Hotel was one of many hotels in town destined to become rooming hoses during the Great Depression. The building still exists as the Bluebird Hotel.

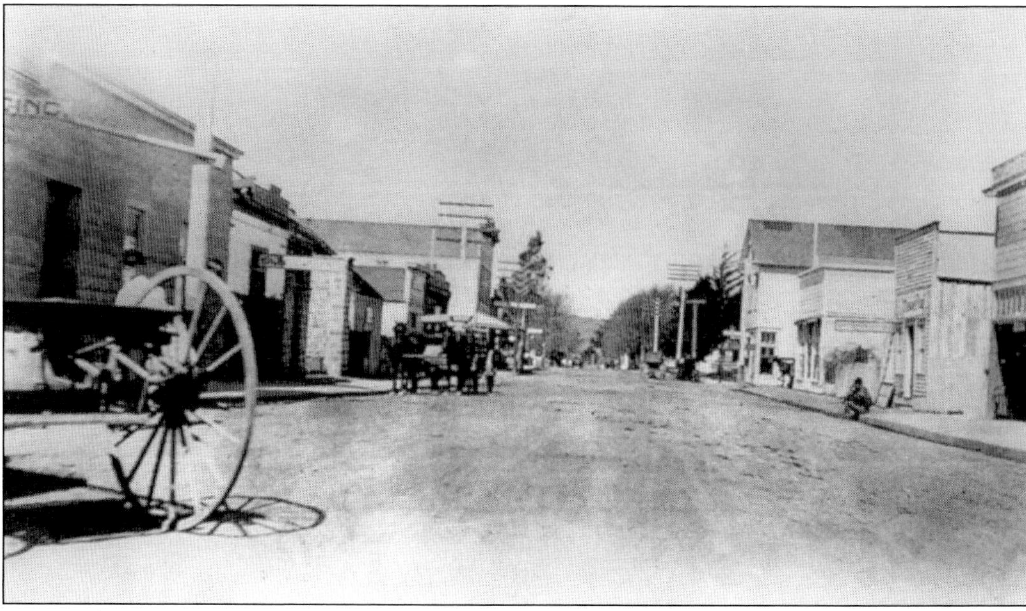

In 1903, horses remained the preferred mode of travel even though automobiles were becoming popular. At that time, cars were still considered something of a curiosity. It was not unusual to have herds of horses, cattle, or sheep driven through town.

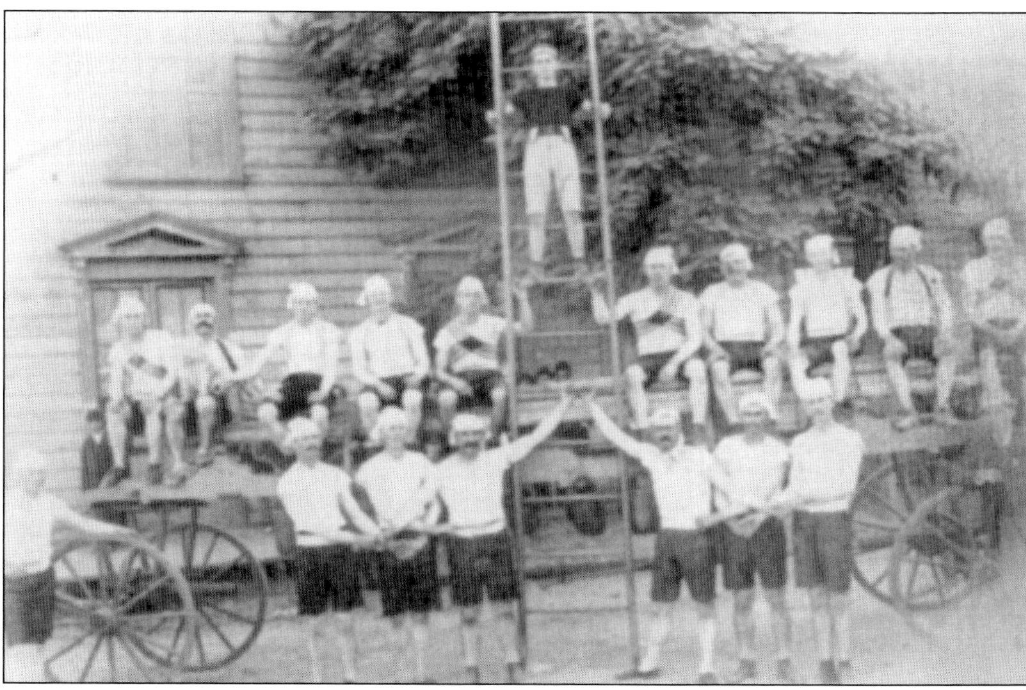

The San Juan Hook and Ladder Company is pictured at a firemen's muster in 1882. The firemen would compete annually with fire companies from other towns for prizes. The events involved the men pulling the "Eagle," the town fire wagon, in a race with other groups. Additional events included ladder climbing and hauling buckets of water. San Juan received trophies in 1882 and 1884.

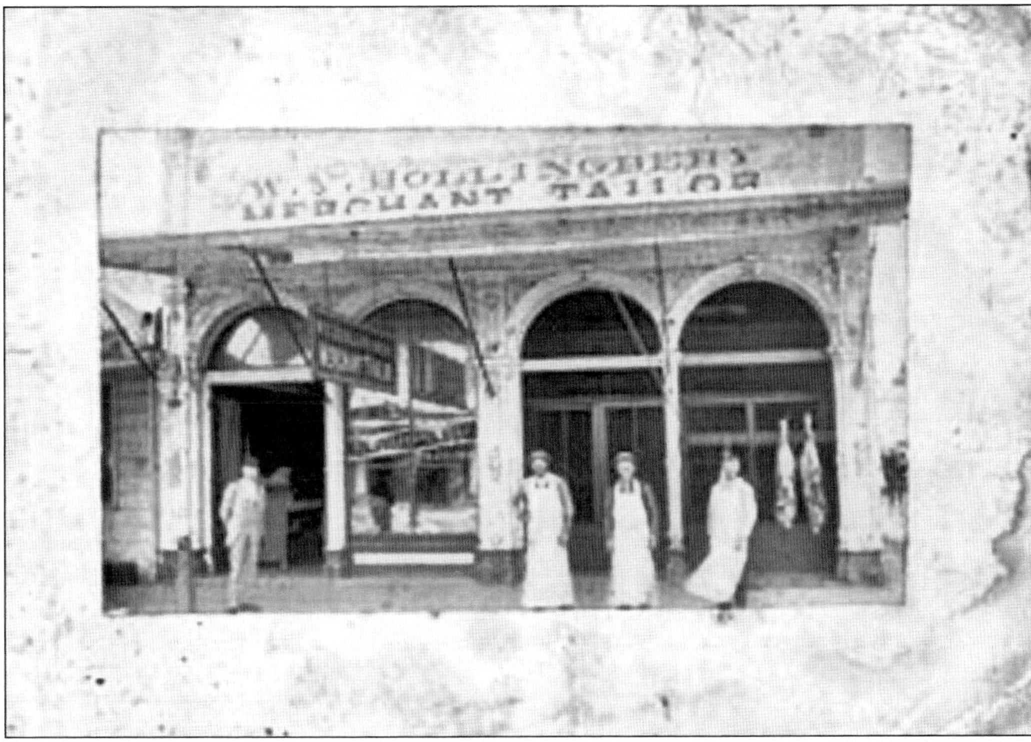

In its heyday, San Juan boasted several businesses that covered five to six blocks along Third Street. These businesses included this tailor shop as well as general stores, meat markets, bakeries, barbershops, restaurants, shoe stores, dressmakers, drugstores, hotels, and blacksmith shops.

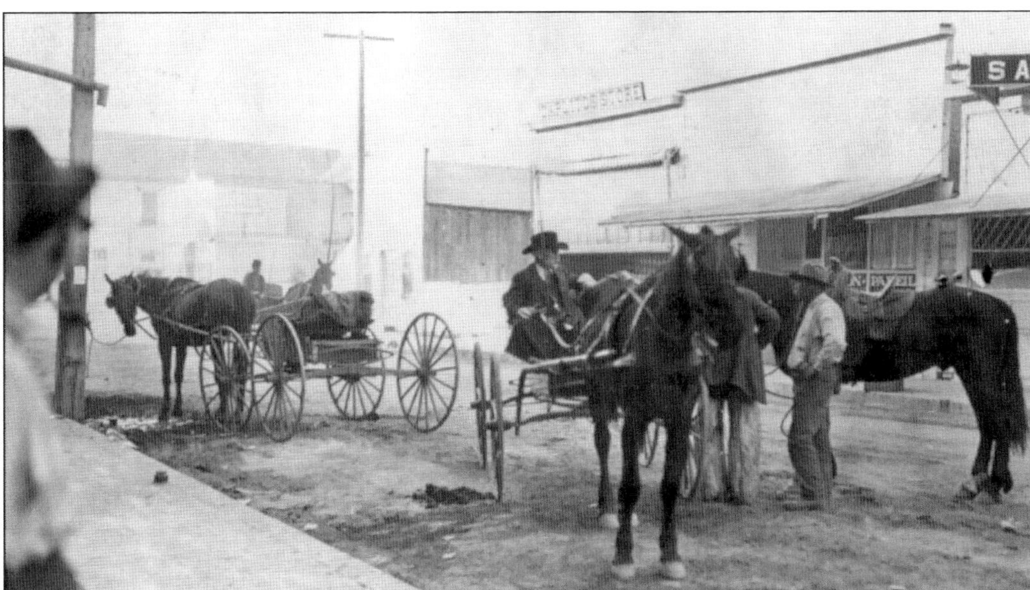

This 1894 photograph of Third Street shows the congestion that could occur with the number of carriages used during the average day.

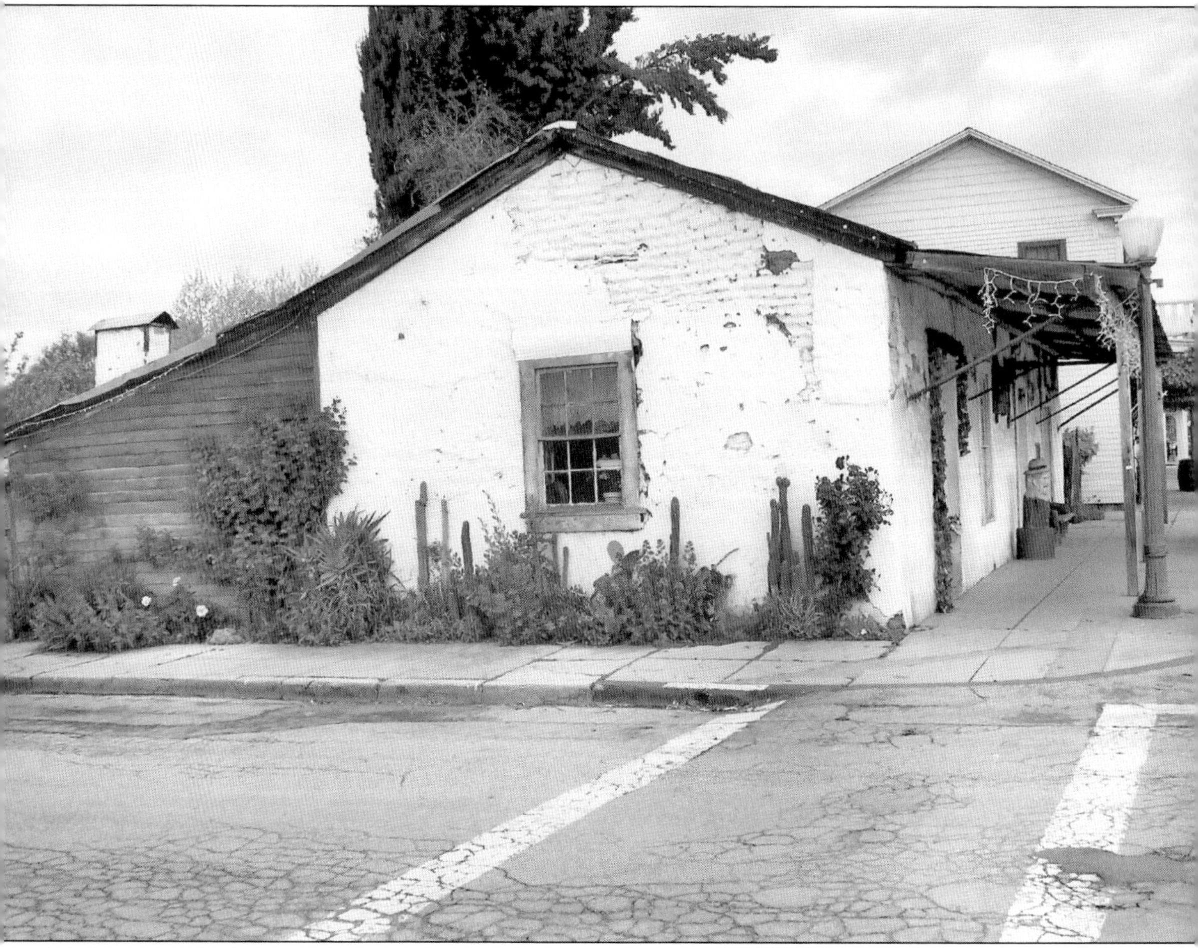

The Juan de Anza Adobe was built in 1834 as the family residence. By 1850, it was being used as a commercial building. This continued until 1933, when it housed the first antique store in San Juan. This building is listed on the National Register of Historic Places in the United States.

Five

San Juan Bautista State Historic Park

In 1928, a delegation from the California State Parks Commission toured the area and was invited to visit the Castro-Breen Adobe by Mayor Frank Abbe. For some time, there had been talk of tearing down a few of the buildings surrounding the plaza, but local citizens, concerned about their historic value, wanted them saved. A group of citizens decided to go to Sacramento and petition the parks commission to purchase the buildings and save them from demolition.

During the Great Depression, there was little money for preservation, yet in 1933, $33,000 was appropriated by the state for the plaza buildings. In 1934, the final deeds were signed and filed, and the park was born. The result was the purchase of the Plaza Hotel and the Castro-Breen Adobe, as well as the entire block where they were located. Included in the purchase was three quarters of the block containing the Plaza Hall–Zanetta House and the Plaza Stable. Other purchases brought smaller areas surrounding the plaza, creating the present park boundaries.

The buildings have all been retrofitted for earthquake safety and restored to create a time capsule representing the Mexican and Gold Rush eras in order to complement the Spanish mission. Today visitors come from all over the world to get a taste of California's past. At no other site in California can one experience life during the turbulent years from 1797 to the present. The park is a popular destination for central California's fourth-grade students researching their state's history. Docents in costume demonstrate living history every first Saturday and during the annual Early Days in San Juan Bautista celebration in June.

This chapter will be divided into the primary buildings surrounding the historic plaza: the Plaza Hall–Zanetta House, the Plaza Stable, the Plaza Hotel, and the Castro-Breen House. The book will conclude with a look at some of the wonderful docents who do so much to bring the past back to life at San Juan Bautista. Their dedication provides the human warmth that means so much to the visitor. The authors dedicate this book to all of those who give their time to making a visit to San Juan Bautista State Historic Park a wonderful adventure.

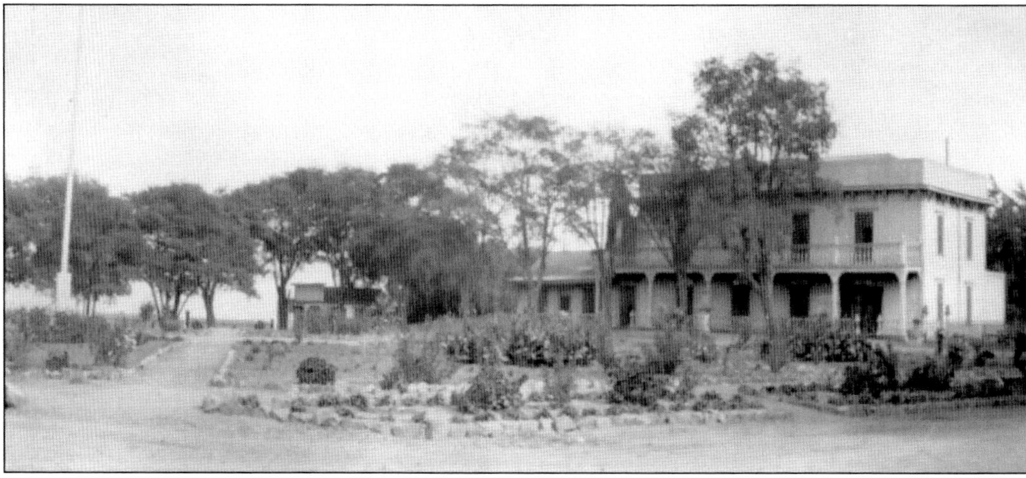

The Plaza Hall–Zanetta House, pictured in 1910, was originally an adobe built between 1797 and 1798 by the Spanish for the unmarried Mutsun Indian girls. When secularization occurred in 1834 and Mexico confiscated the mission property, the structure was abandoned until General Castro established a military presence in 1839. The military housed its horses and grain in the building, which soon fell into disrepair and was abandoned. In 1868, Angelo Zanetta purchased the ruins and salvaged the adobe bricks to rebuild the walls. The building was to be offices for the new county of San Benito, but in 1870 Hollister became the seat instead. Hotel owner Zanetta added a one-story extension for a wine cellar, kitchen, and dining room and moved his family from the hotel, freeing rooms there for rent. The second floor became the Plaza Hall, which was used for meetings, dances, and other special events.

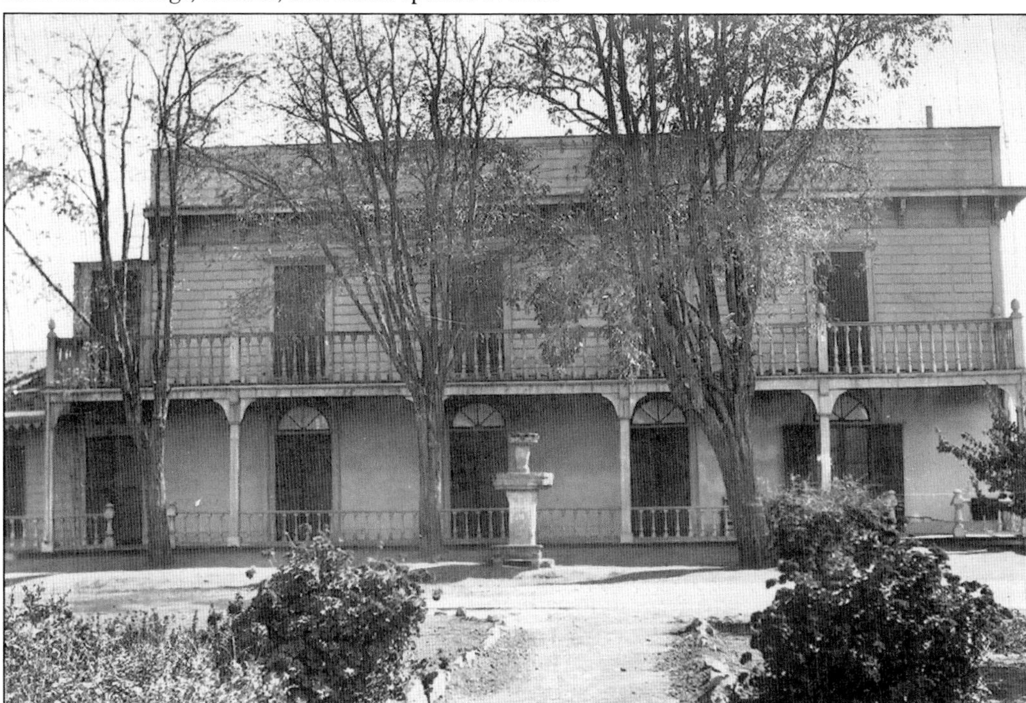

Over the years, the site was landscaped with paths that crossed from one building to another. Zanetta planted black locust trees around the plaza in the 1880s.

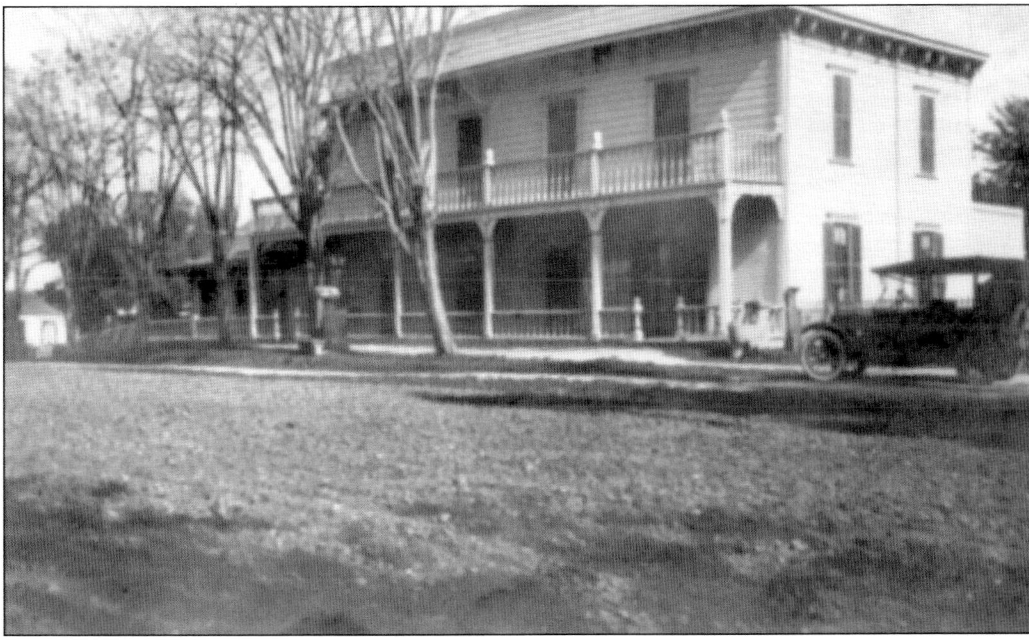

This 1917 photograph of the Plaza Hall shows the full growth of the locust trees planted in front of the building.

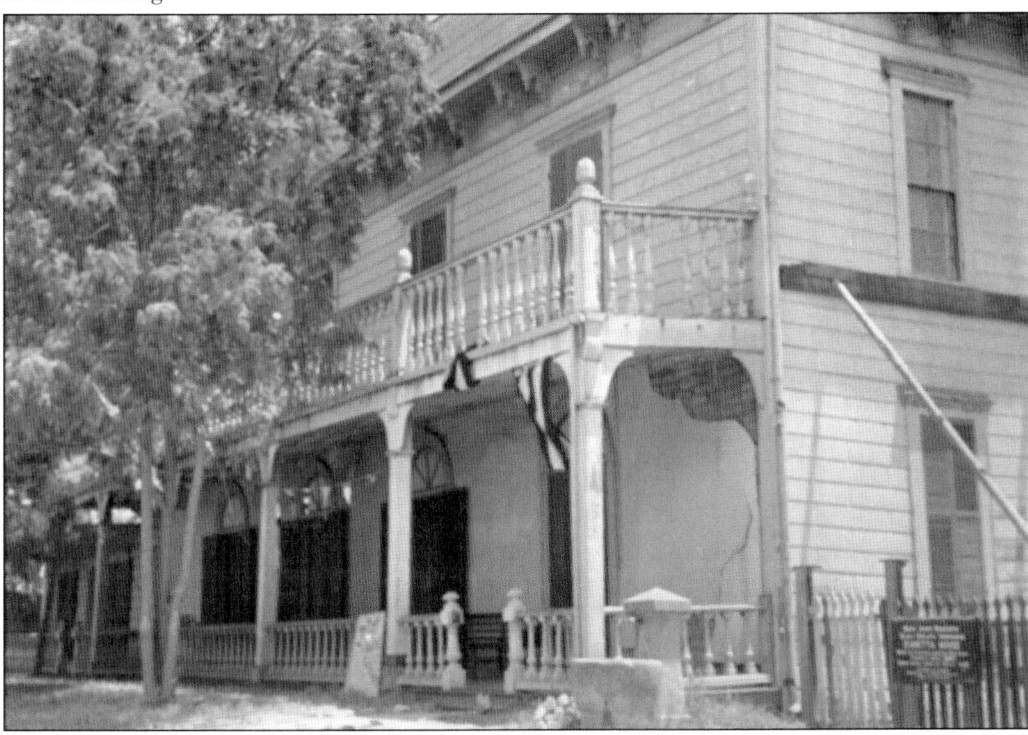

When the park system purchased the plaza in 1933, the Plaza Hall had to be stabilized and propped up with metal rods. The plaster was falling off and many interior repairs had to be completed before the building could be opened to the public. Today the structure is furnished as it was when the Zanetta family lived there in the last quarter of the 19th century.

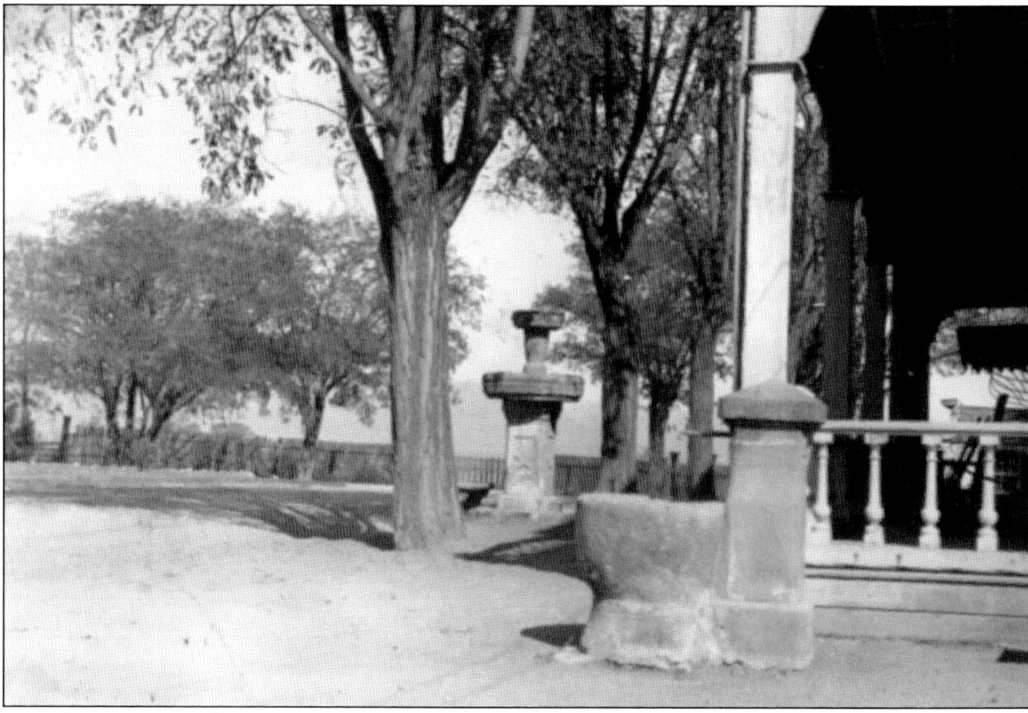

Angelo Zanetta had this fountain and bench placed in front of the building, proudly carving his name on both. The fountain inscription reads, "Erected, A. Zanetta, 1870."

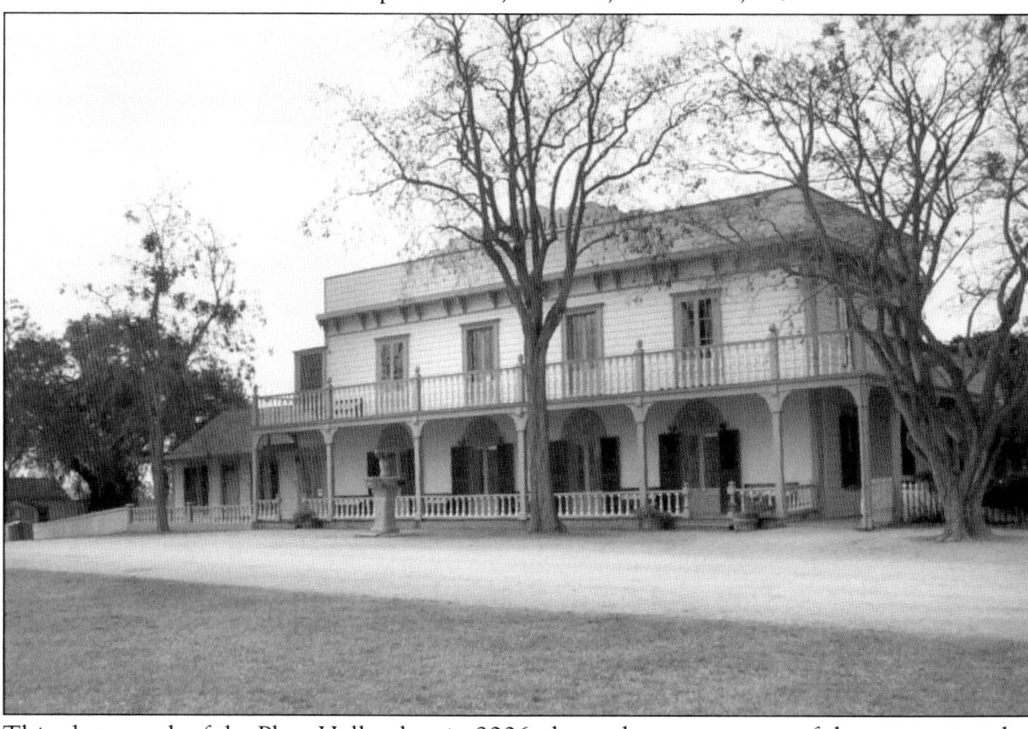

This photograph of the Plaza Hall, taken in 2006, shows the present state of the restoration that was completed in 2005. Further work is planned on the side stairs and the windows.

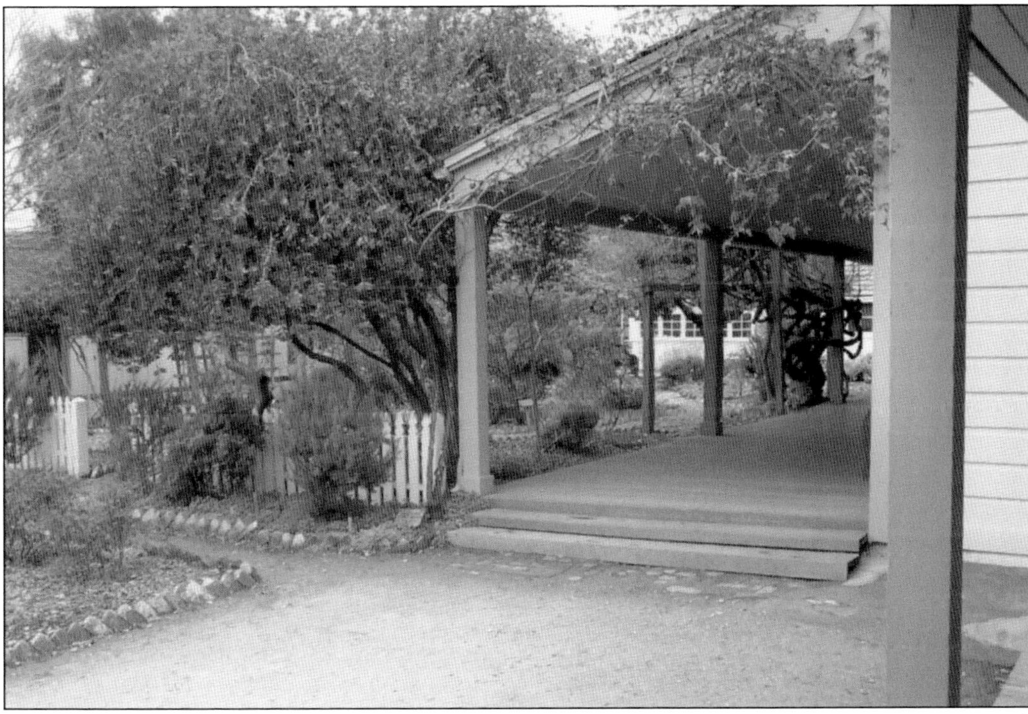

The long covered back porch was a favorite place to spend warm summer evenings. A very old wisteria spreads across the porch, displaying beautiful, aromatic clusters of blossoms in spring.

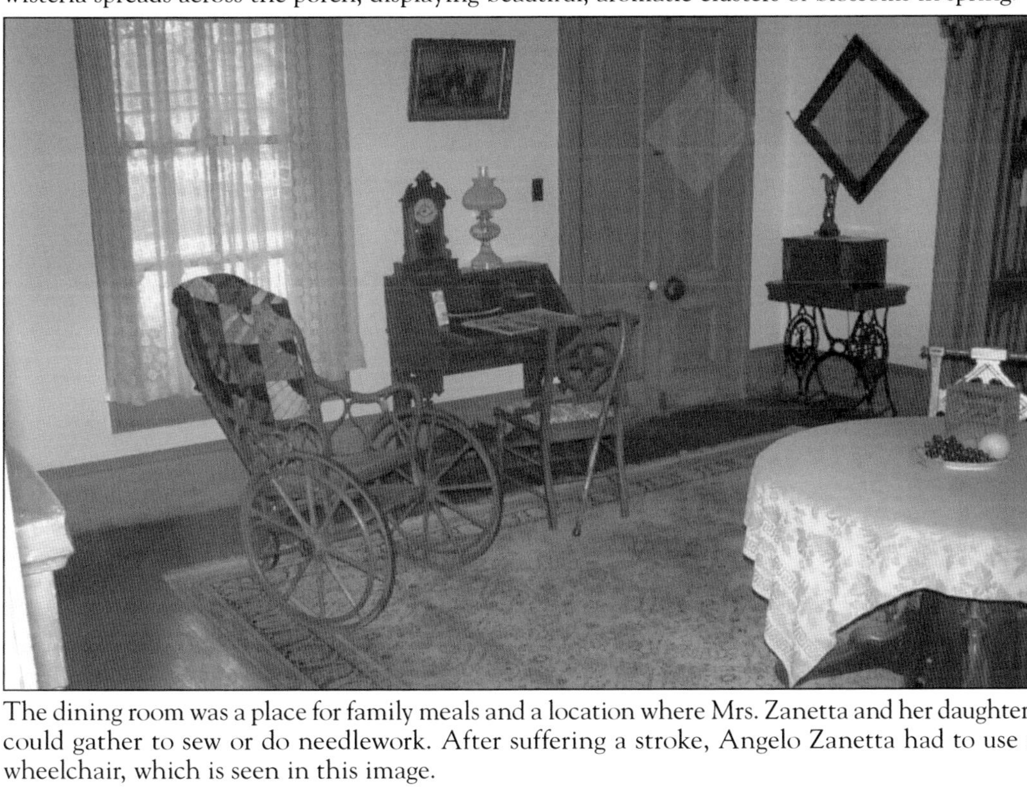

The dining room was a place for family meals and a location where Mrs. Zanetta and her daughters could gather to sew or do needlework. After suffering a stroke, Angelo Zanetta had to use a wheelchair, which is seen in this image.

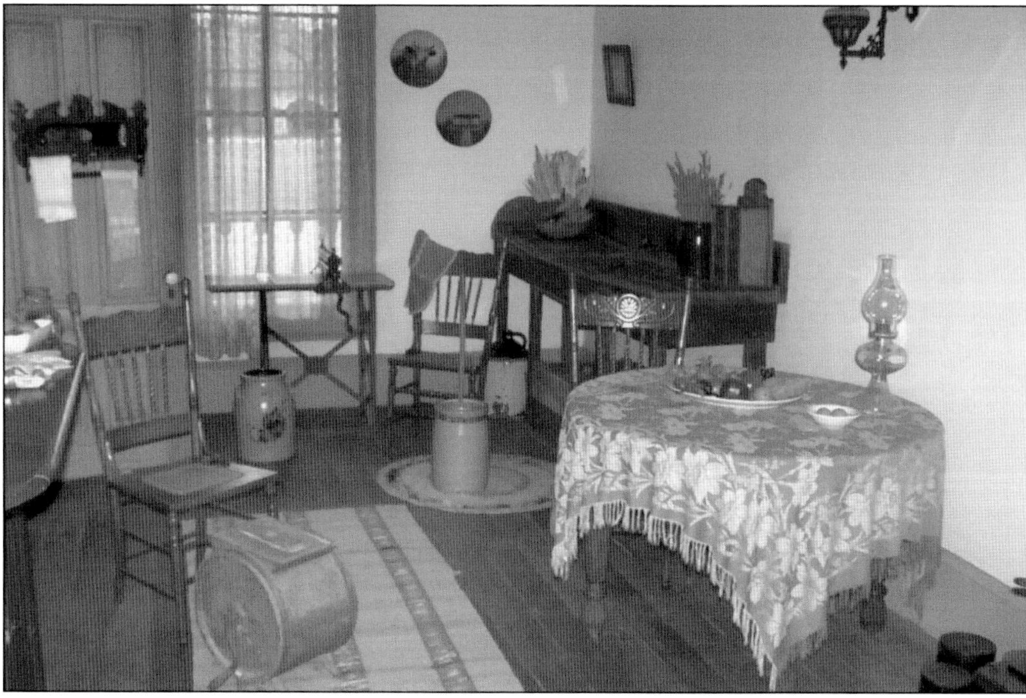

The kitchen, as it is furnished today, displays many of the original accessories, including the butter churn. Mrs. Zanetta was a good cook, but by the time the family moved into the house, cooks and maids had been hired to care for them.

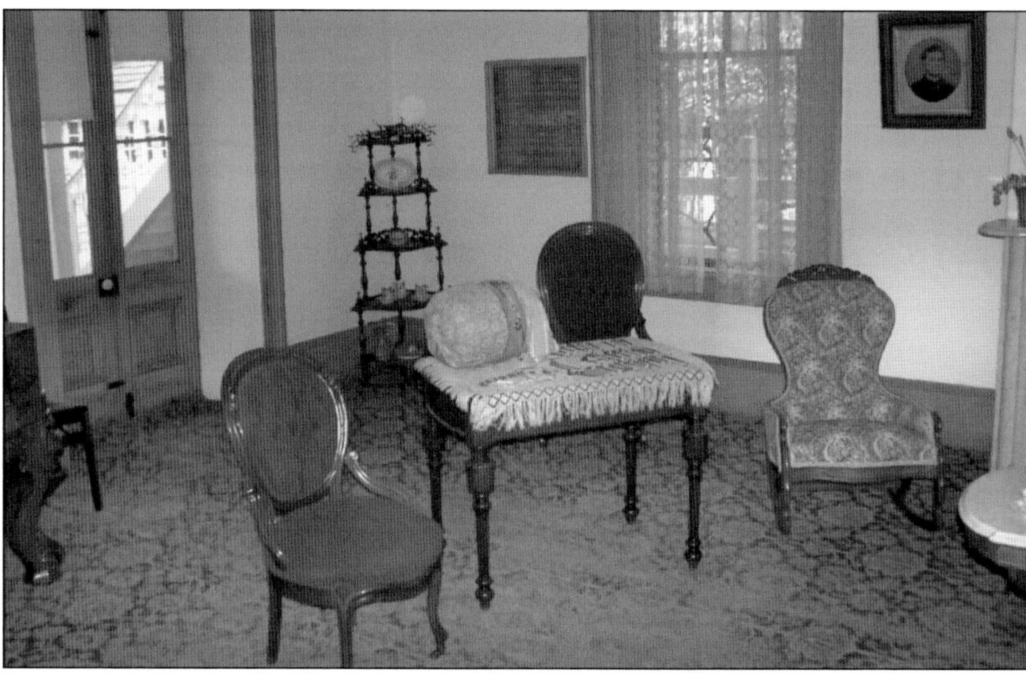

The parlor had originally been planned as the judge's office when the building was to be the county courthouse. The room became the main parlor and was used for afternoon tea as well as social events.

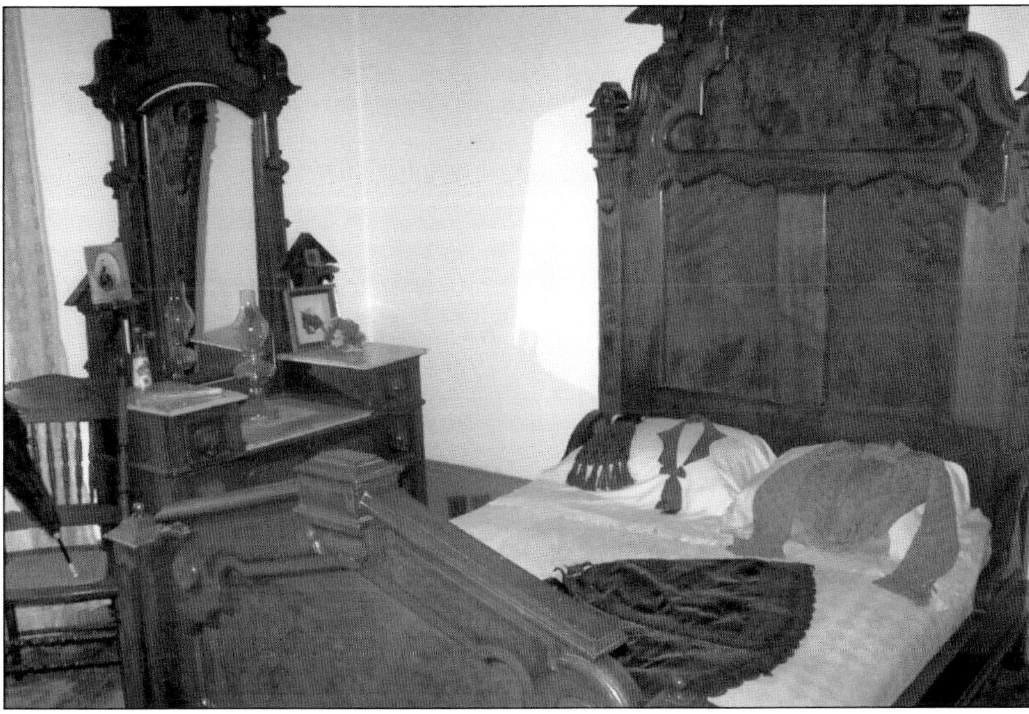

There were five bedrooms in the house. These two photographs show the original beds and wardrobes used by the family. Each spring, all the heavy furniture was moved for cleaning, a job few would want to do today.

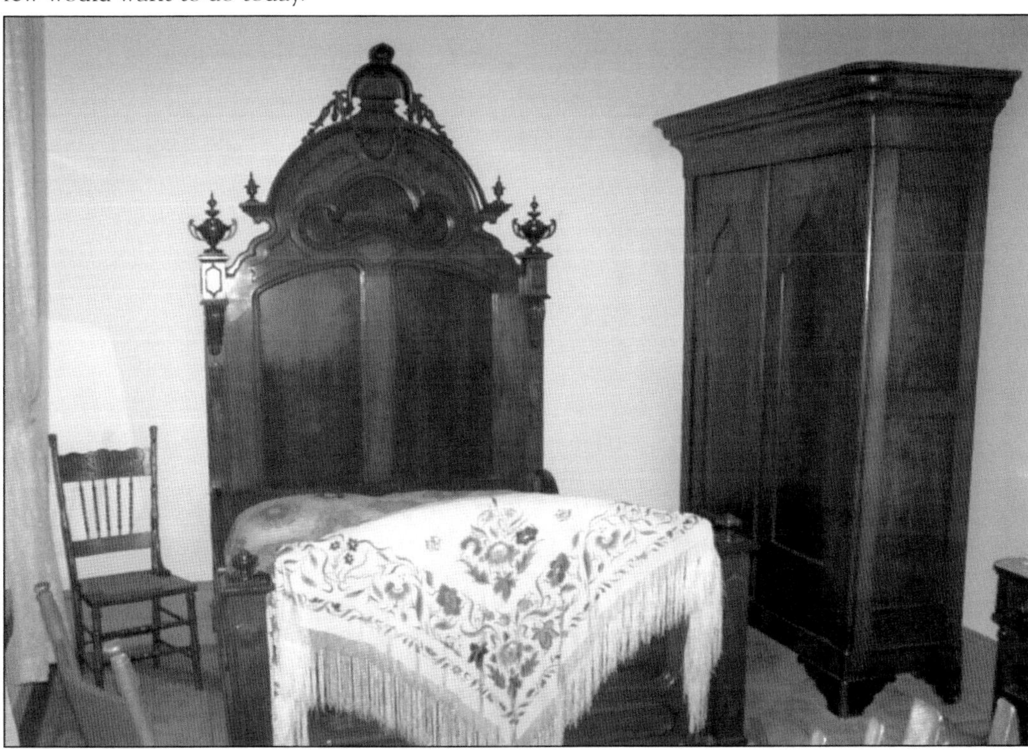

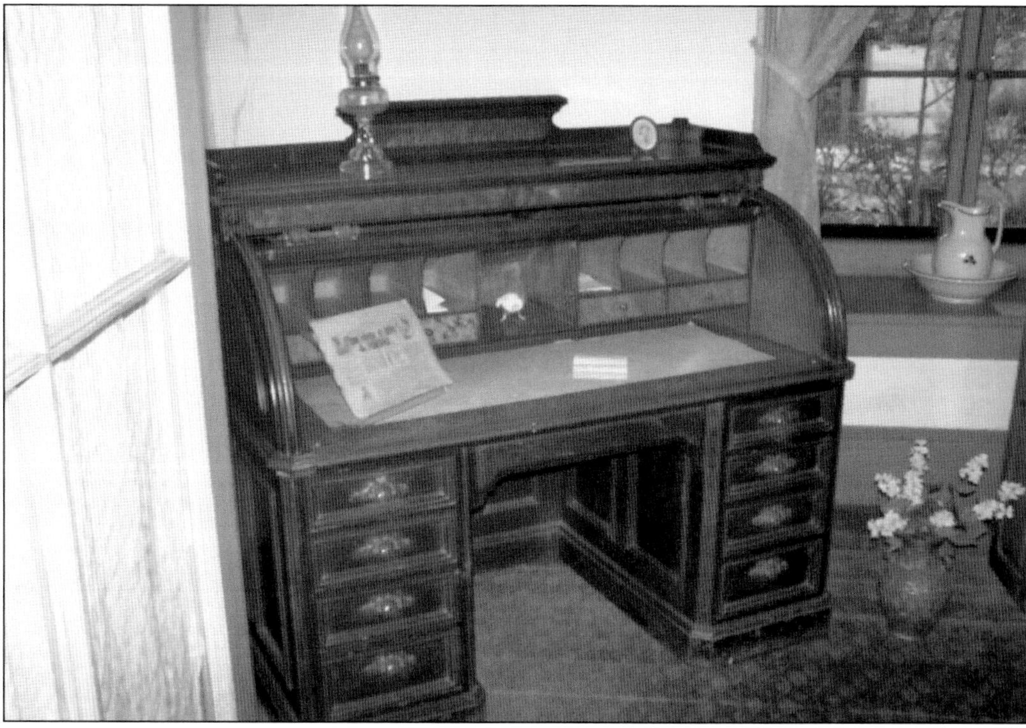

Shown here is a Flint family desk. Angelo often used this room as an office.

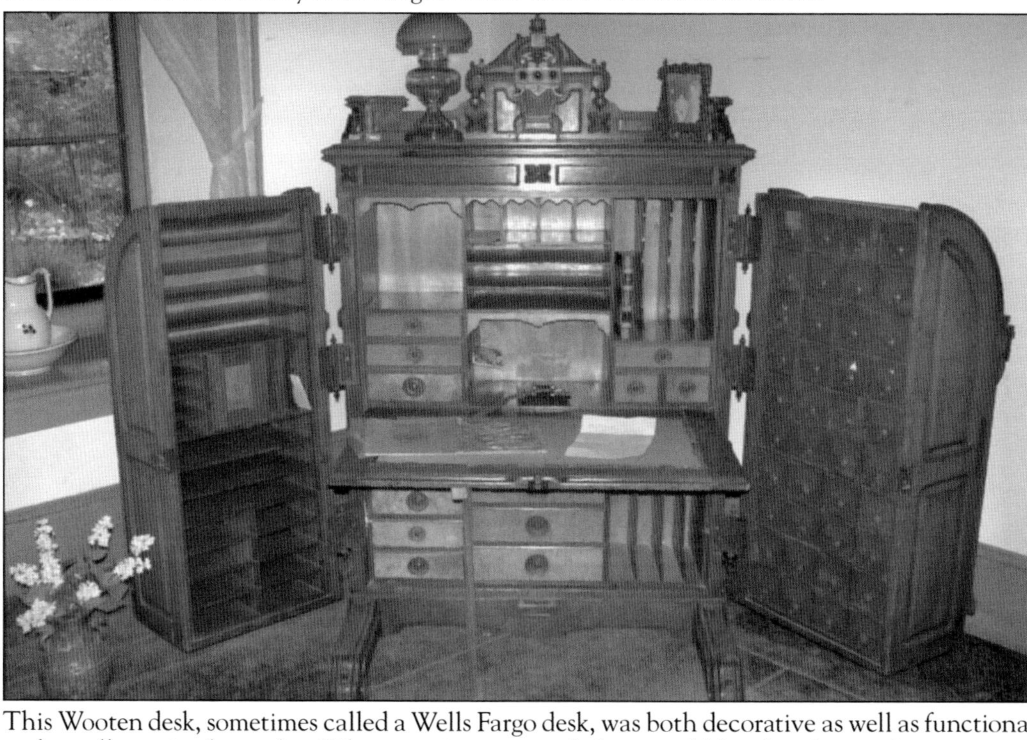

This Wooten desk, sometimes called a Wells Fargo desk, was both decorative as well as functional and usually sat in the parlor. When not in use as a desk, it could be closed to make a compact and attractive piece of furniture.

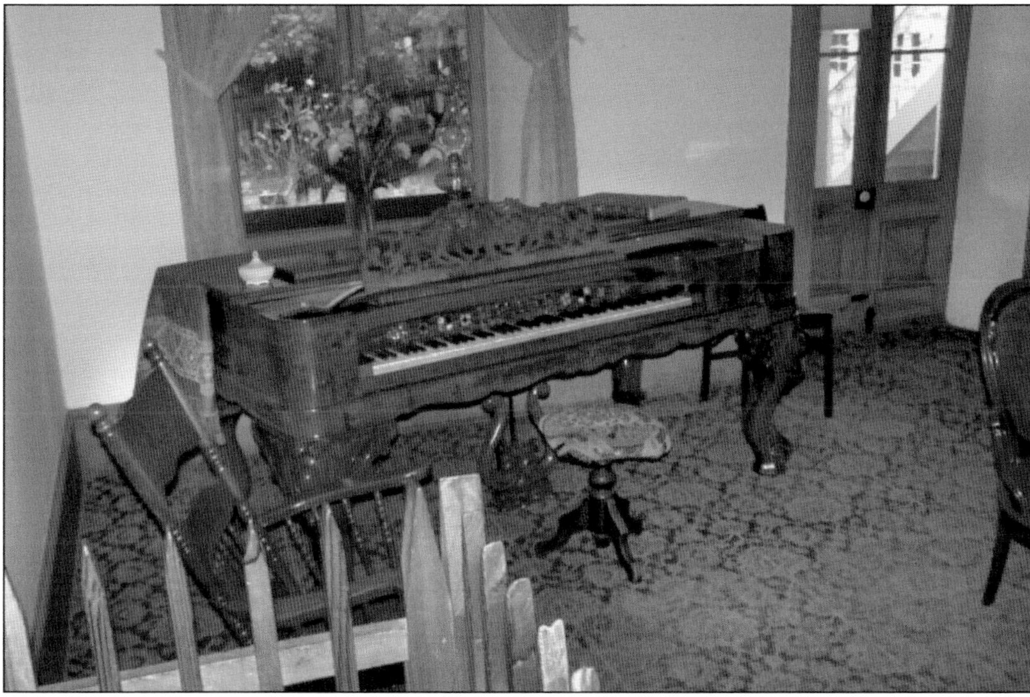

This fine old Fisher piano, created around 1860, belonged to accomplished musician Victoria Zanetta. Guests were often entertained by Victoria, who also played the organ in the mission. Today docents keep the piano tuned and play it for special events.

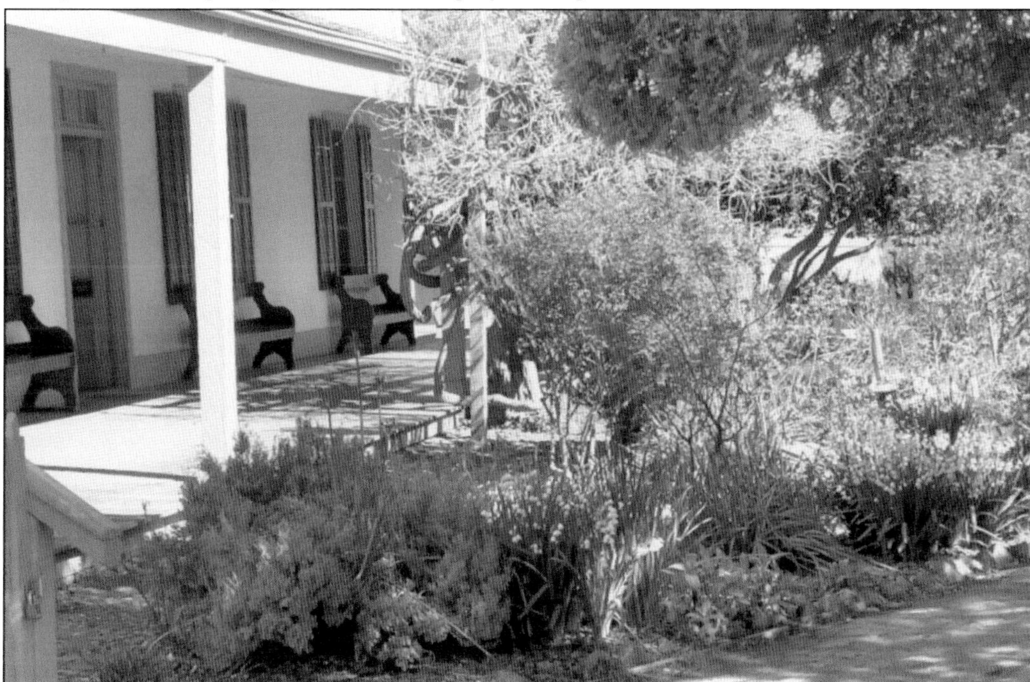

The garden behind the Zanetta house features many old roses and wisteria vines. The large rear porch can be seen in this photograph.

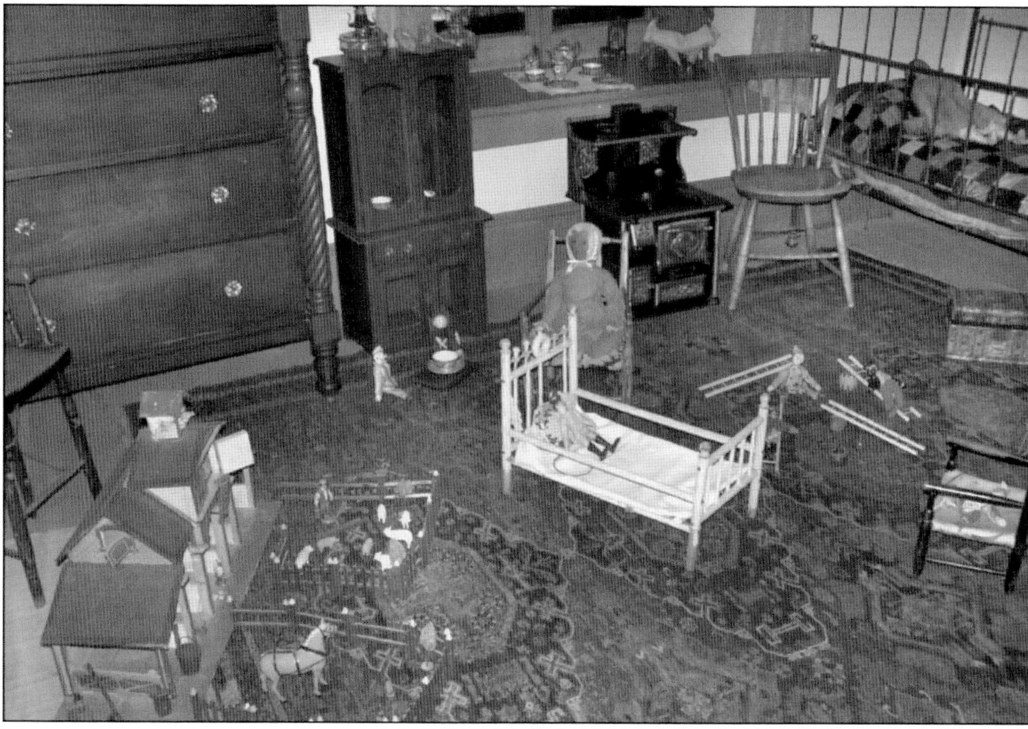

This bedroom is furnished as a child's room. There are dolls, cradles, and a tea set, as well as a miniature stove with pots, pans, and oven doors that open. The miniature barn with all the farm animals, including a horse and wagon, must have delighted a child of the 1870s.

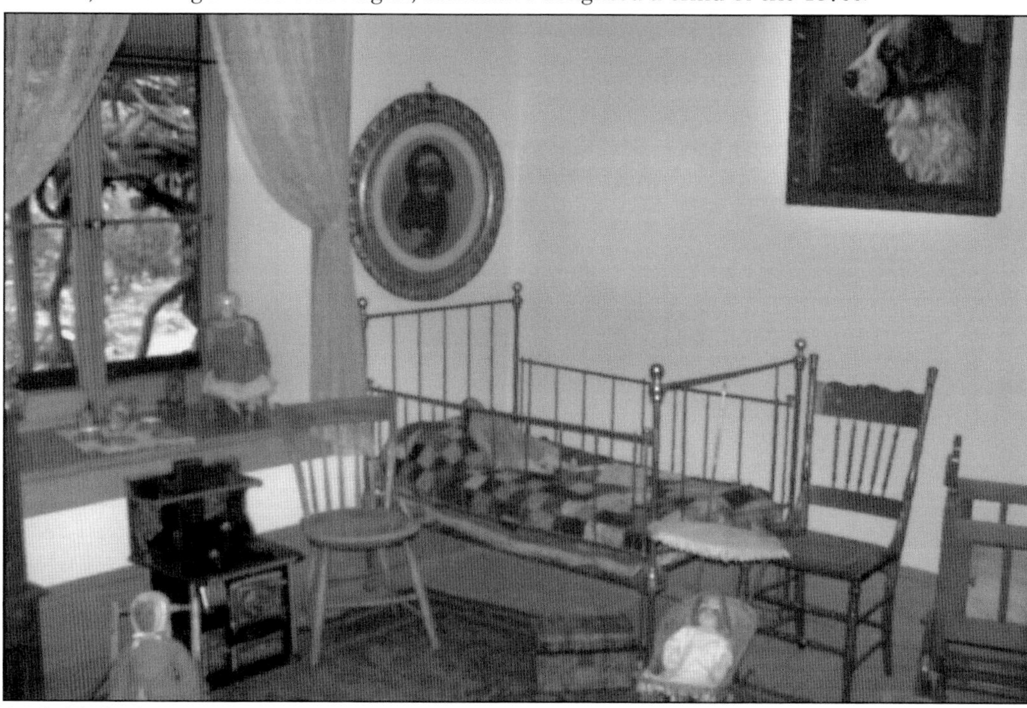

A child's bed sits in the toy room used by members of the Zanetta family.

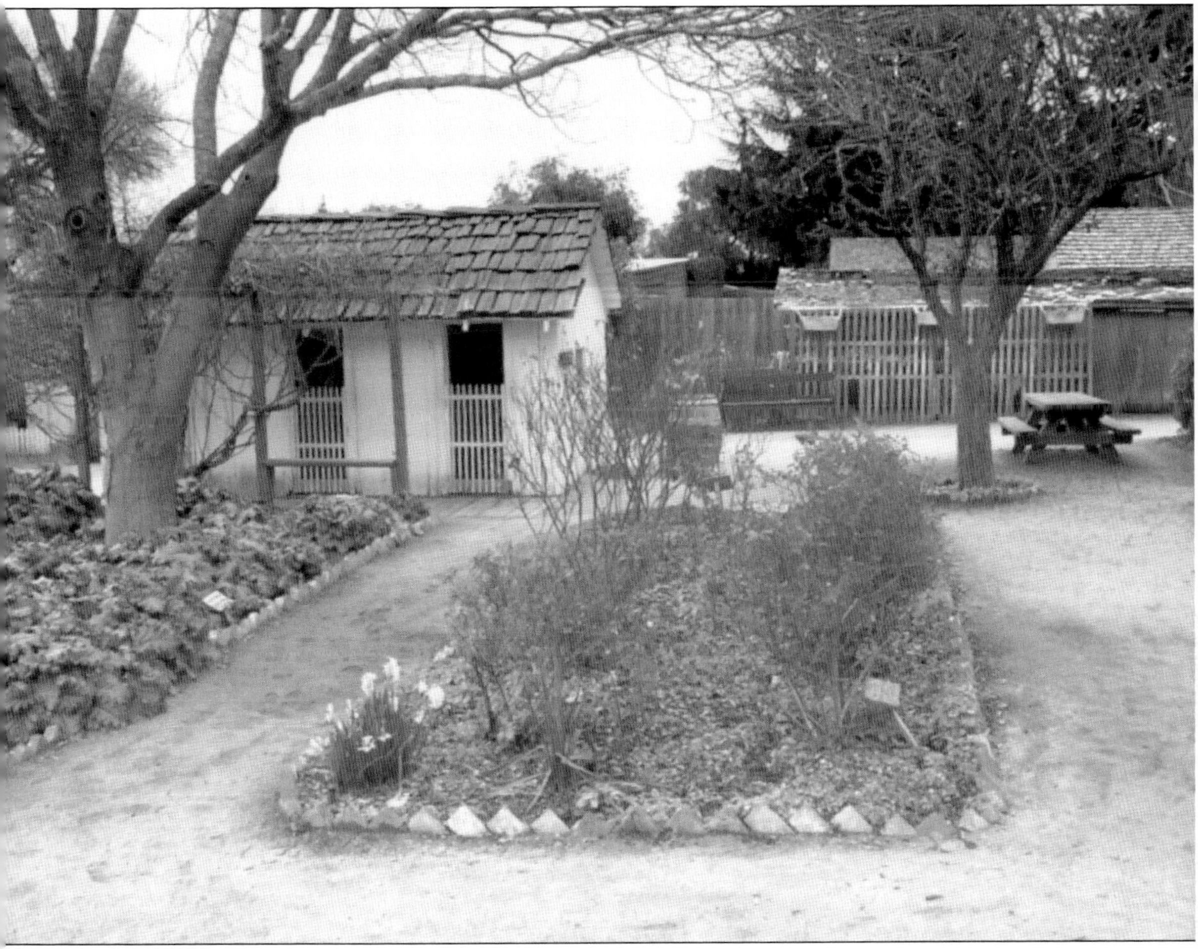

The old washhouse located behind the Plaza Hall–Zanetta House consists of three rooms: a washroom, a bathing room, and an outhouse. It was built in the early 1950s as a reconstruction from memory of the original as provided by Clara Zanetta, the daughter-in-law of Angelo Zanetta.

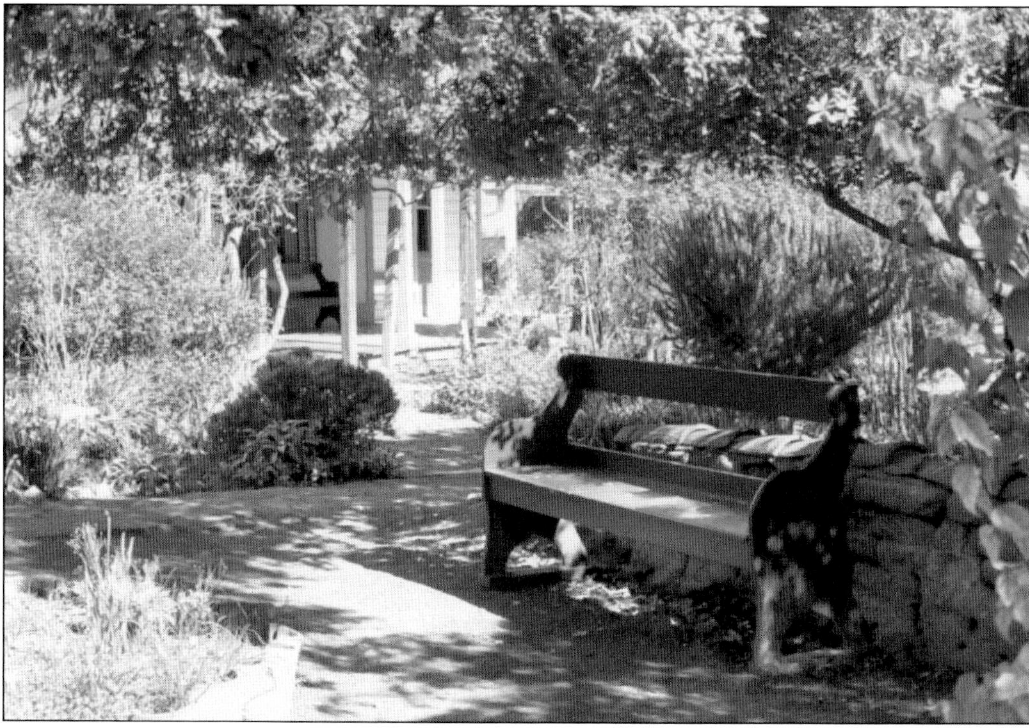

The garden behind the house is full of meandering paths with beds of old roses, lilacs, and wisteria. Mrs. Zanetta planned the garden in the latter quarter of the 19th century.

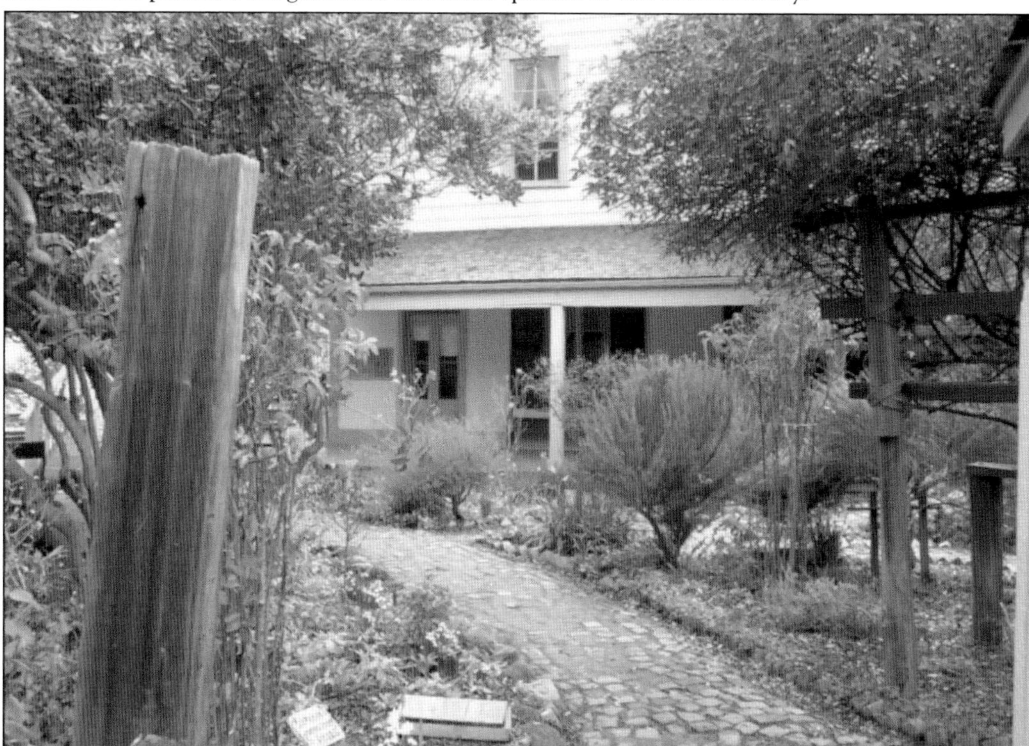

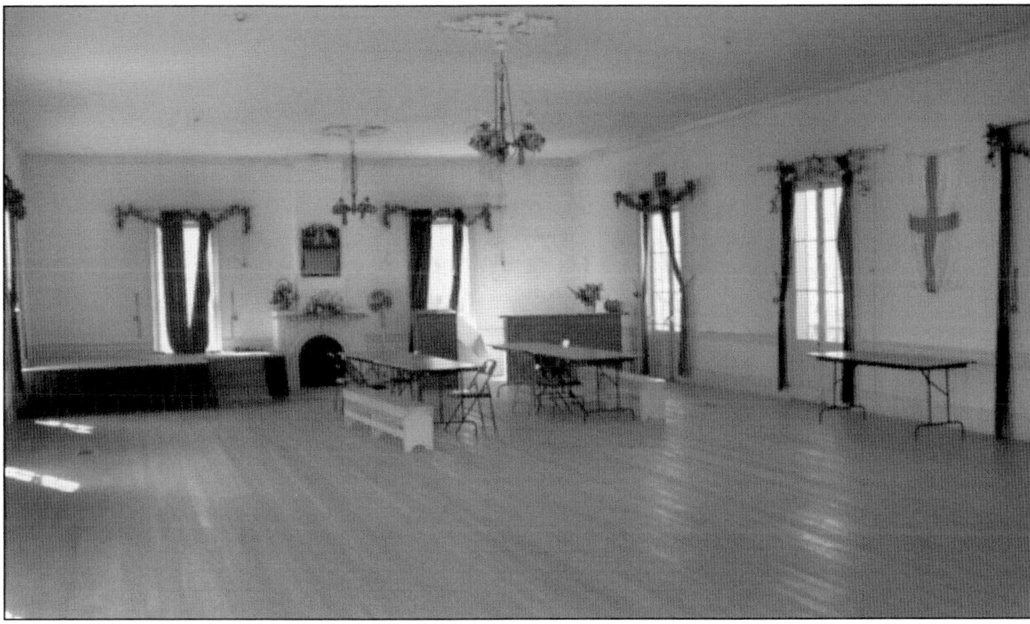

The second floor of the Plaza Hall originally had a springboard floor, which was installed when the building was constructed in 1868. This room was slated for trials when the building was to have been the county courthouse. When Hollister became the county seat, the room became the largest in town available for parties, dances, and theatrical events. Many a grand ball was held here.

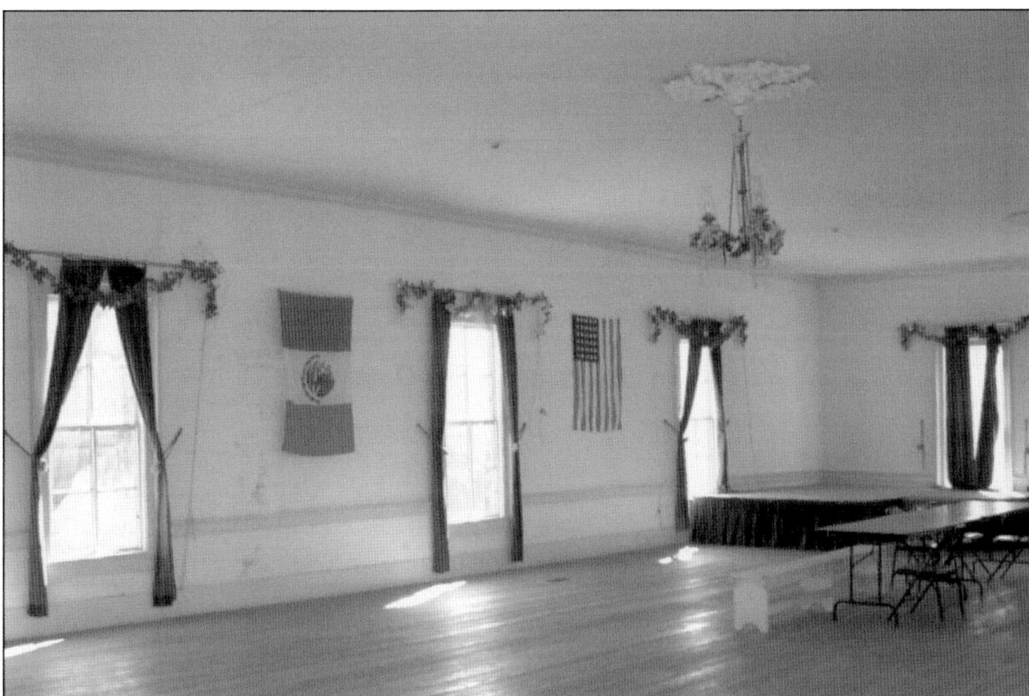

This view of the room shows the 30 stars on the American flag. California was the 31st state but there were no 31-star flags for almost a year, so the 30-star flag had to suffice.

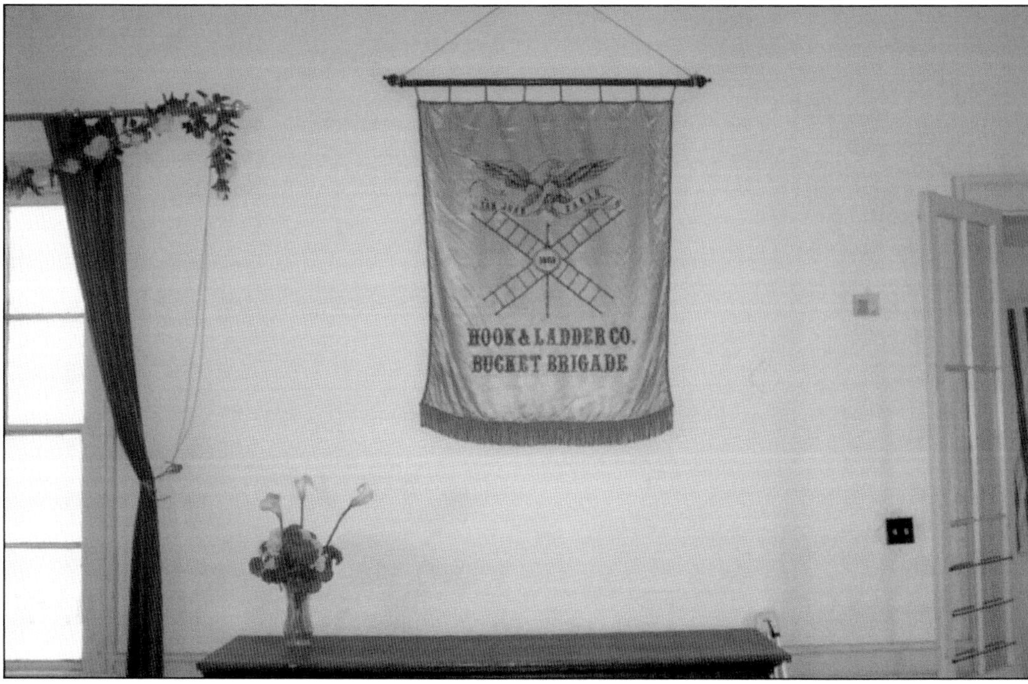

The San Juan Bautista Hook and Ladder Company created this banner in 1869, when the group was dedicated as a fire-fighting contingent in the community.

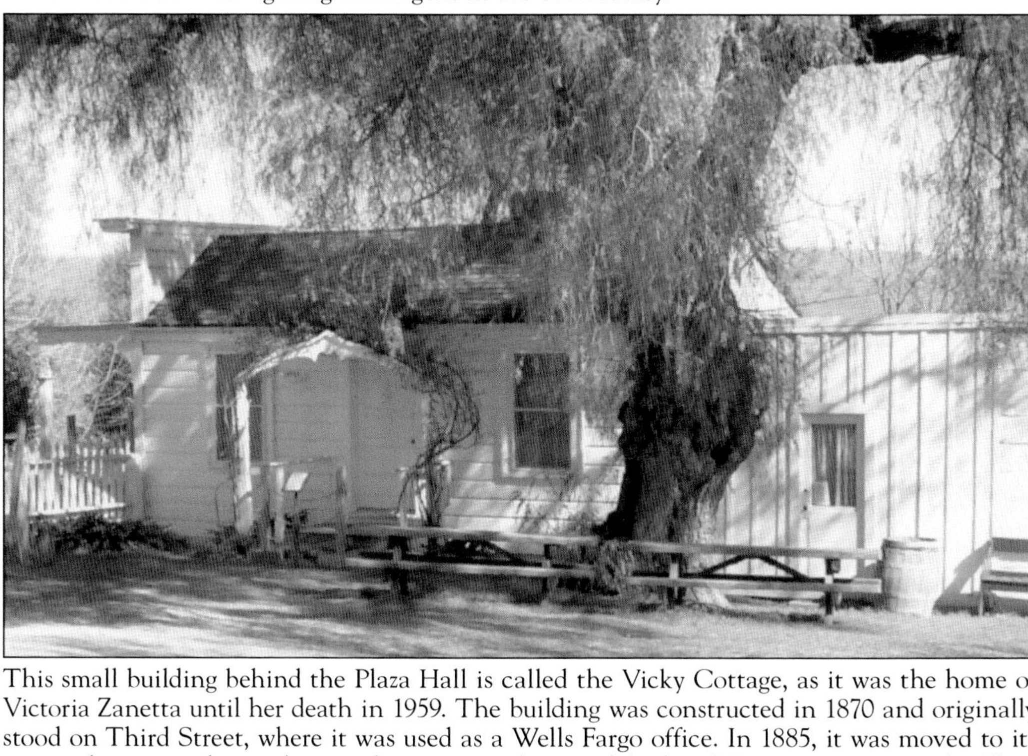
This small building behind the Plaza Hall is called the Vicky Cottage, as it was the home of Victoria Zanetta until her death in 1959. The building was constructed in 1870 and originally stood on Third Street, where it was used as a Wells Fargo office. In 1885, it was moved to its present location, where it became home to employees of the hotel. It now serves as park offices and has not yet been restored to its original interior.

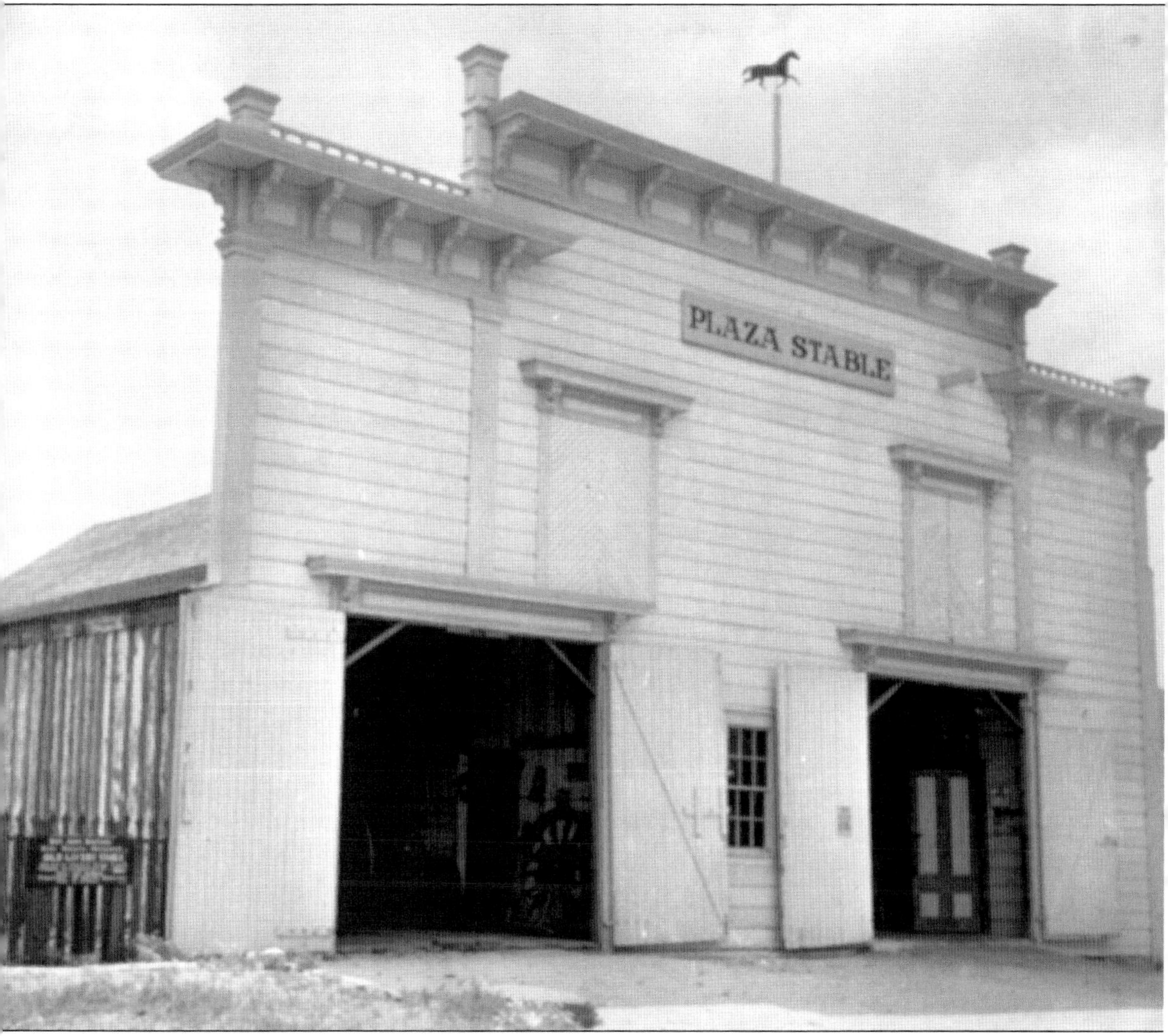

In 1870, John Comfort, partner of Angelo Zanetta, purchased this property, and he built the stable in 1874. The stable handled extensive stage and wagon traffic during San Juan's busiest years. The loft was used to store hay, which was dropped down through chutes to the individual stalls. There are 23 single stalls and two box stalls.

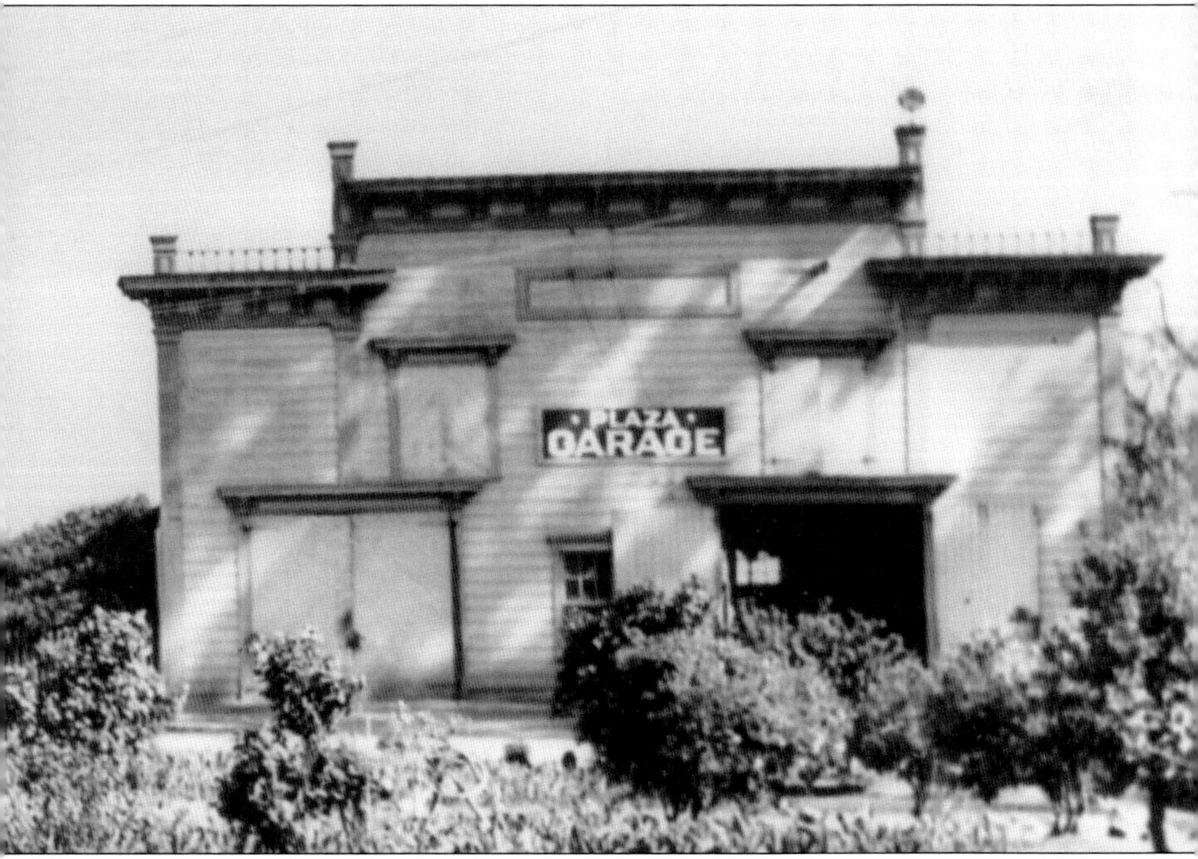

During the early 1930s, the stable became the parking garage for the guests of the Plaza Hotel. The building was restored to its original state in 1956.

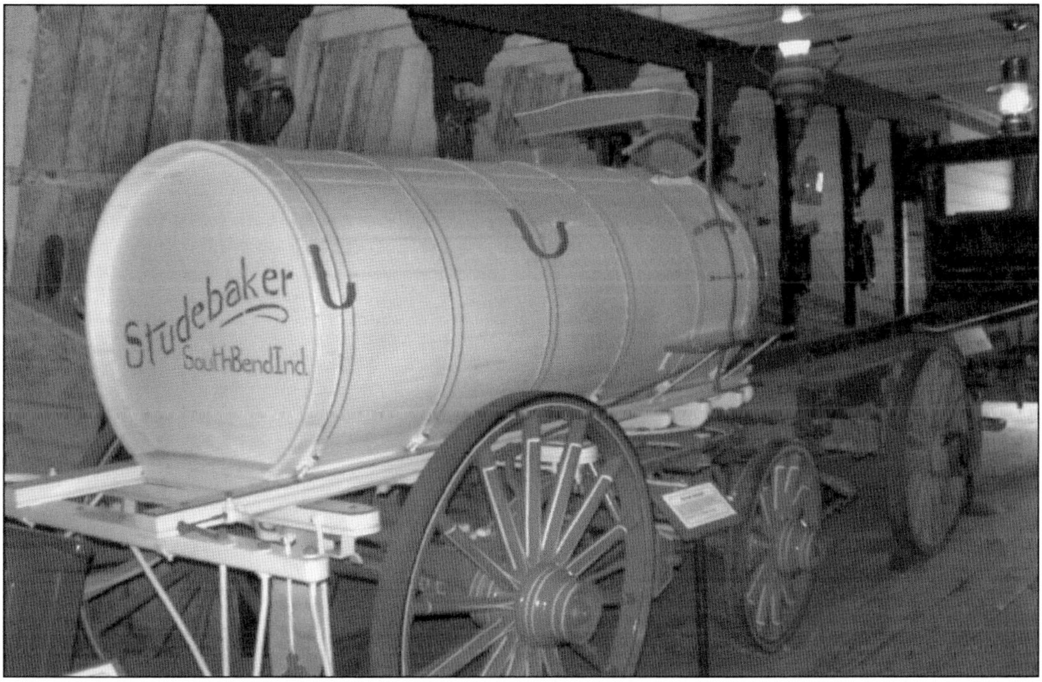

The city streets were very dusty during the summer months, when horses, cattle, and sheep were often driven through town. After many complaints from local businessmen, the city fathers decided they would hire a water wagon to keep the dust down. For $25 a month, the streets were watered several times a day. The wagon owner had to pay for maintenance of the wagon, supply the horses, and pay for animals' feed and grain. Below is the tack room in the stable.

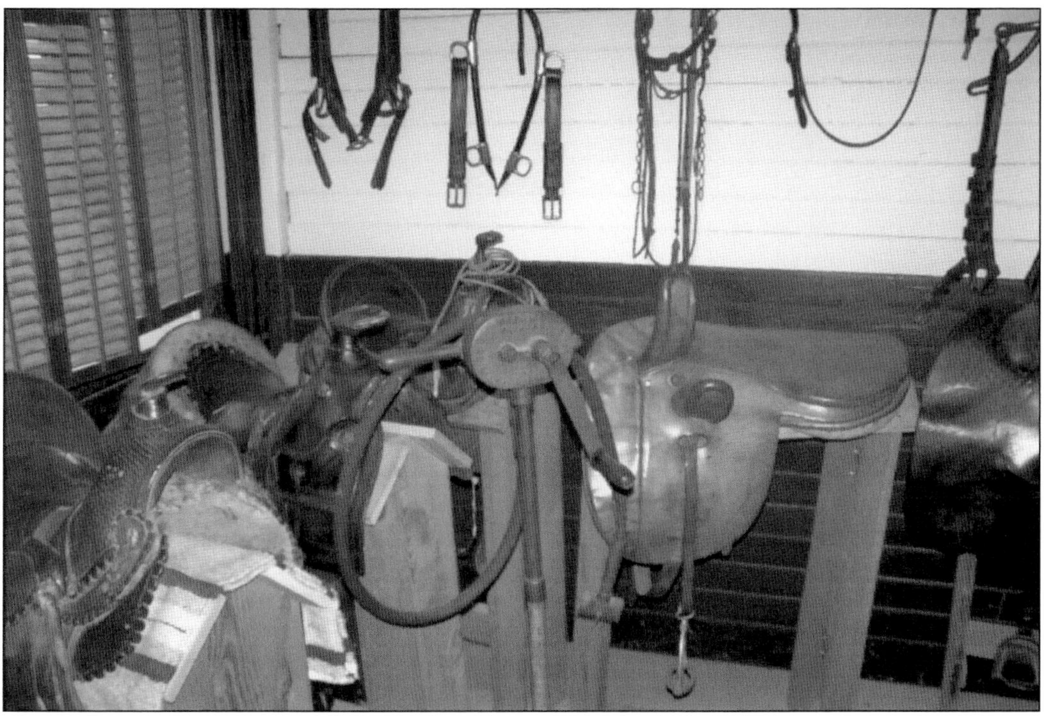

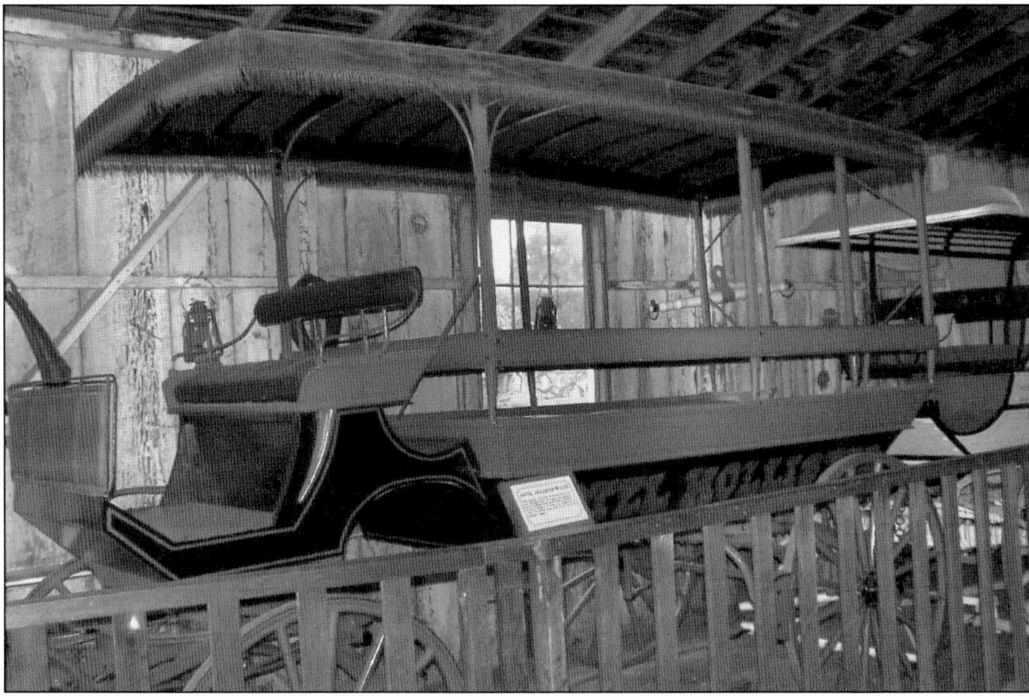

The Hollister Hotel wagon carried passengers from the hotel to and from the train depot. The seats ran the length of the wagon, and a stair at the rear allowed passengers to step directly from the train platform. The wagon only traveled four blocks and was provided as a service to hotel patrons. Baggage was transported in a separate wagon. Below is the carriage of Sen. William Raston.

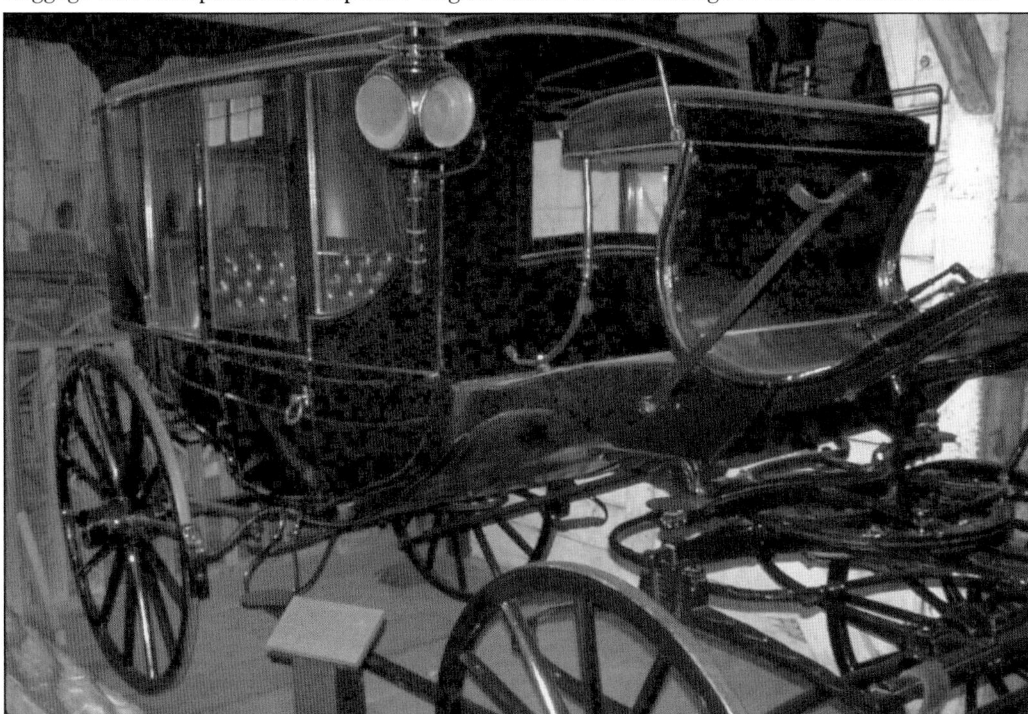

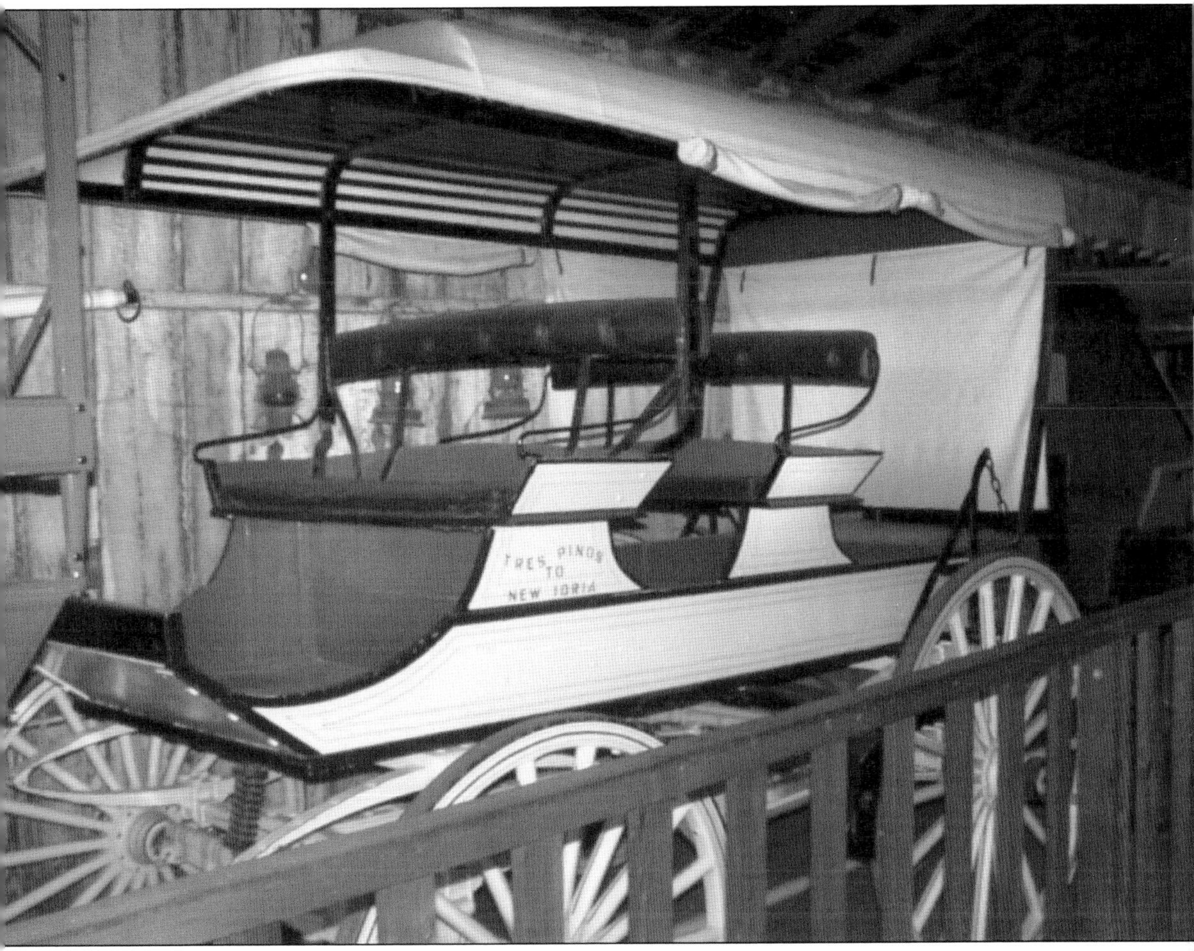

The Tres Pinos Stage ran from the town of Tres Pinos to the New Idria quicksilver mines some 50 miles to the south. Many townspeople gathered in the streets as the stage rolled in to see who and what was aboard. The dirt road climbed many hills and crossed streams; passengers were often asked to get out and walk up the steep hills and along the rain-filled streams.

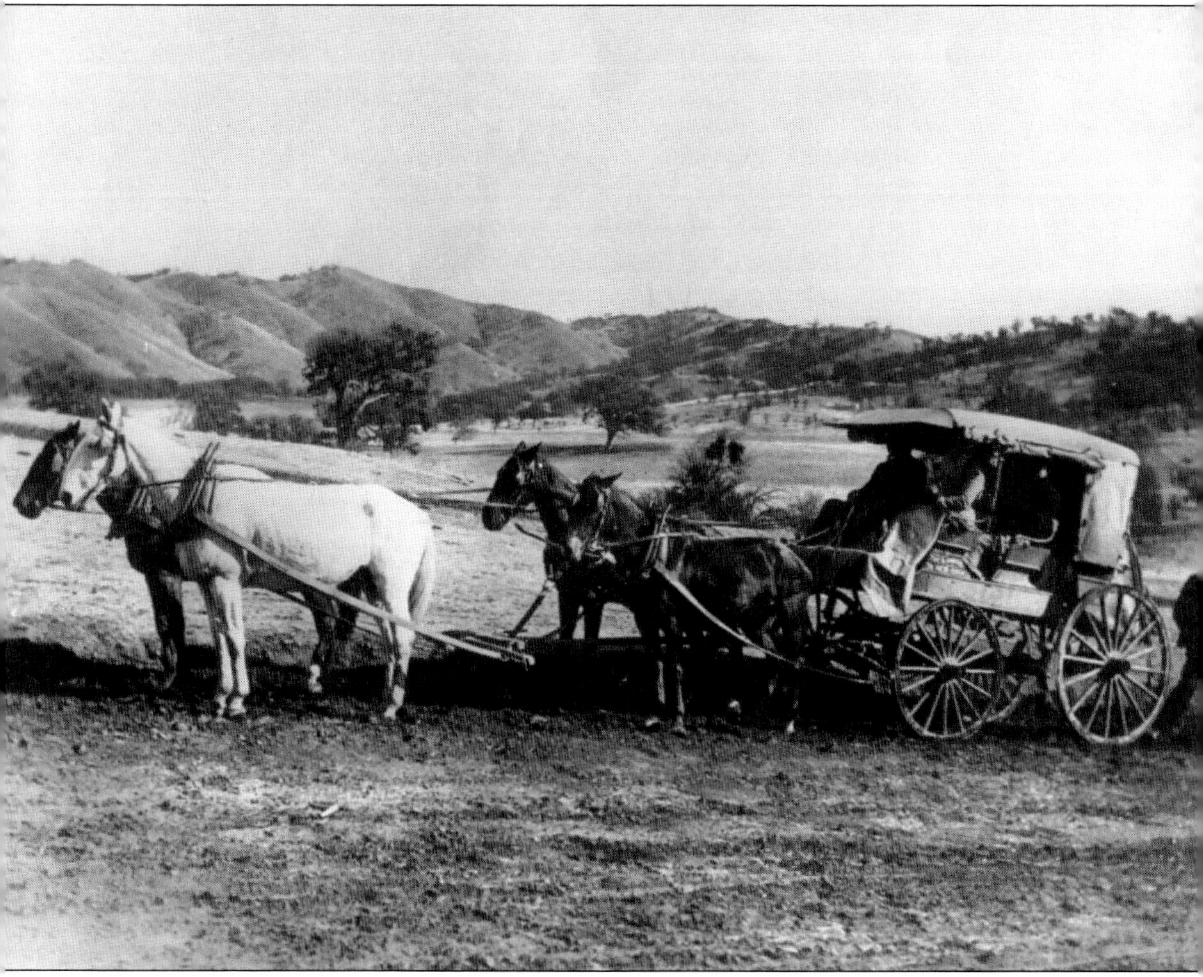

A. J. Fruits owned and operated the Tres Pinos Stage. This 1900 photograph shows the typical terrain traveled and the crowded conditions.

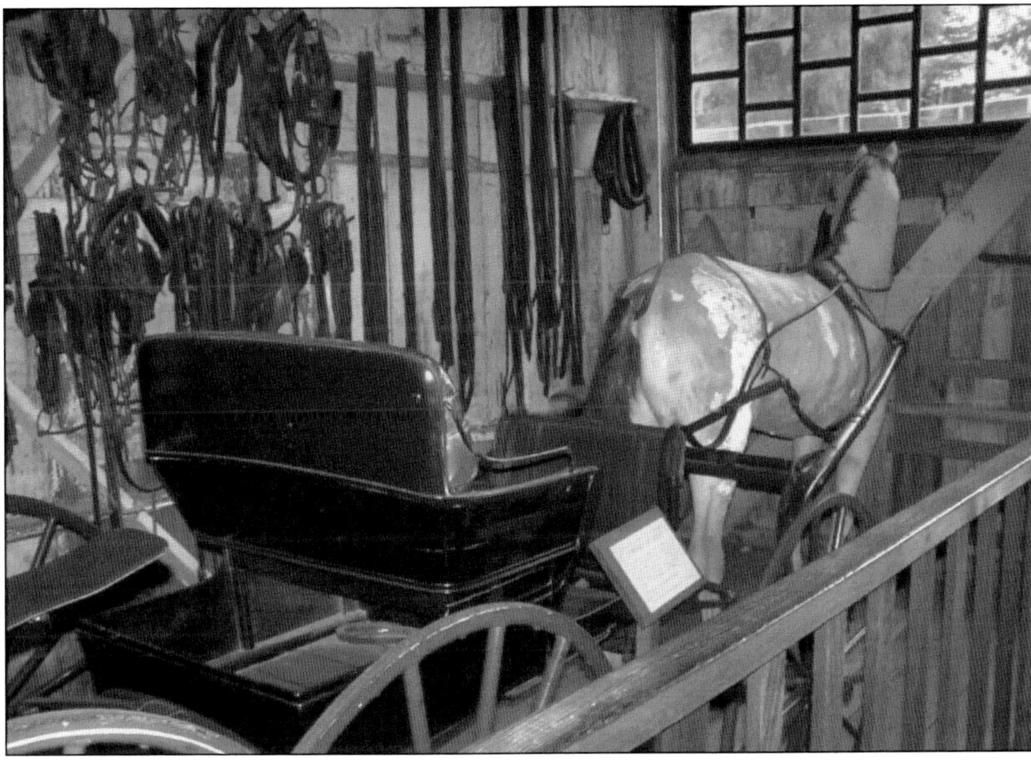

This carriage and manikin were used in Alfred Hitchcock's *Vertigo*. Kim Novak sat in the carriage before she left the stable and entered the mission. The year 2007 is the 50th anniversary of the movie's release.

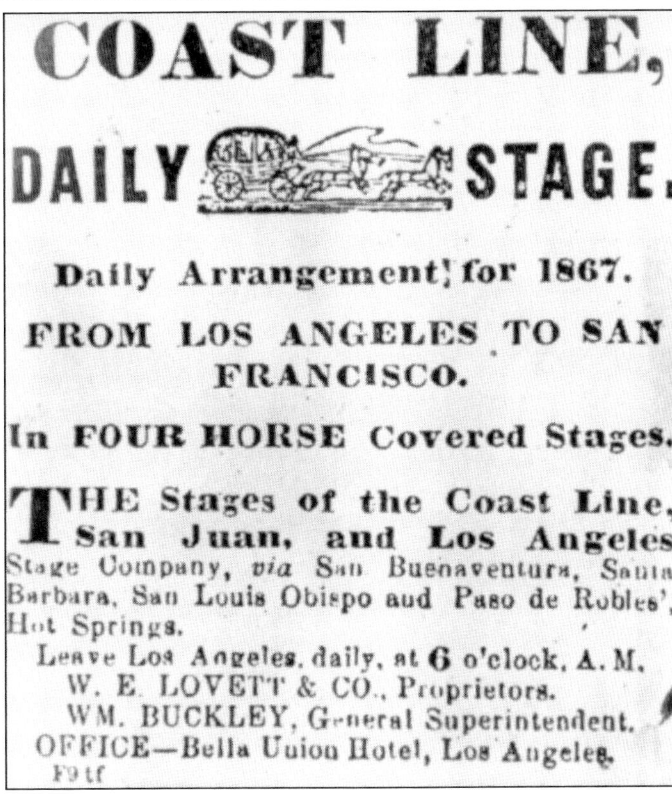

W. E. Lovett, a relative of Thomas Flint, owned the Coast Line Stage. This advertisement was seen throughout California.

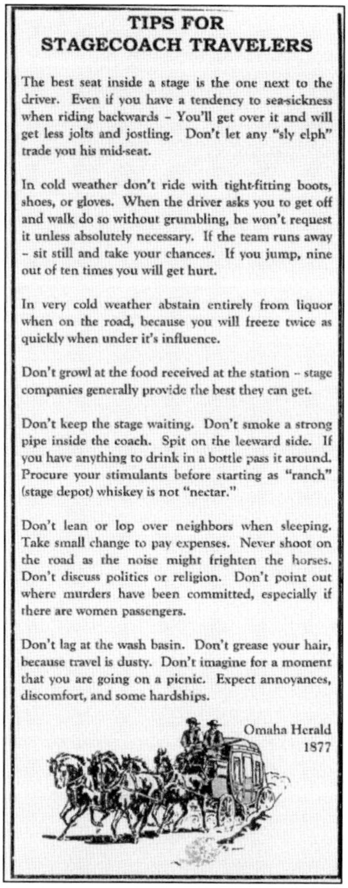

TIPS FOR STAGECOACH TRAVELERS

The best seat inside a stage is the one next to the driver. Even if you have a tendency to sea-sickness when riding backwards - You'll get over it and will get less jolts and jostling. Don't let any "sly elph" trade you his mid-seat.

In cold weather don't ride with tight-fitting boots, shoes, or gloves. When the driver asks you to get off and walk do so without grumbling, he won't request it unless absolutely necessary. If the team runs away - sit still and take your chances. If you jump, nine out of ten times you will get hurt.

In very cold weather abstain entirely from liquor when on the road, because you will freeze twice as quickly when under it's influence.

Don't growl at the food received at the station - stage companies generally provide the best they can get.

Don't keep the stage waiting. Don't smoke a strong pipe inside the coach. Spit on the leeward side. If you have anything to drink in a bottle pass it around. Procure your stimulants before starting as "ranch" (stage depot) whiskey is not "nectar."

Don't lean or lop over neighbors when sleeping. Take small change to pay expenses. Never shoot on the road as the noise might frighten the horses. Don't discuss politics or religion. Don't point out where murders have been committed, especially if there are women passengers.

Don't lag at the wash basin. Don't grease your hair, because travel is dusty. Don't imagine for a moment that you are going on a picnic. Expect annoyances, discomfort, and some hardships.

Omaha Herald
1877

This poster was given to all patrons when they boarded the Coast Line Stage. It contained the code of conduct expected of passengers.

The San Juan Eagles Hook and Ladder Company's fire truck, built in 1869, is one of the oldest vehicles of its type in California. A crew of 16 men was used to propel the truck, which carried several ladders as well as buckets of water. These ladders were strong enough to hold four or five men of the bucket brigade as they passed water up to the burning roof.

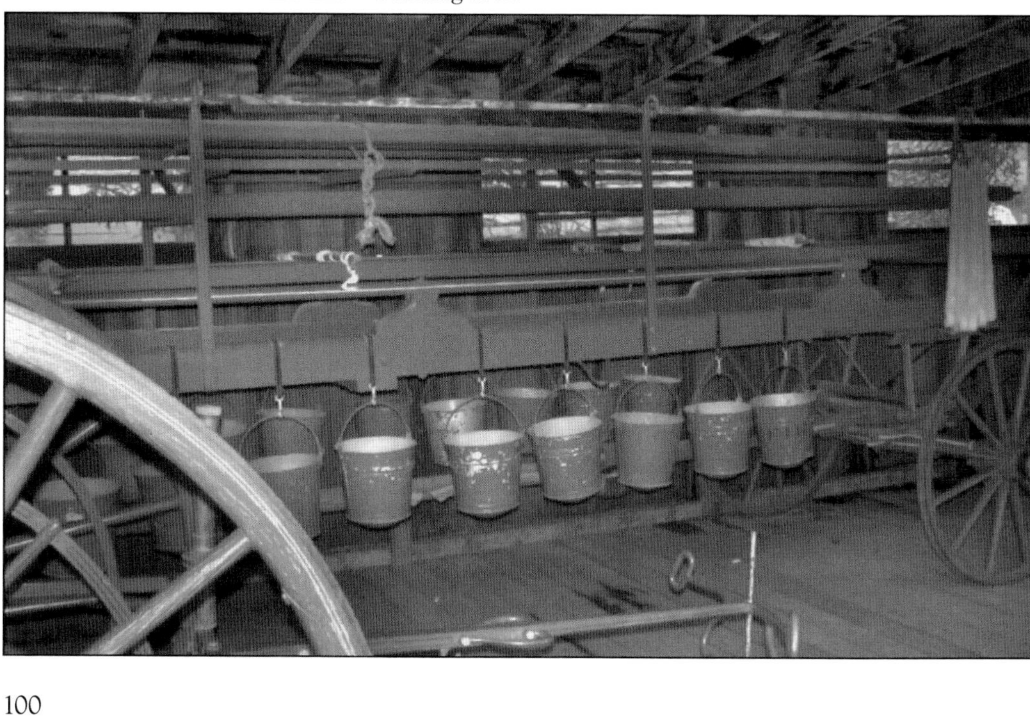

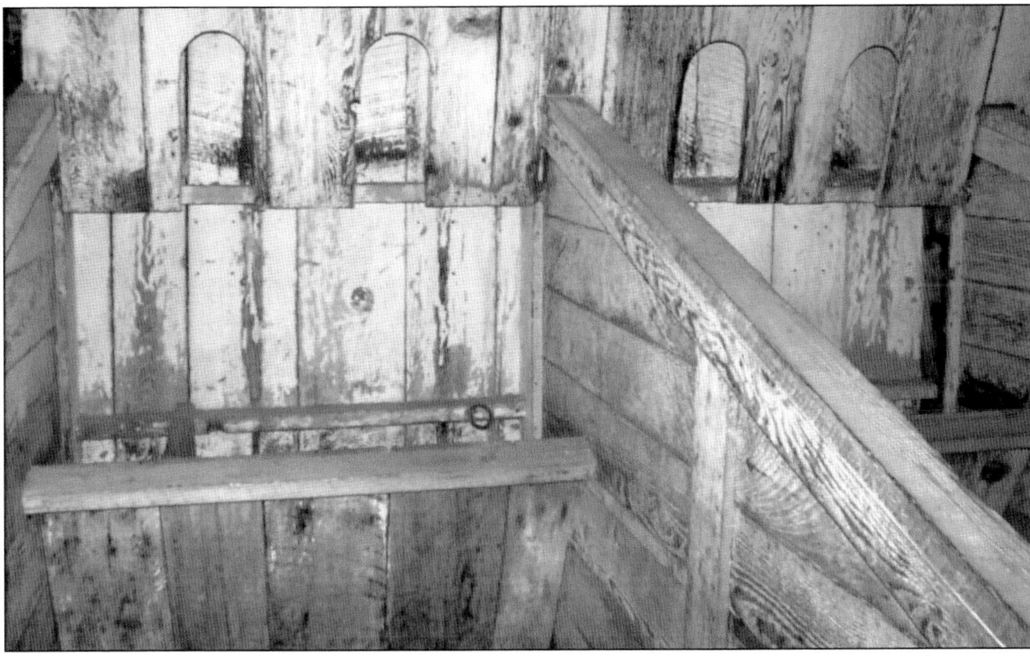

The stable's original stalls had chutes that delivered hay and grain from the loft to the waiting trough. This was a single stall, which did not allow the horse to lie down when sleeping. The stalls were made of rough redwood that was coated to prevent splintering.

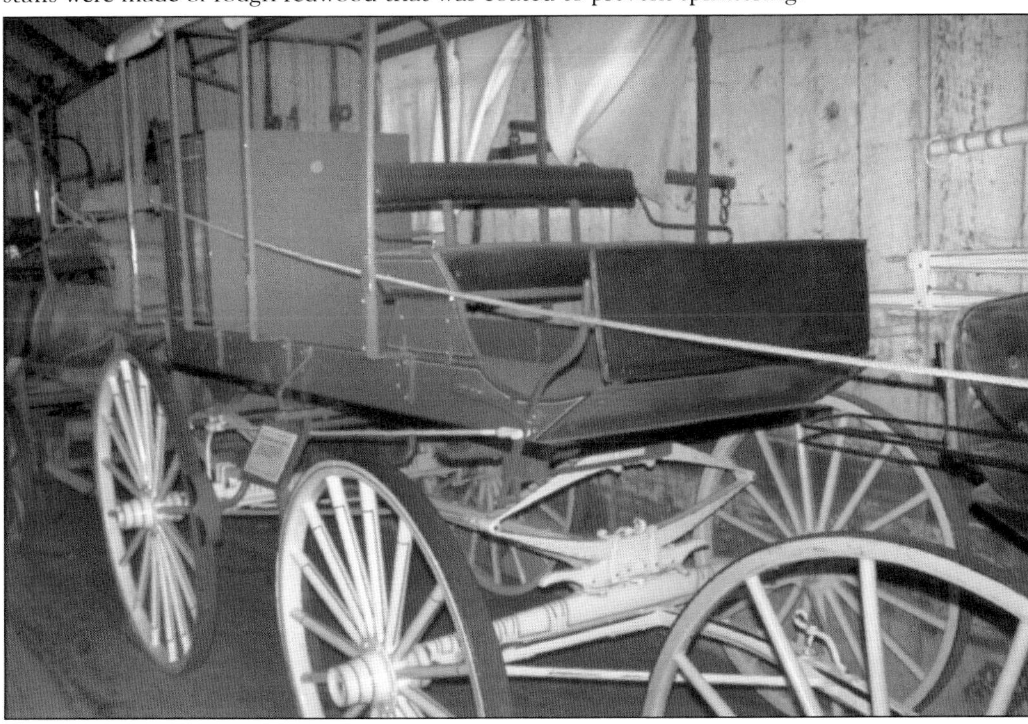

This original chuck wagon dates to the last quarter of the 19th century. It has a large metal-lined box in the rear that kept food hot when it was carried to the fields. Supplies could be brought from a large kitchen in order to provide the men with quick meals.

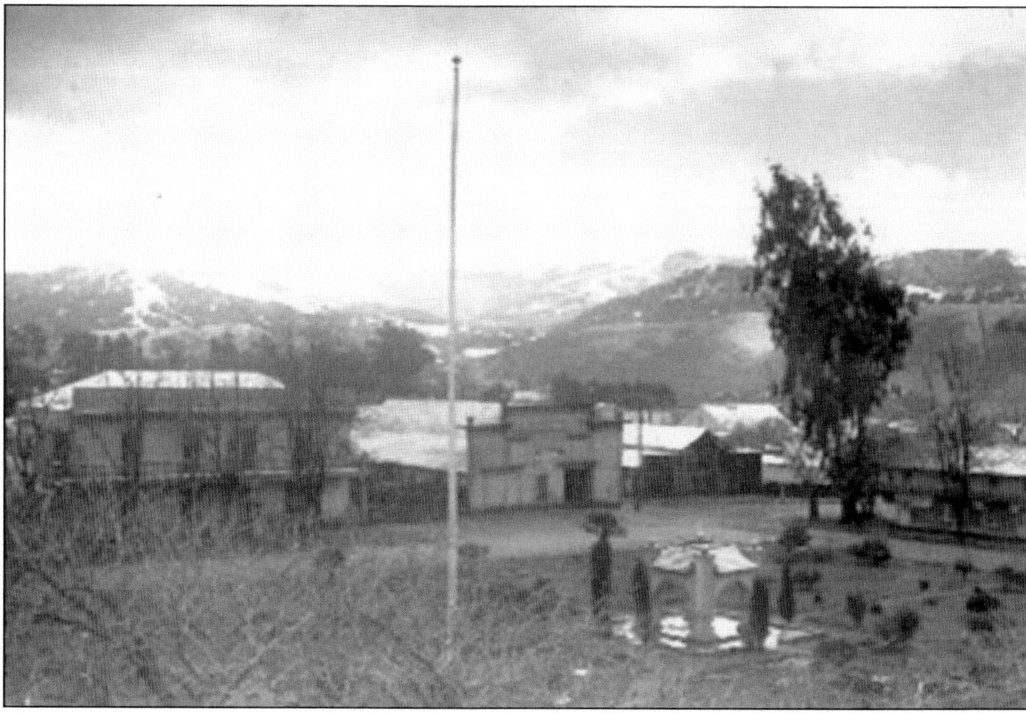

This view of the plaza and stable was likely taken from a balloon. Dating to the early 20th century, the winter scene marks a rare snowfall on the surrounding hills.

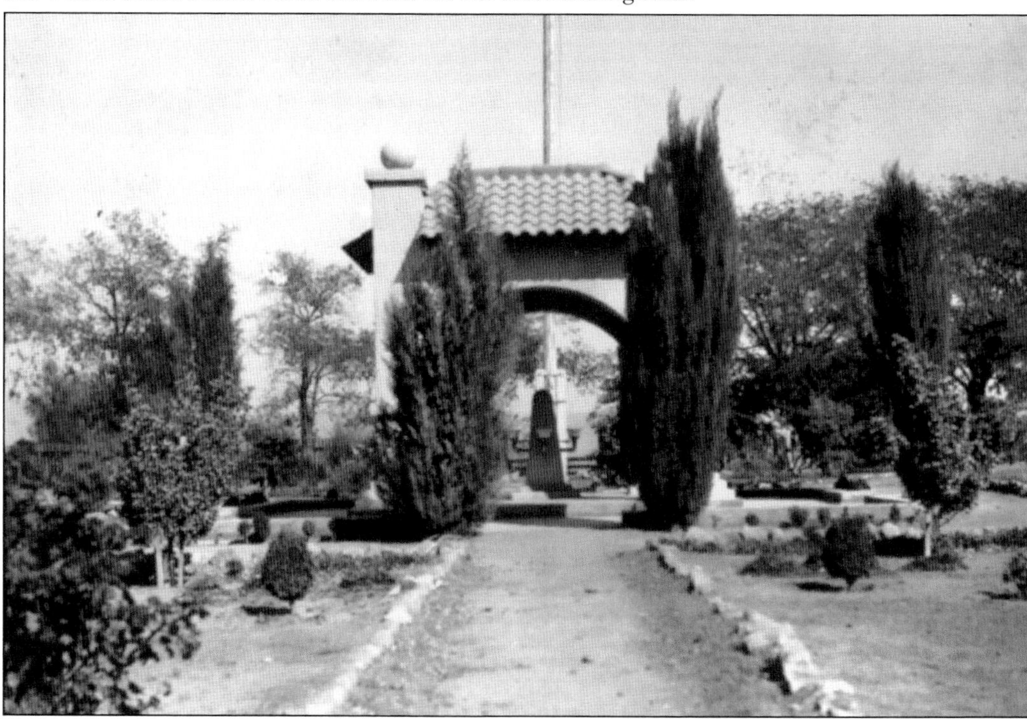

This early-20th-century photograph of the plaza shows the fountain dedicated to a local World War I soldier..

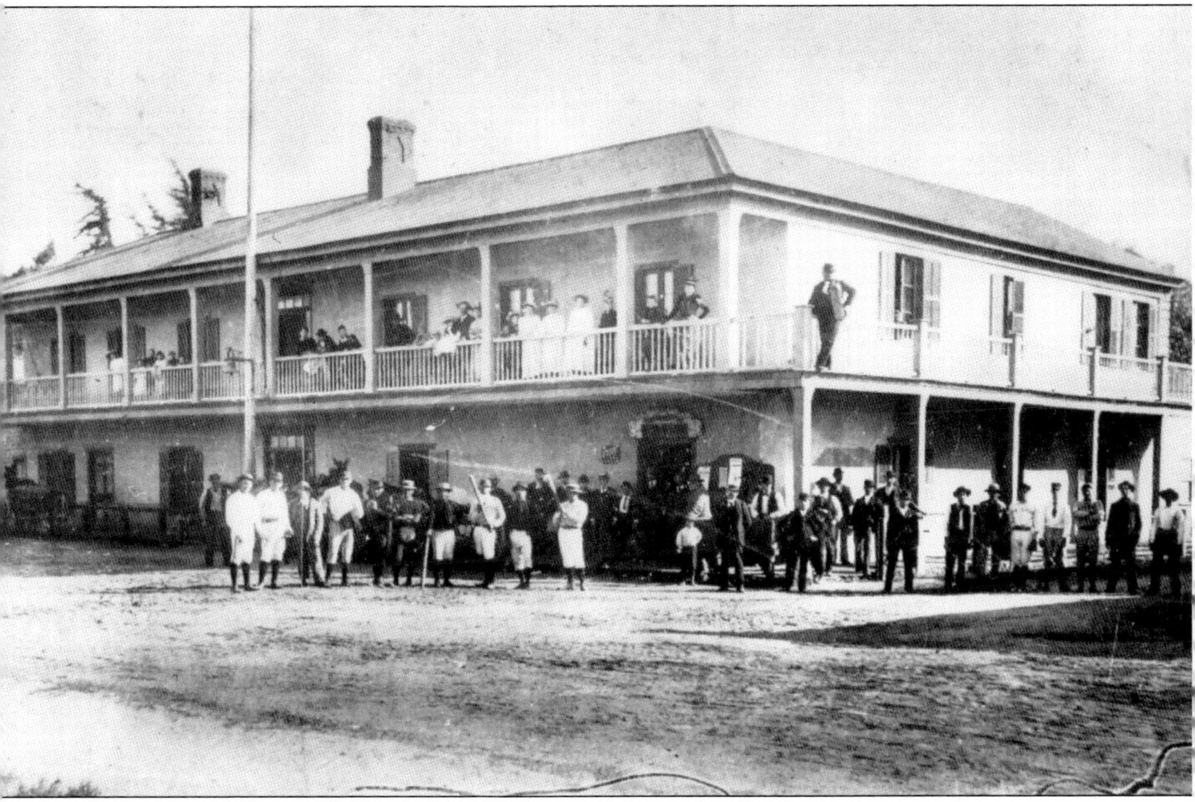

The Plaza Hotel was built on the ruins of the original Spanish soldiers' guardhouse of 1813–1814. When Angelo Zanetta purchased the old guardhouse, he added a second floor and remodeled the first floor. It became the Plaza Hotel and opened in 1856. In this 1890s photograph, townspeople pose with the hometown baseball team.

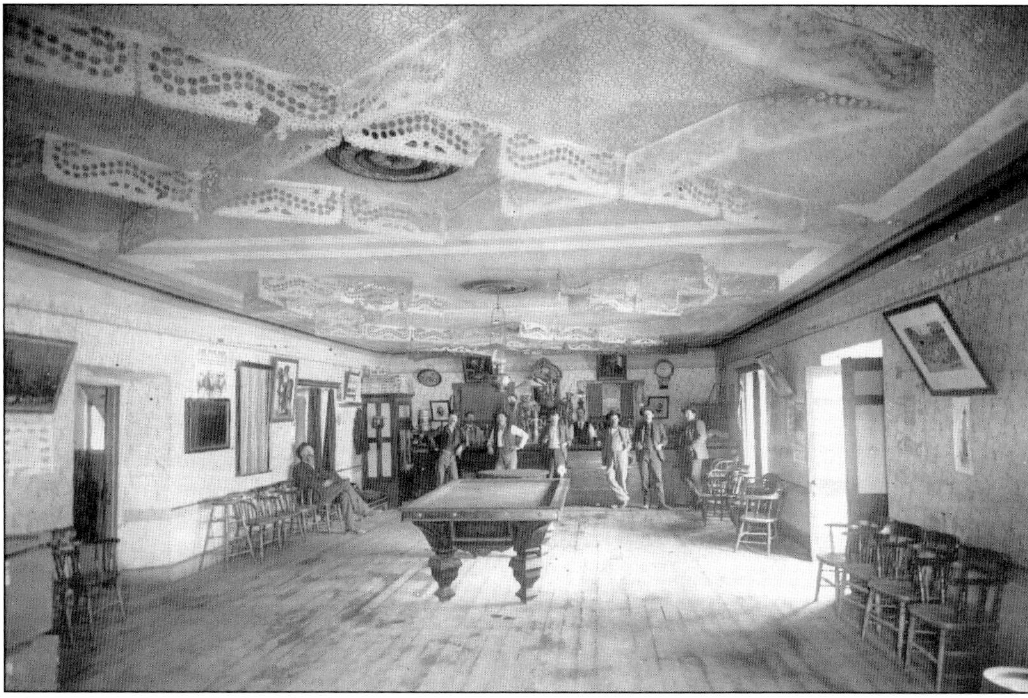

This image shows the hotel saloon in 1898. Today the barroom has been restored to this scene, including the ornamental stencils, or *papel picado*, displayed during celebrations. The pool table was shipped around Cape Horn specially for this room. During the Spanish era, the space was used as the barracks for soldiers.

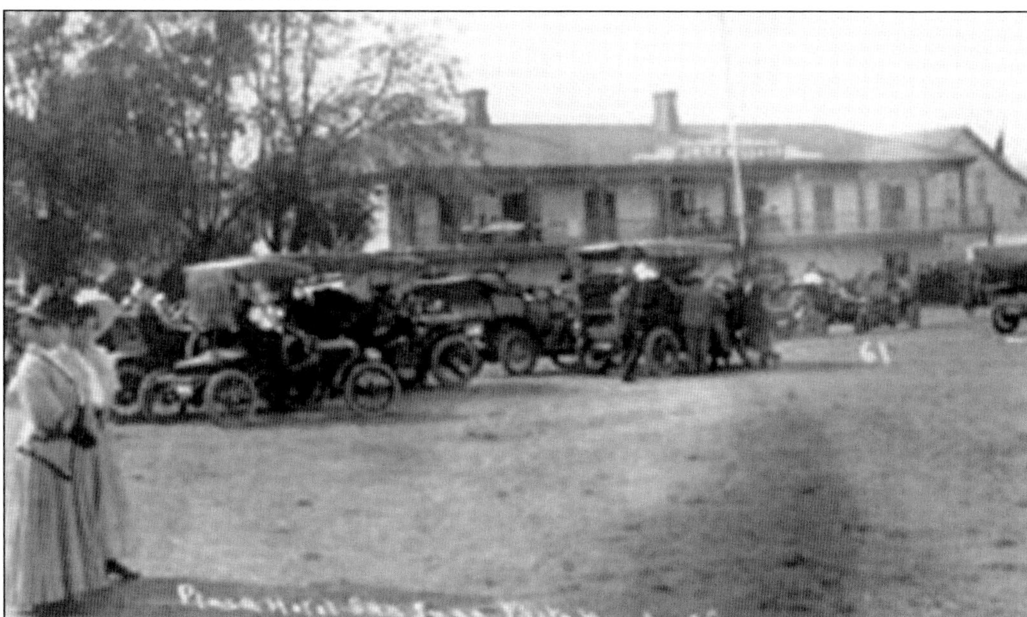

People celebrate the first fiesta at the Plaza Hotel in 1906 to raise money to restore the mission, which was damaged in the earthquake. The annual fiesta of San Juan Bautista is still held on June 24, the feast day of St. John the Baptist.

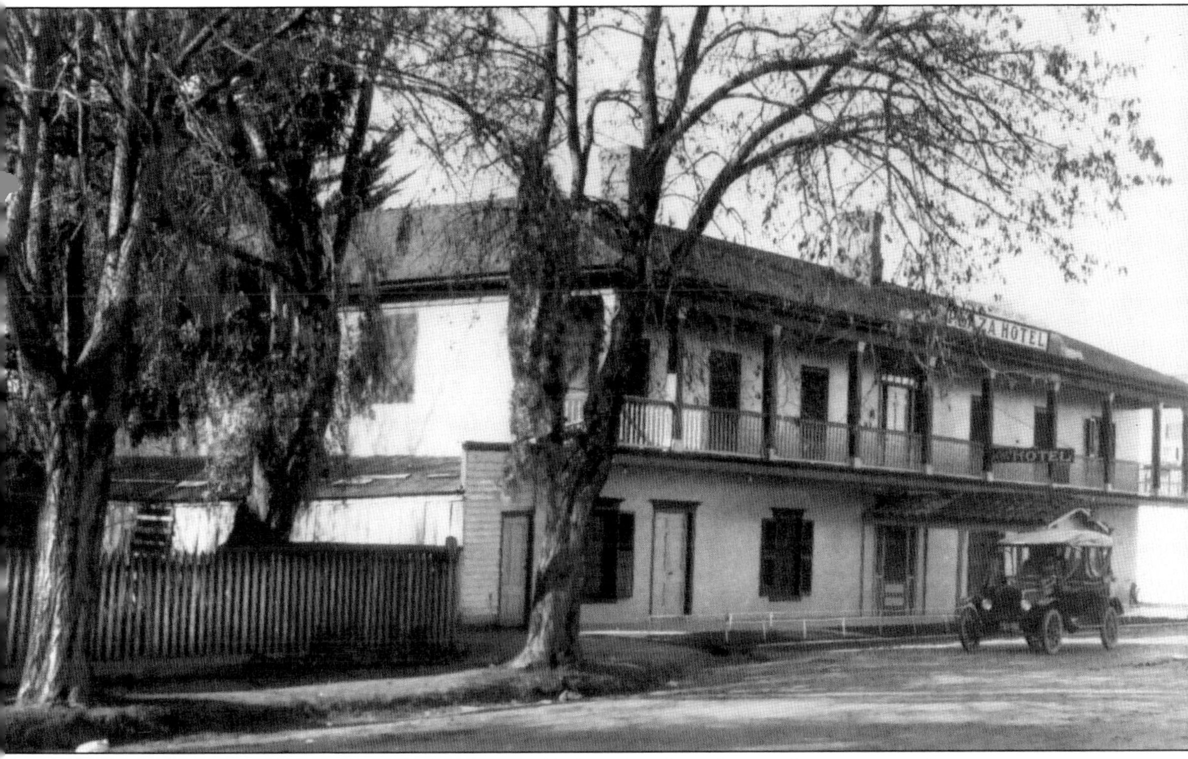

This view of the Plaza Hotel was taken in 1917, shortly after the roads were paved.

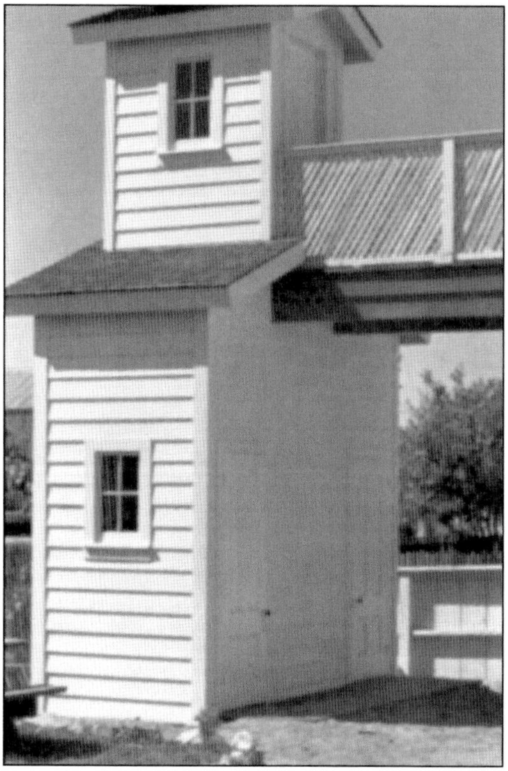

The outhouse for the Plaza Hotel was restored in the 1980s. In its day, it was the height of luxury, since men would use the ground floor and women used the second floor. The latticed walkway on the second floor provided women with a sense of privacy, something lacking in most outhouses of the period. Before this replica was built, archeologists dug into the old pit and found several hundred small medicine and pocket whiskey bottles. They also found a few wire glasses, a gold wedding band, and 16 assorted upper and lower dental plates.

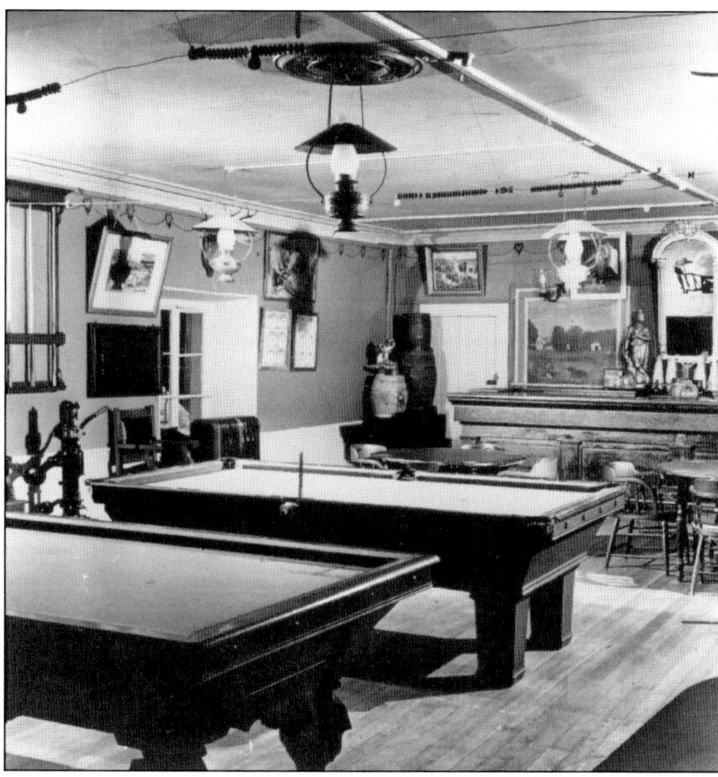

Taken in the 1950s, this photograph of the barroom shows many of the original items, including the hanging lamp and the billiard table in the foreground.

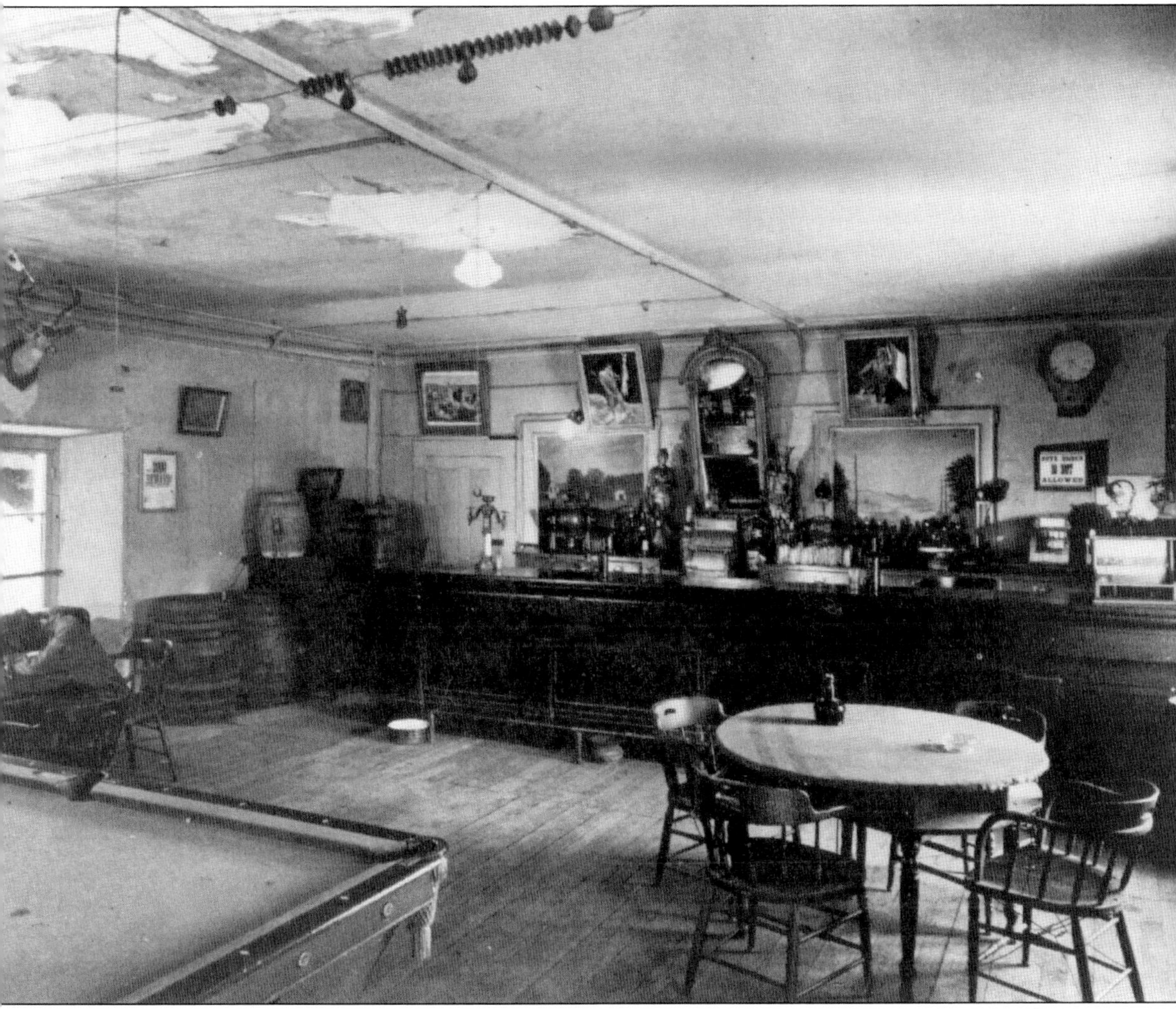

This 1940s image of the barroom reveals many of the original paintings, mirrors, and statues that decorated the back bar. These items are still found in the barroom today.

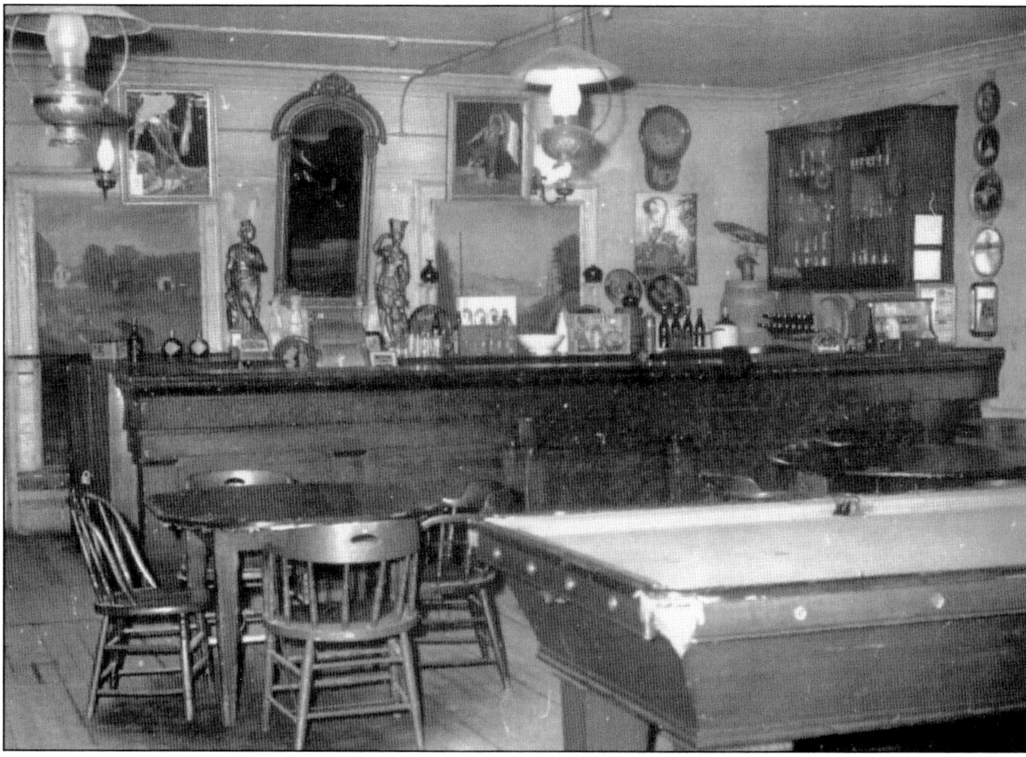

This is another view of the Plaza Hotel barroom before the restoration of the 1980s.

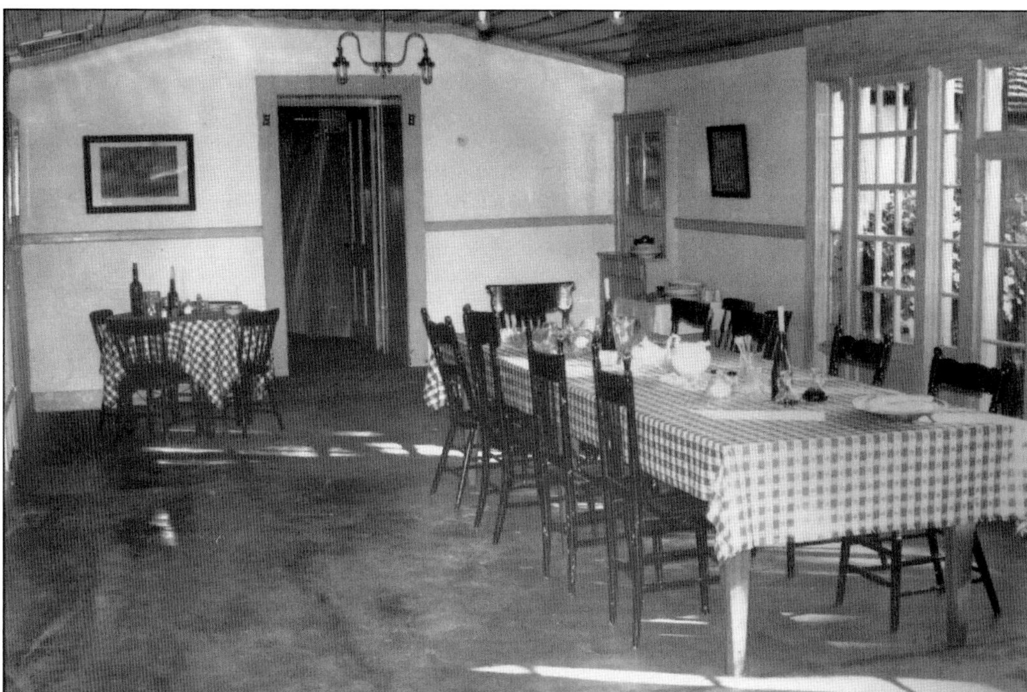

The Plaza Hotel's dining room is pictured before its restoration in 1976.

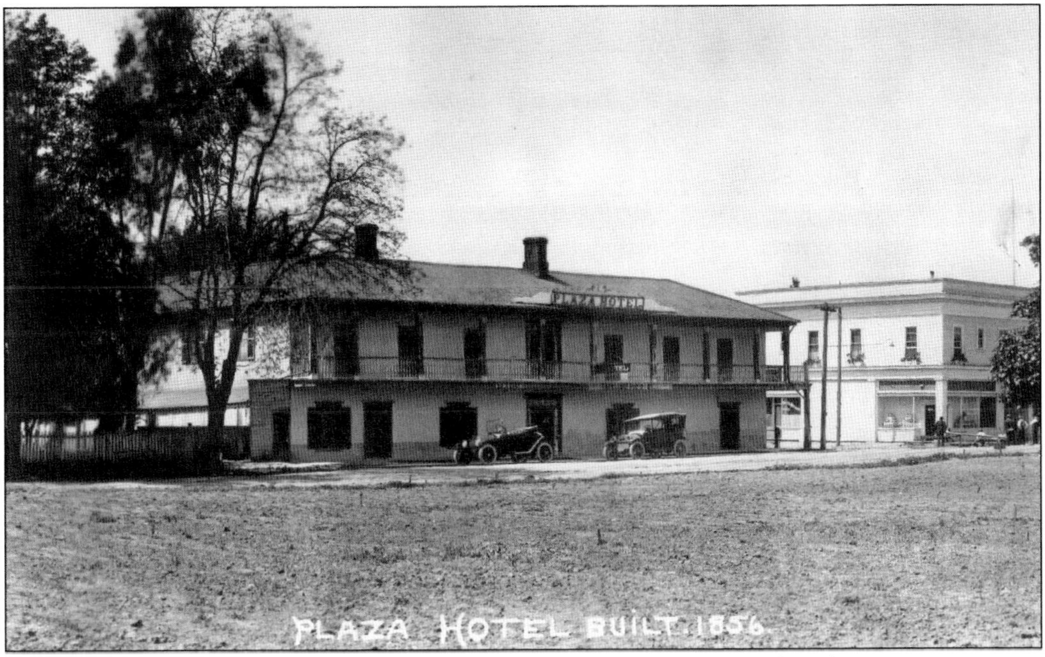

The Plaza Hotel, with the Mission Hotel in the background, is pictured in the 1920s.

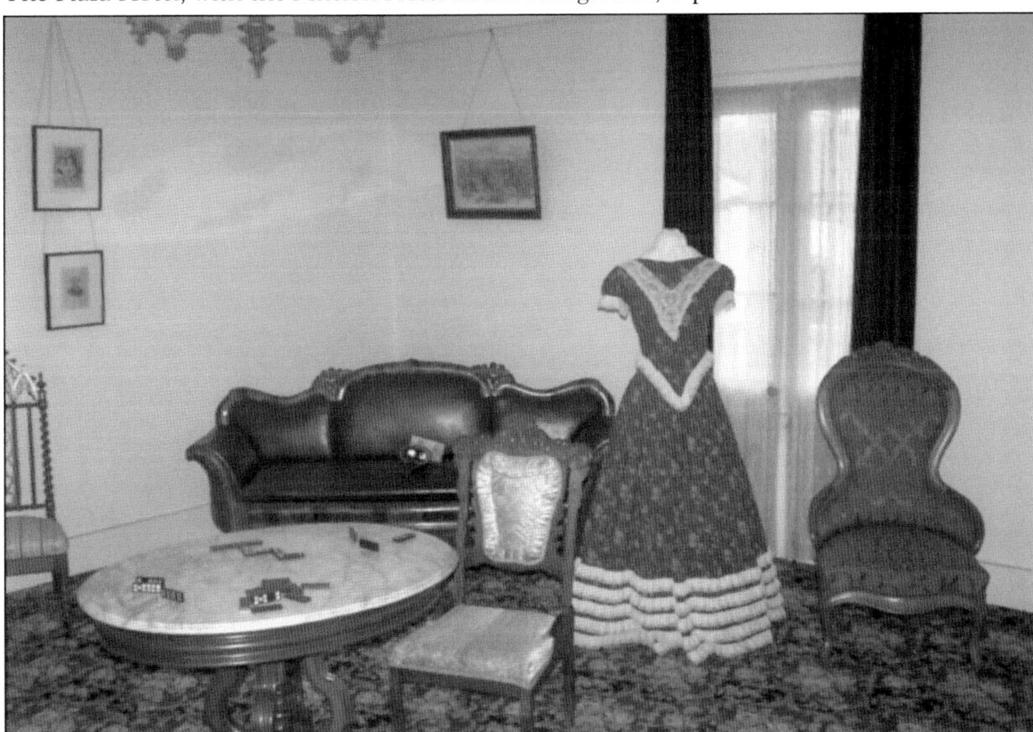

The ladies' parlor on the second floor was reserved as a private place for female guests. Women were not allowed in the saloon, so this room provided the ladies with a place to enjoy their drinks and unlace their corsets. When an unescorted lady came to the hotel, she was directed here and registered as a guest.

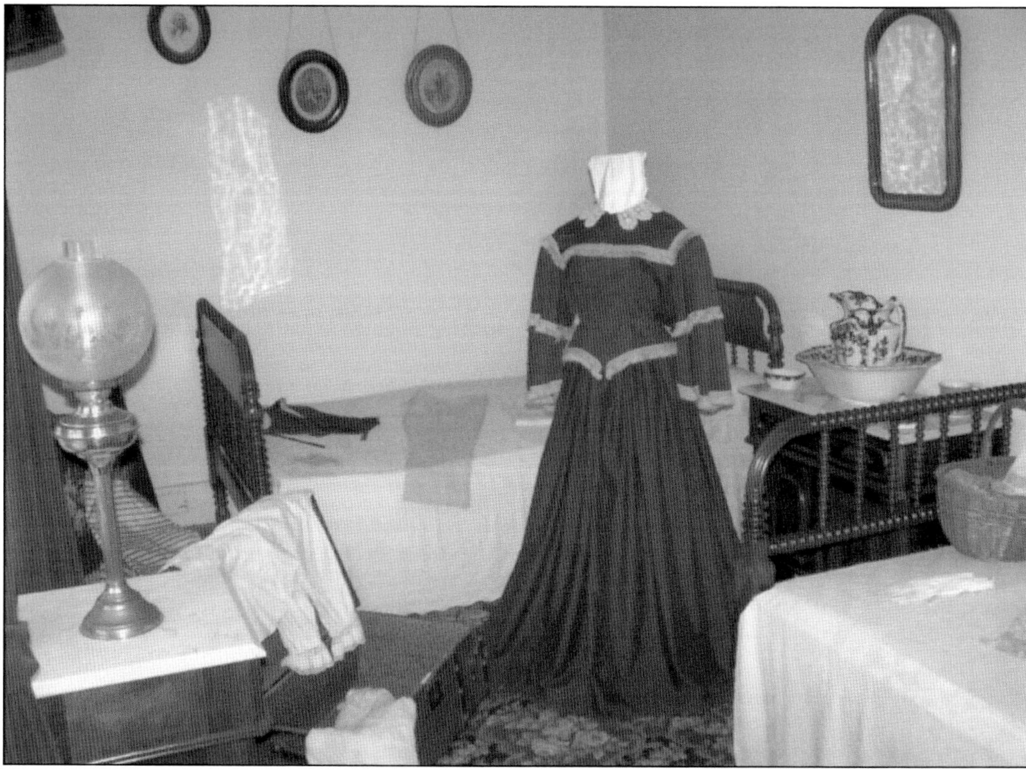

This second-floor guest room displays the original furnishings of the day. When men came to the hotel—either single or with family—they would register in the barroom. It was common for single men to share a room if the hotel was busy.

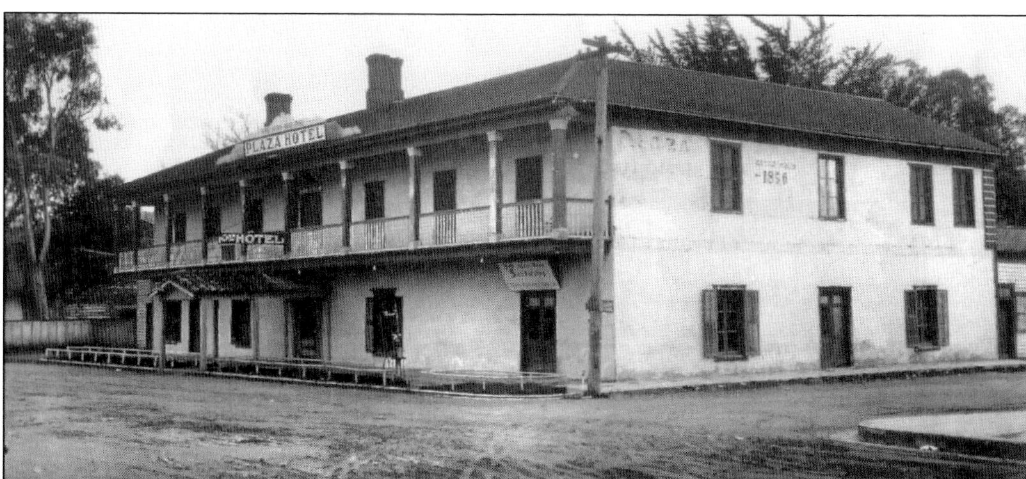

The Plaza Hotel is pictured in this *c.* 1900 view showing the porch roof over the front door. The porch was removed after a short time because it was thought to detract from the original appearance of the building.

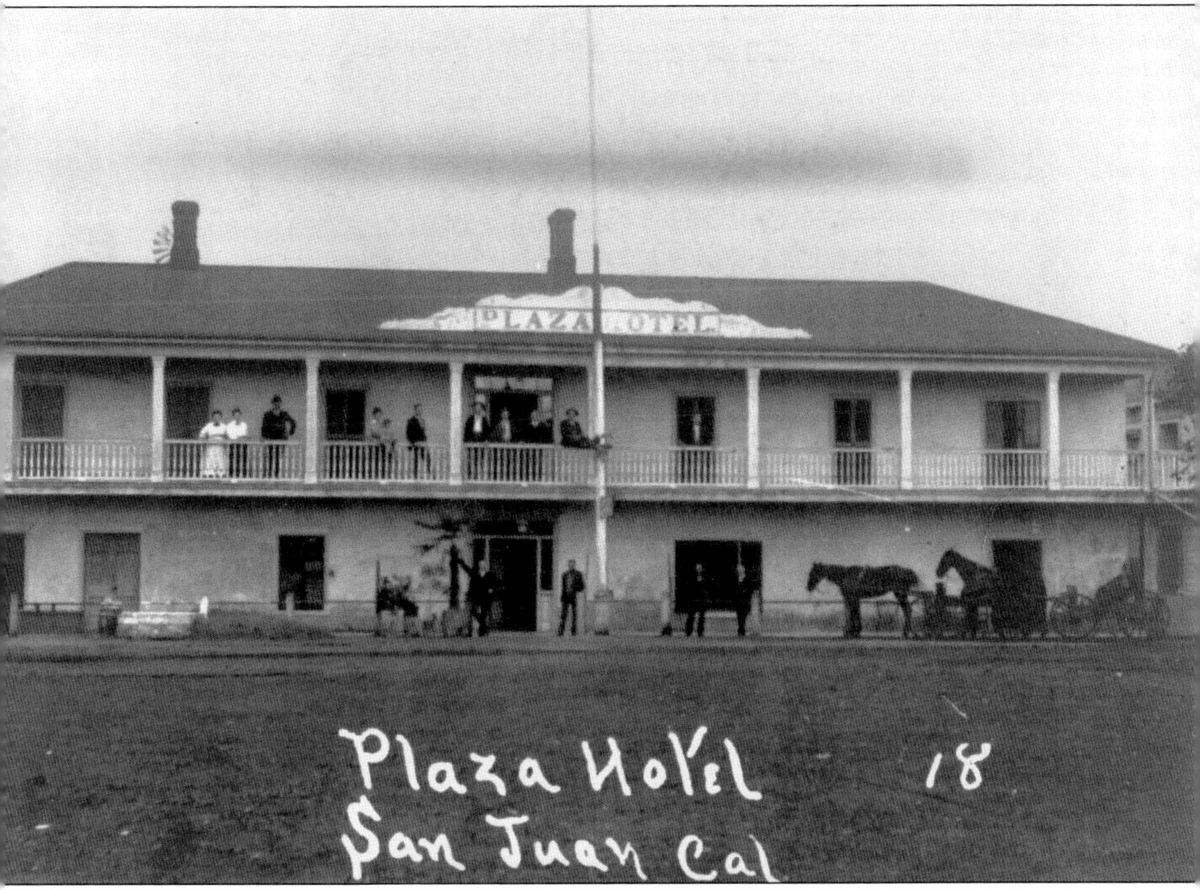

This photograph of the Plaza Hotel was taken in the late 1800s.

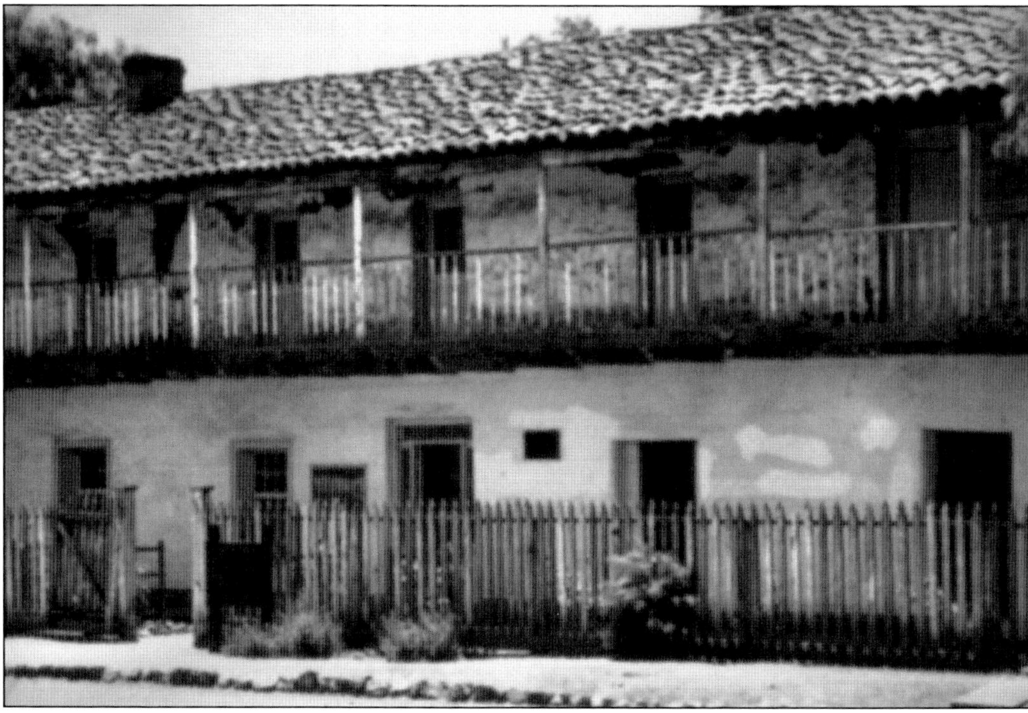

This photograph depicts the Castro-Breen Adobe on its front, or plaza, side in the 1940s. The front fence had been restored by this time, although much work was still needed in order to stabilize the building.

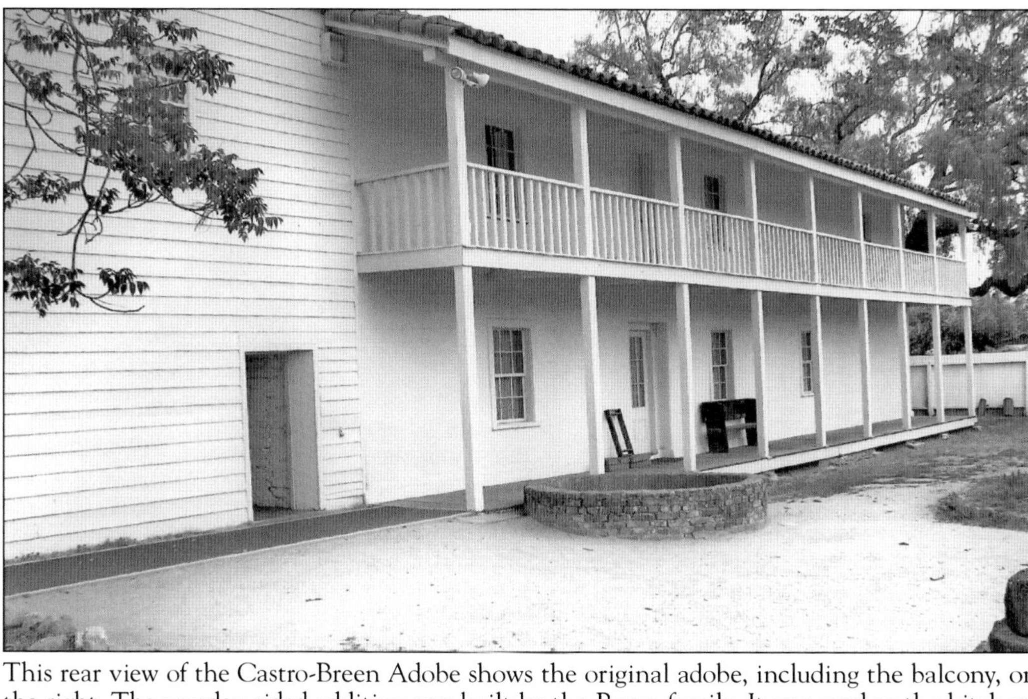

This rear view of the Castro-Breen Adobe shows the original adobe, including the balcony, on the right. The wooden-sided addition was built by the Breen family. It was used as the kitchen. The circular cistern or water storage tank can be seen in the foreground.

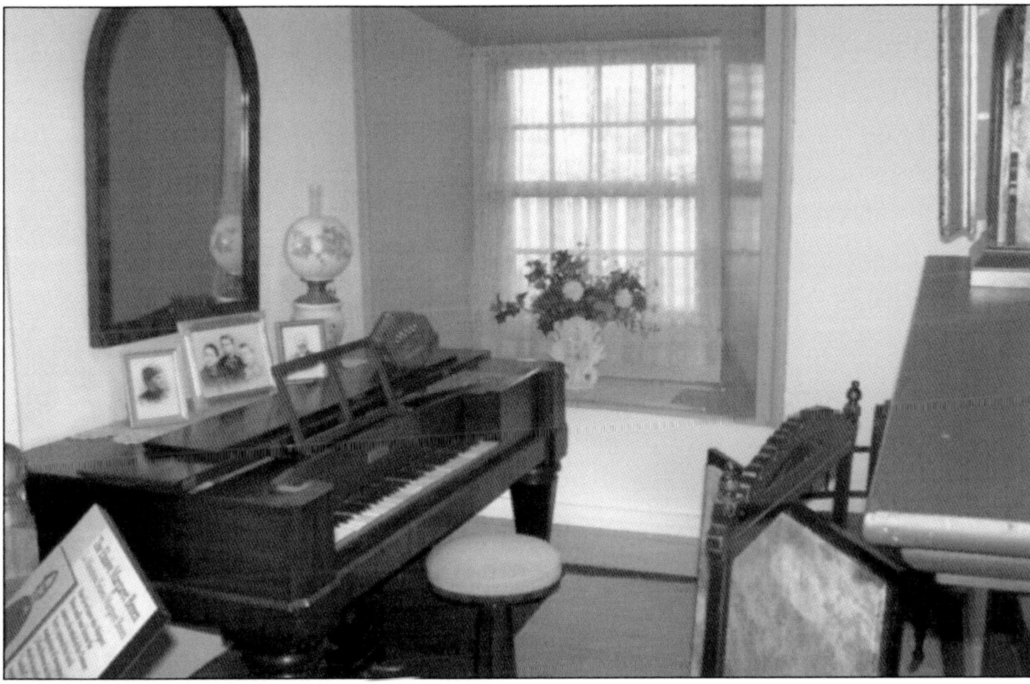

The Breen family purchased this piano after they had bought the house in December 1848 from the Castros. The piano, played by the Breen children, has been kept in excellent condition by the park staff.

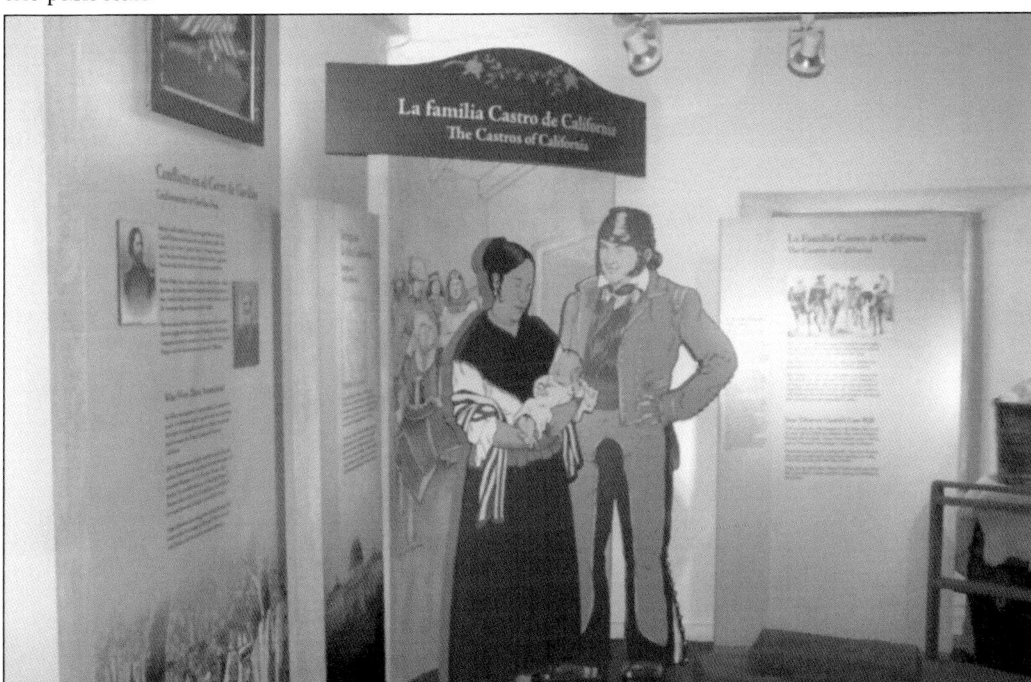

This room is dedicated to the history of the Castro family. The small photographs on the left are portraits of John C. Fremont and Gen. Jose Castro.

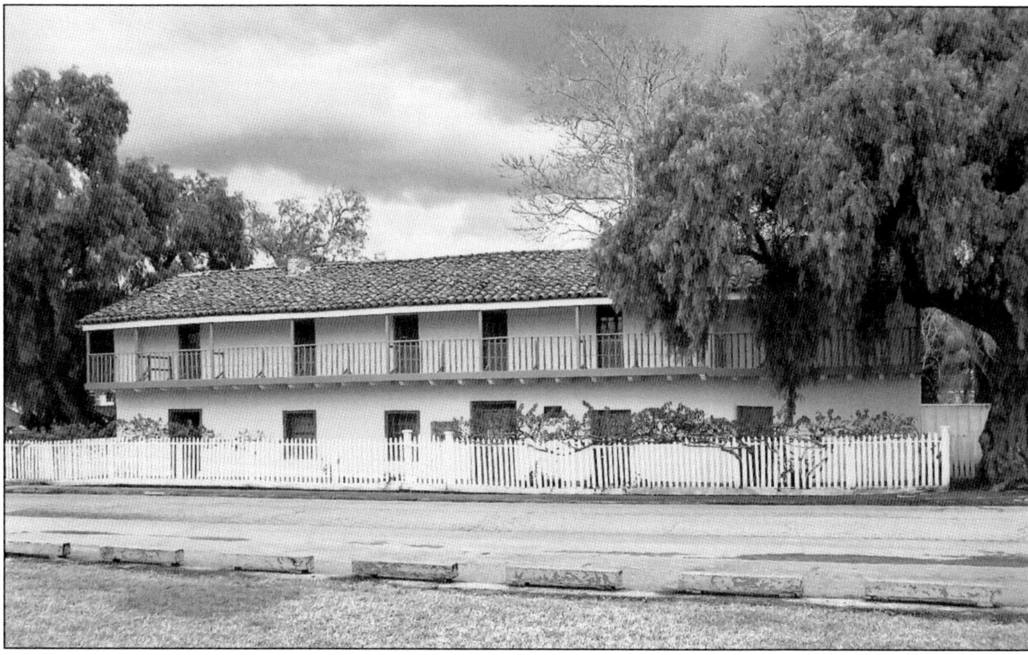

This is a present view of the front of the Castro-Breen Adobe. Great attention was given to an authentic appearance during the seismic retrofitting of 2005–2006. Below is a view of the room dedicated to the history of the Patrick Breen family. The room includes the original desk owned by John Breen (right) and items of clothing that survived the winter of 1846.

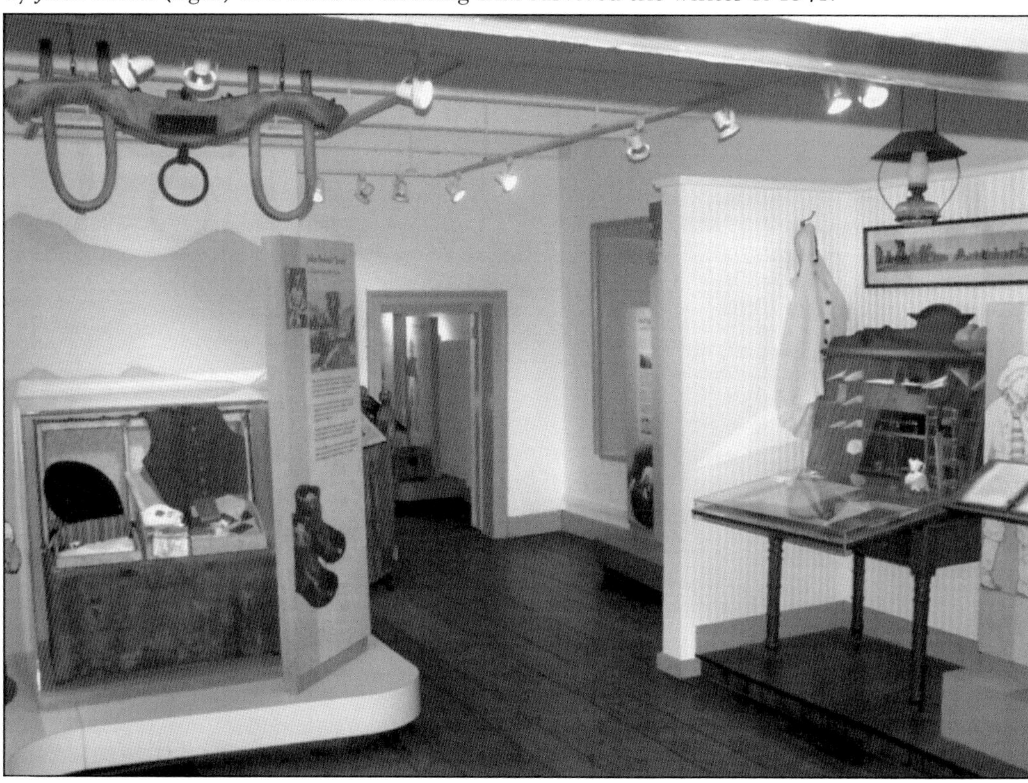

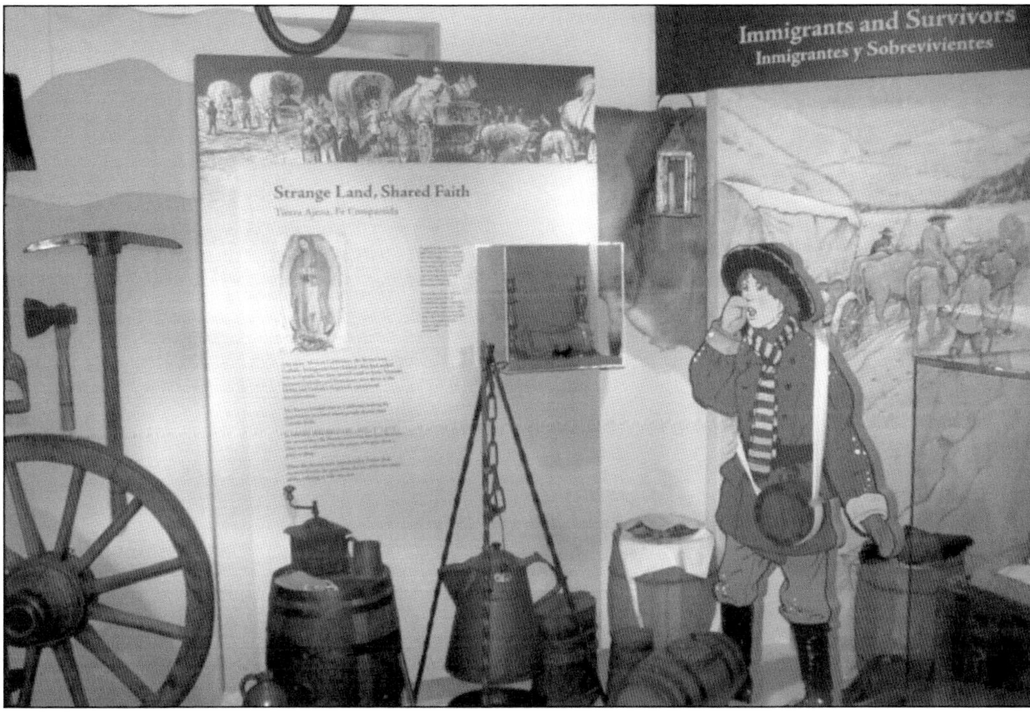

Above is a view of the Breen Room, dedicated to the early settlers who came overland to California during the years before and after the Gold Rush of 1848–1849. The candlesticks in the case belonged to the Breens and were with them during the harsh winter of 1846. Below is the old San Juan jail, built in 1870. It was originally located on Third Street before its donation to the state park in 1954. The building consists of two very small rooms with an attached outhouse. It was frequently used to hold suspects until a trial could be convened by the justice of the peace. It operated until 1941, when it was closed and a new jail built.

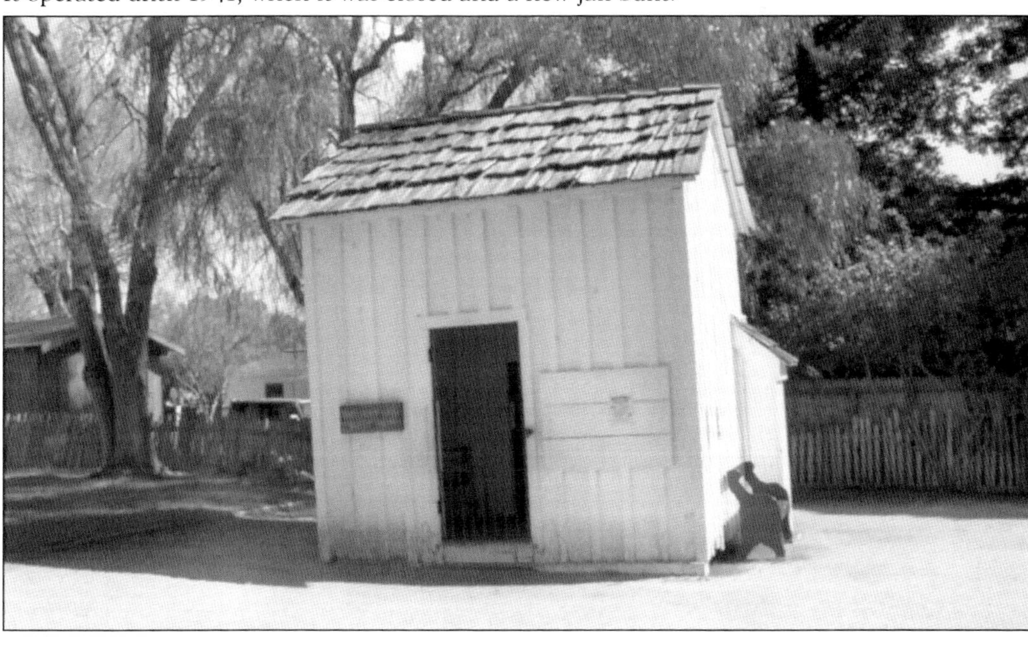

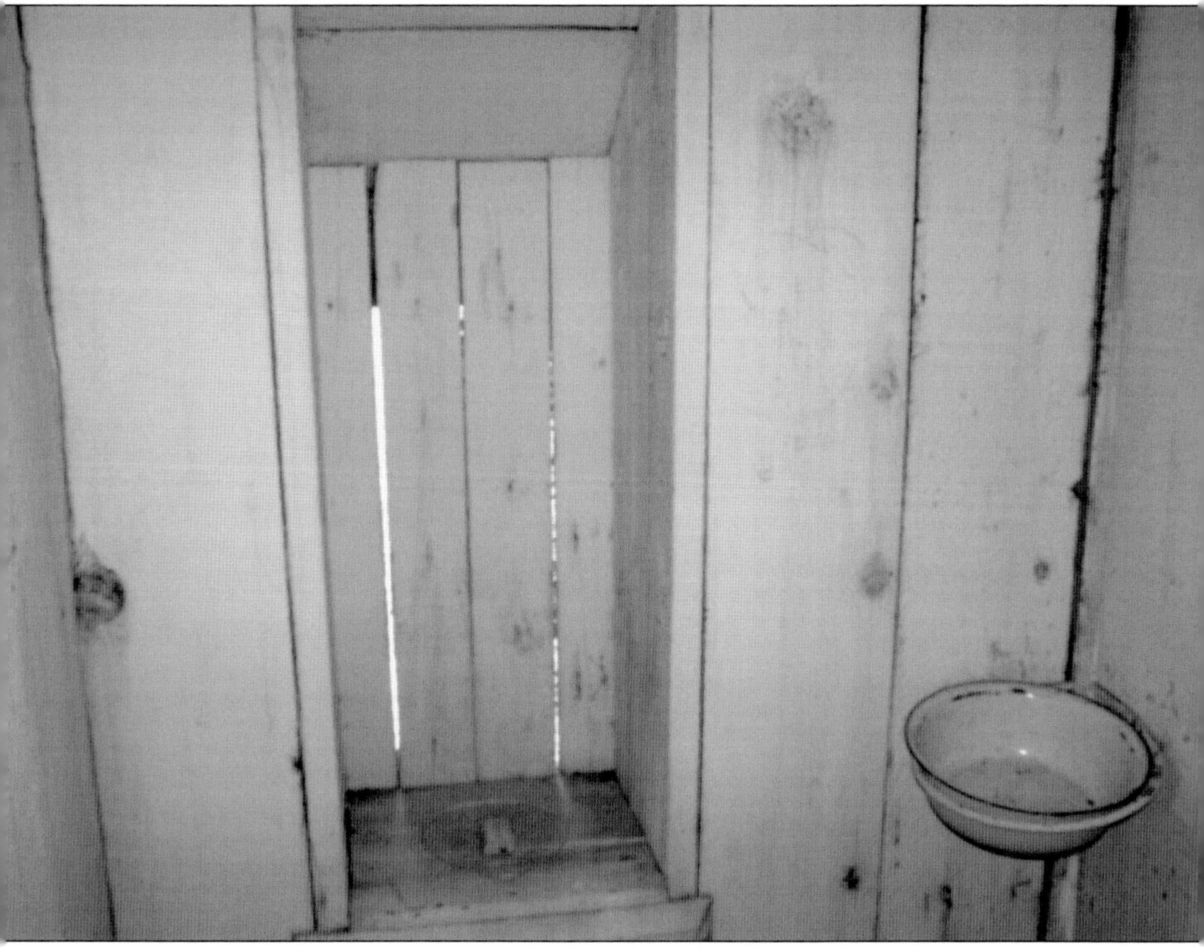

The jail's outhouse is attached to the second room. There is a small cover for the original hole.

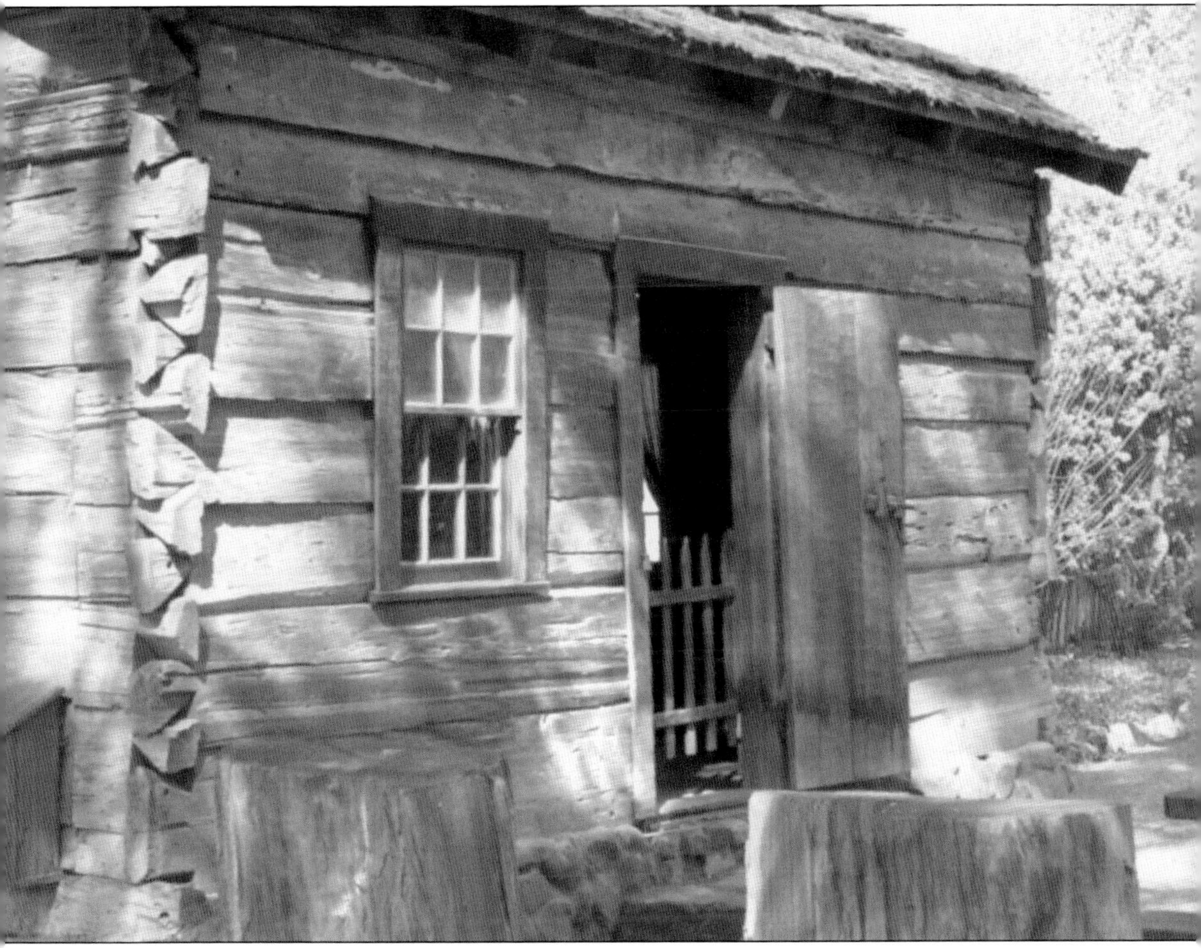

This cabin initially stood at the south edge of town and housed the Francis family. Mr. Francis, a shoemaker, constructed the cabin of split redwood slab planks placed horizontally and dovetailed at the corners. The floor is redwood, and the roof is covered with redwood shakes. When the cabin was moved to its present location, the sandstone fireplace and foundations were replaced.

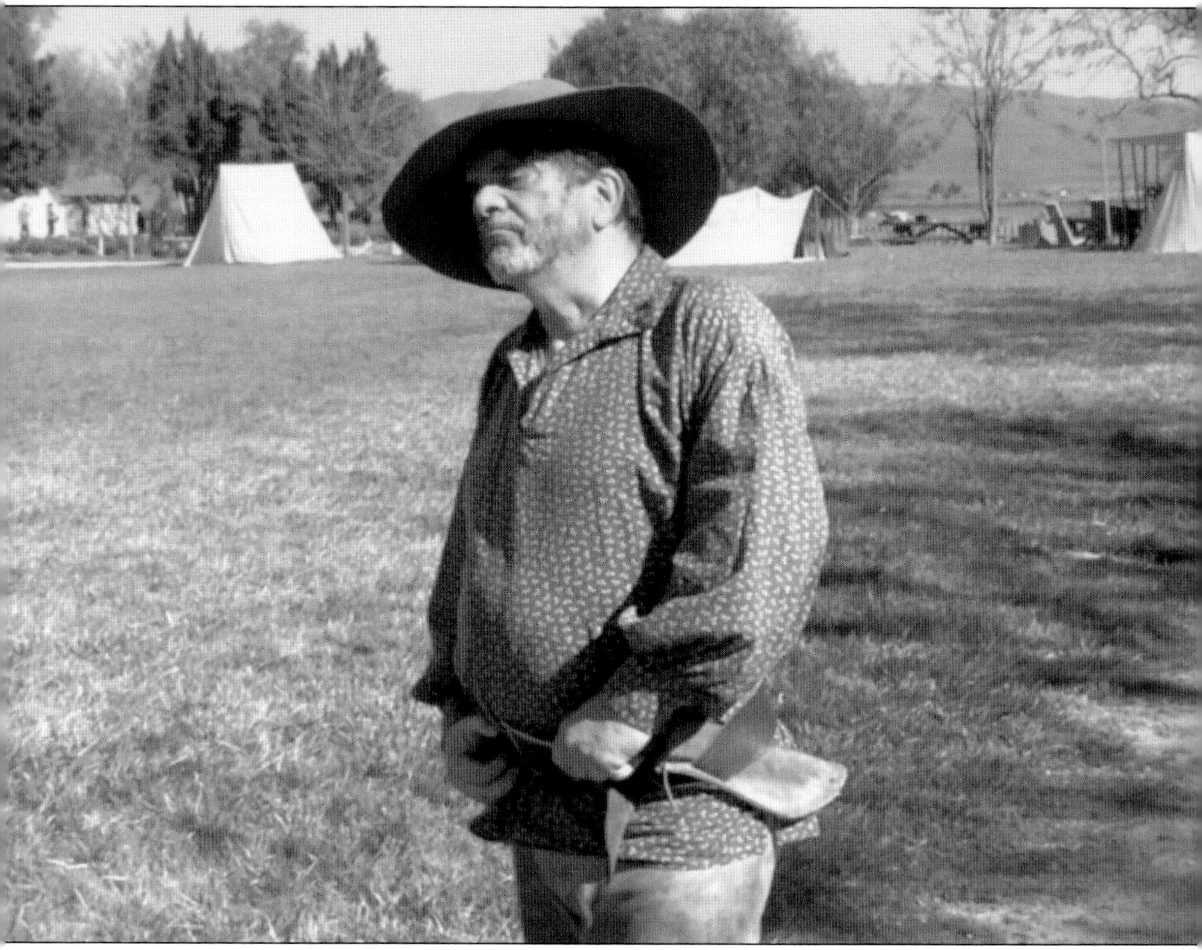

Larry Brown is a member of a group of men and women who portray the Mountain Men era of San Juan Bautista history. The many wonderful volunteer docents at San Juan often dress in costume for historical events.

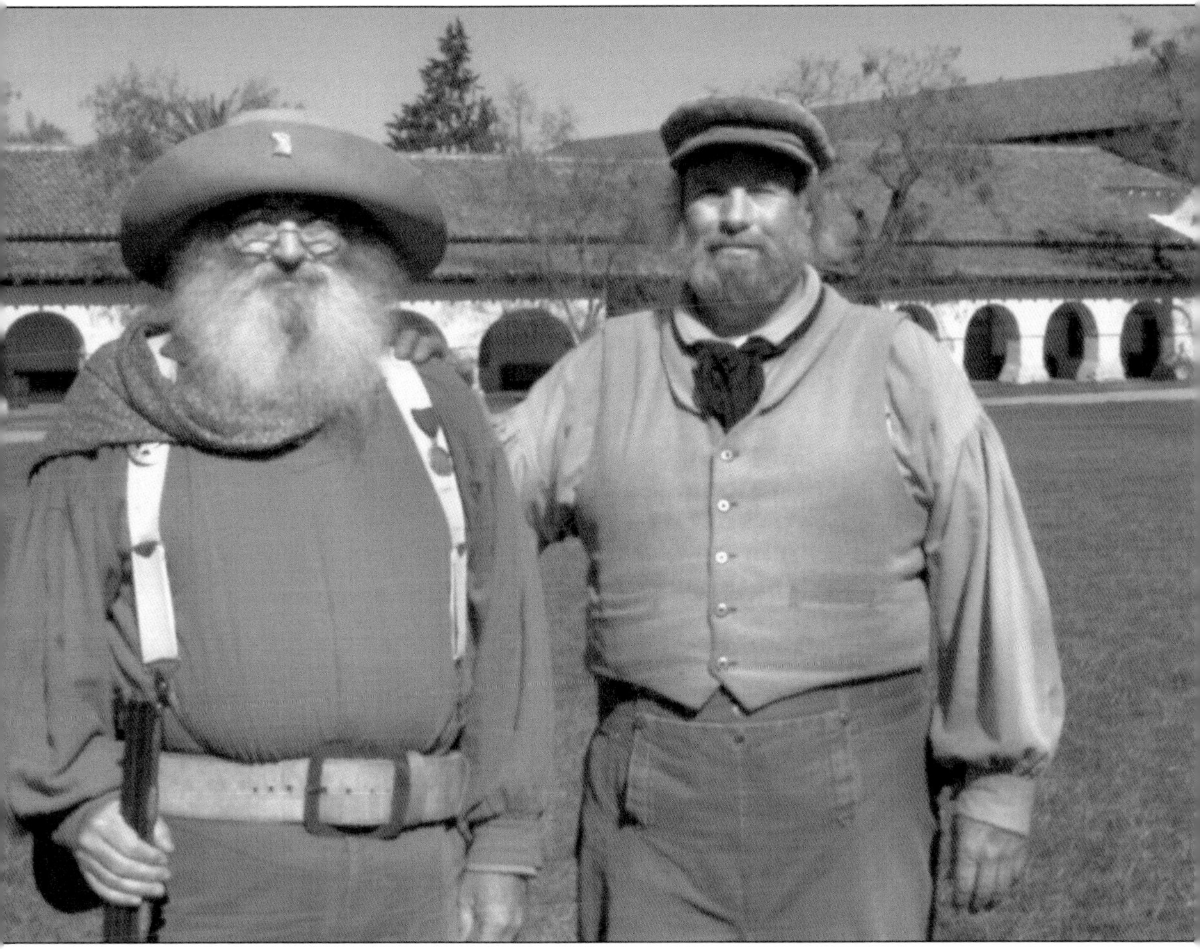

Glen Koehl (left) and Bruce Horttor serve as docents at the San Juan Bautista State Historic Park.

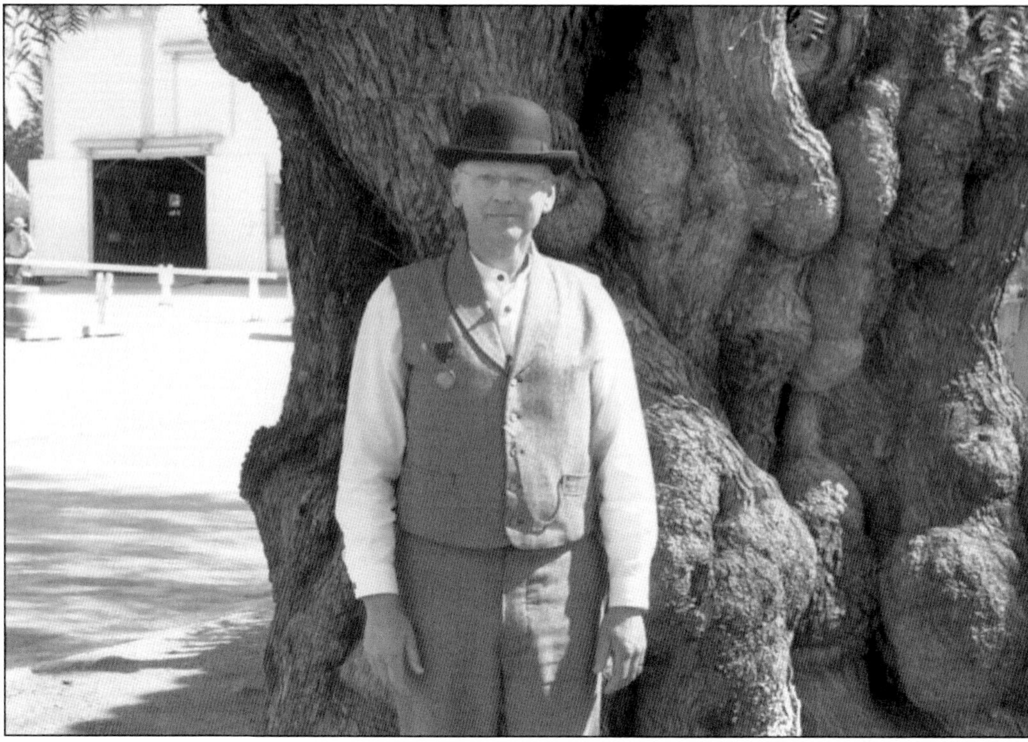

Pictured above is Larry Kellogg, a member of the park staff and a volunteer. The Plaza History Association hosts an annual Grand Victorian Ball during its Early Days in San Juan festival in June. Ladies and gentlemen dress in period costume and dance the waltz and other popular dances of the 19th century. Seen below are guests Libby (left), Joseph (center), and Joanna McMahon.

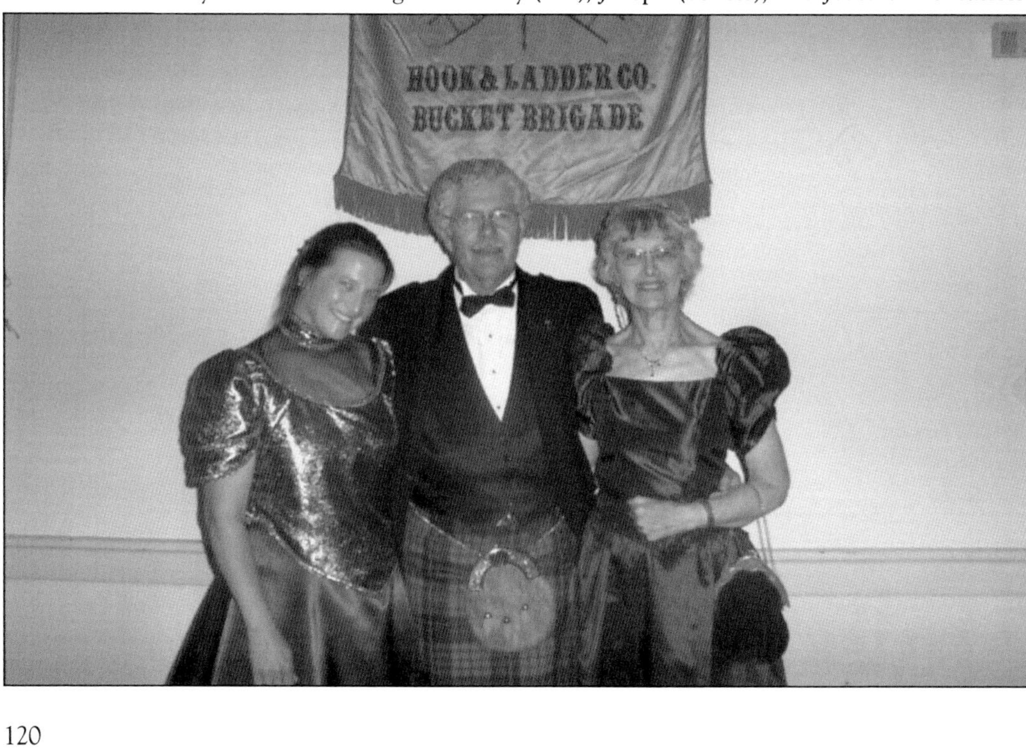

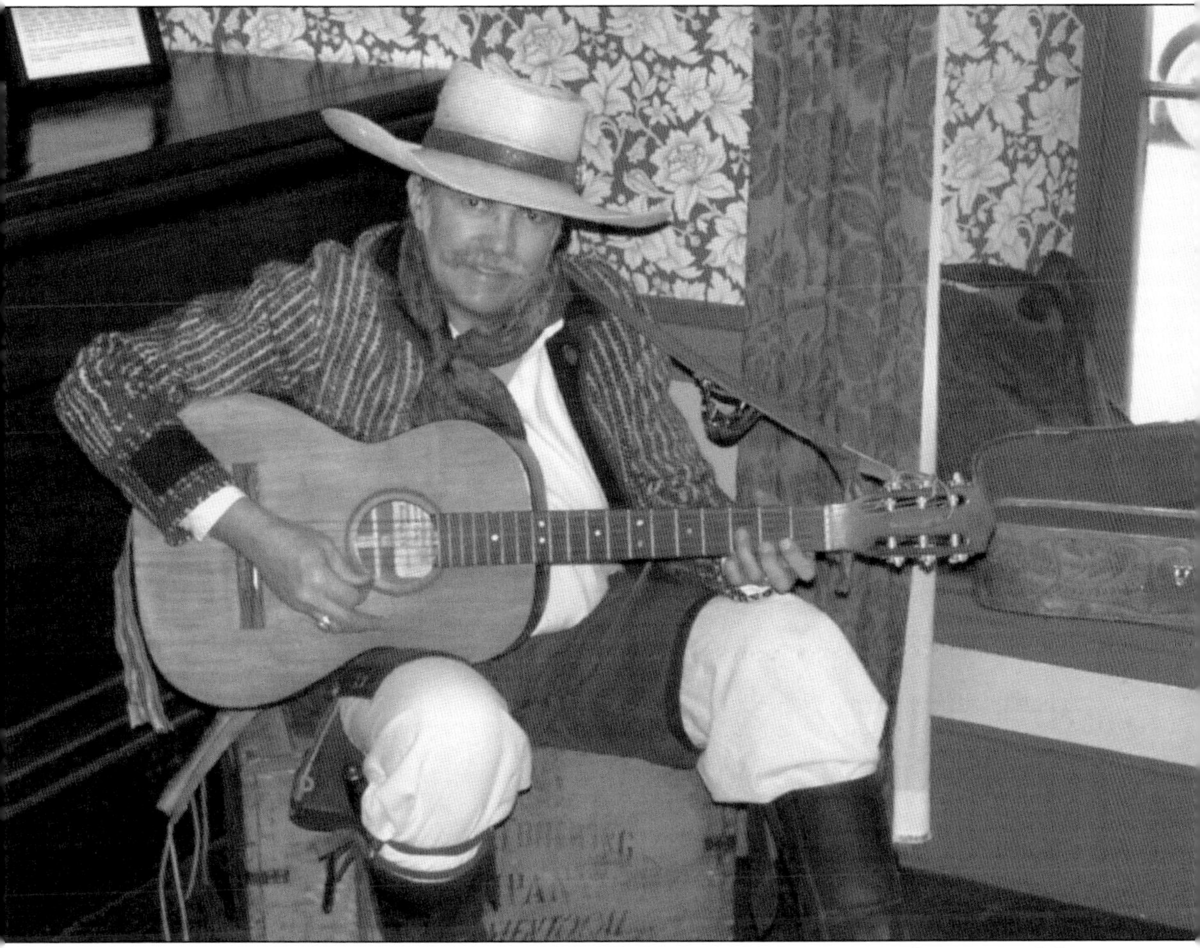

Cisco Jim is another of the park's charismatic volunteers. He entertains visitors from around the globe with his songs.

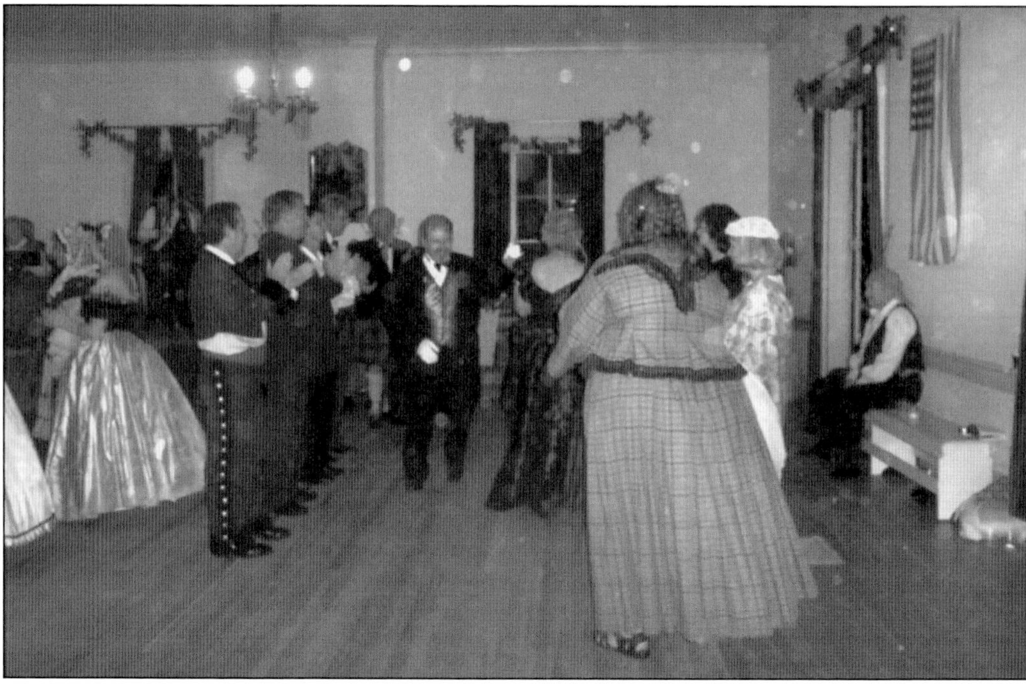

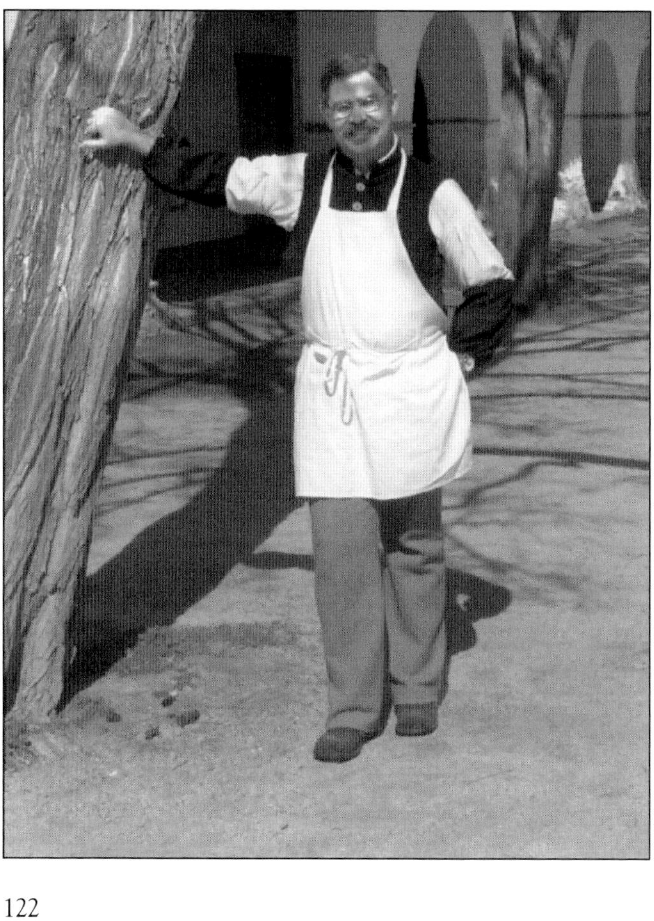

Guests at the Plaza History Association's Grand Victorian Ball dance to a popular tune of the period. The dancers include Jim and Kate Wolf-Pizor and Carlos Zapatta, shown dressed as a Californio.

Robert Groeling, the plaza's bartender, is an expert at serving sarsaparilla and ginger beer.

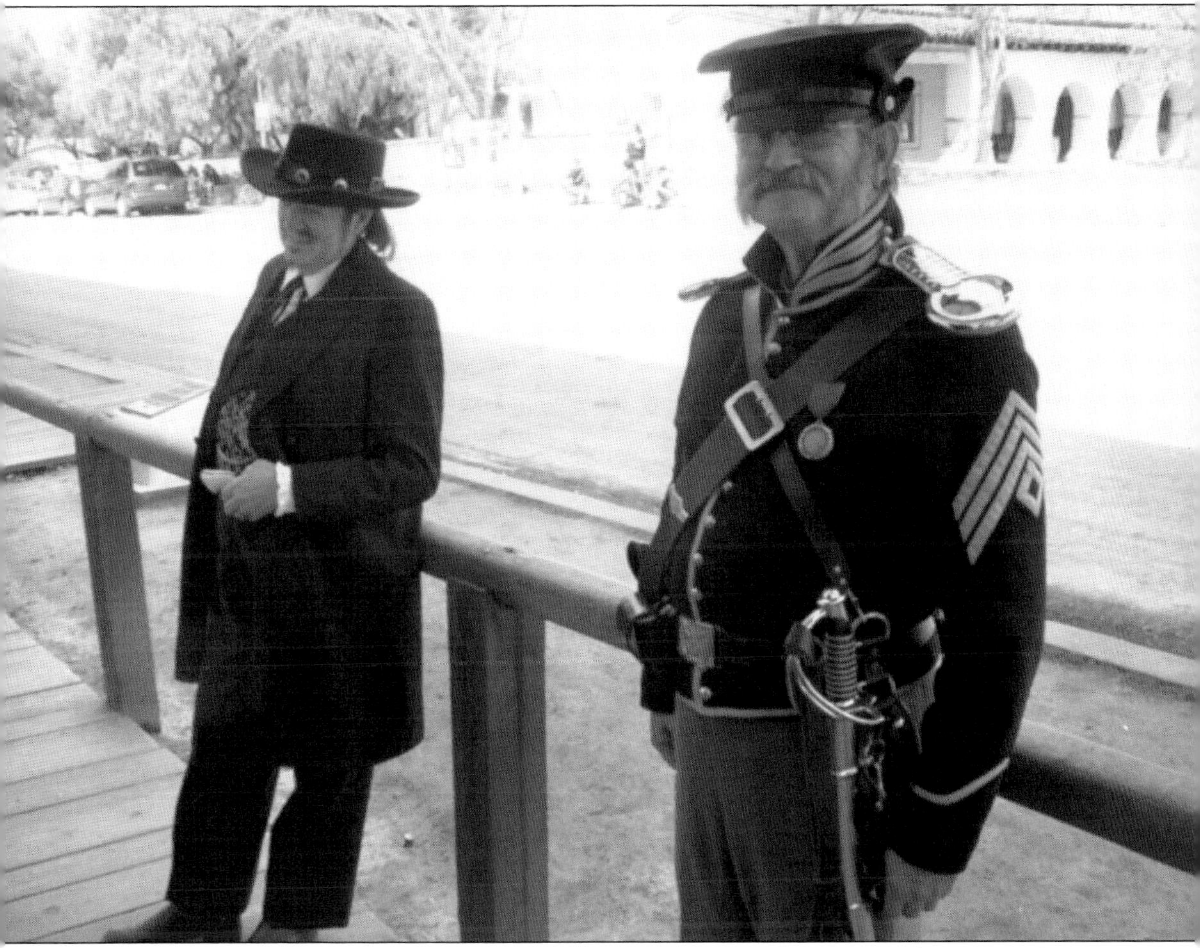

Frank Penninger, dressed in a uniform worn during the Mexican-American War of 1846, stands in front of the Plaza Hotel with San Juan's resident card shark, "High Card Johnny," on the left.

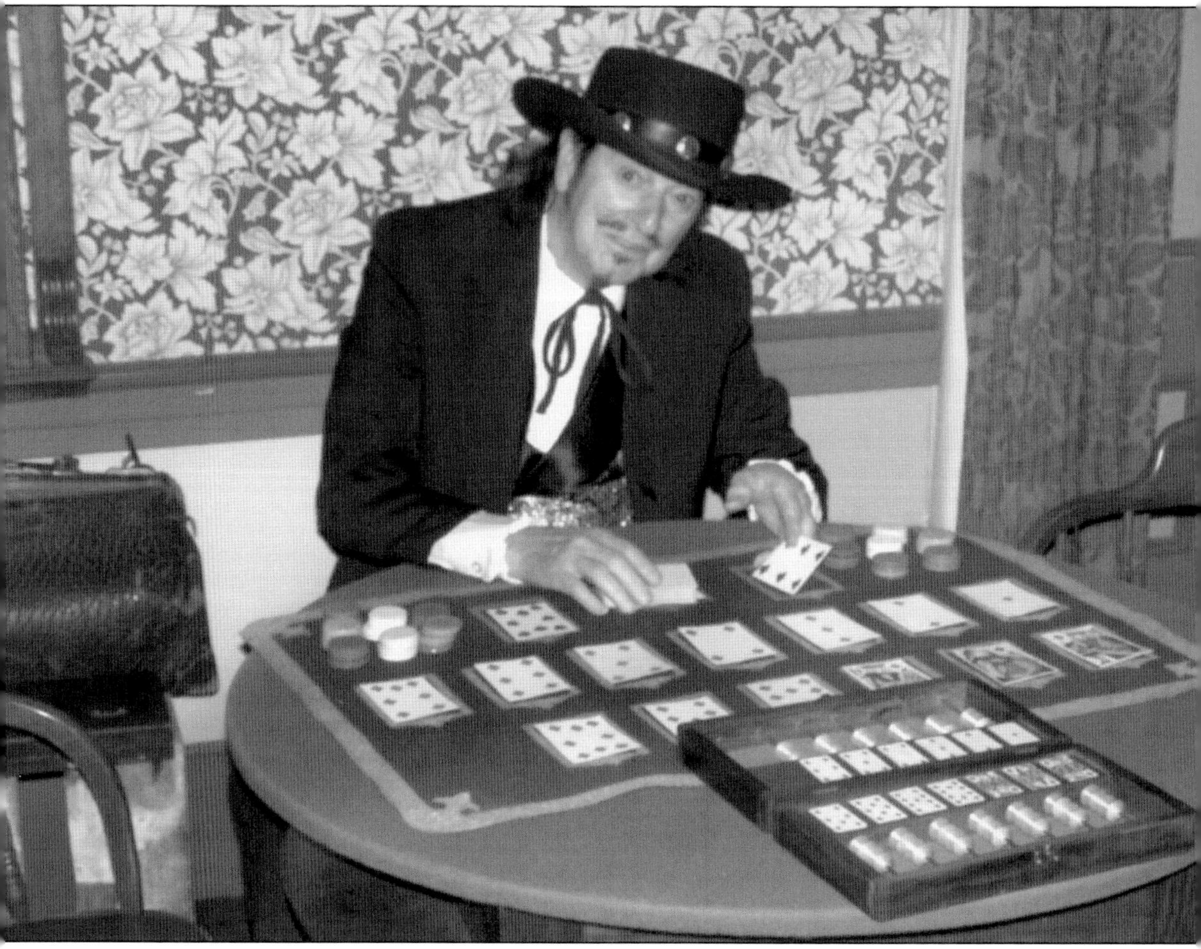

High Card Johnny, at his favorite spot, teaches park visitors how to play cards in the 19th-century style.

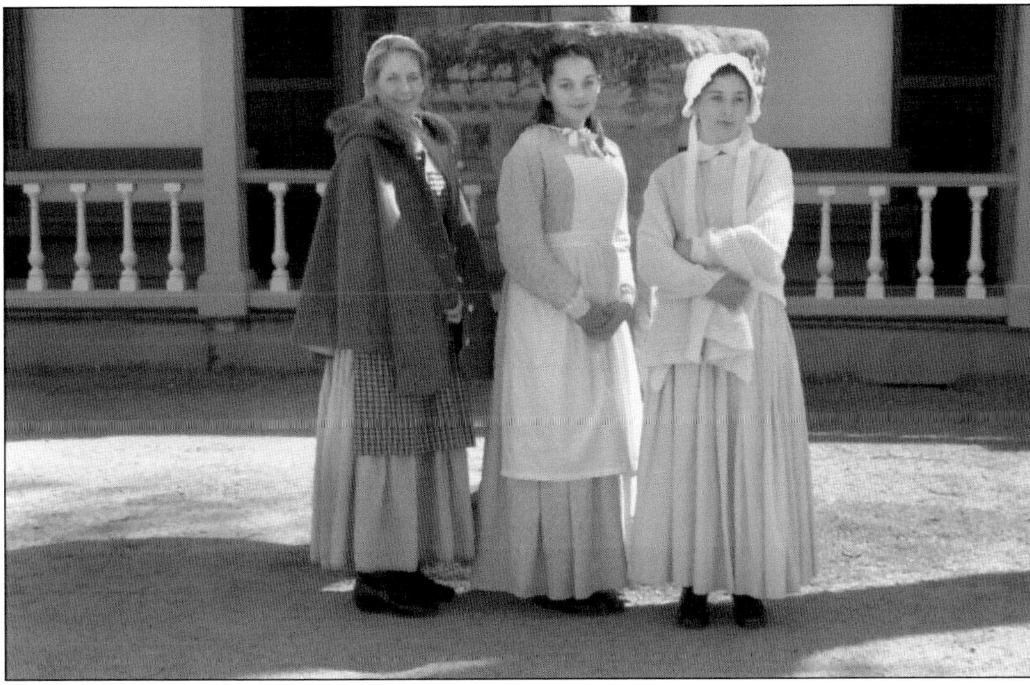

Julie Geiger (left), Lauren Boyd (center), and Jessica Geiger stand in front of the Plaza Hall above. Below is San Juan Bautista's gang of Mountain Men, consisting of Bob Larsen (left) and Jack Swallow Jr.

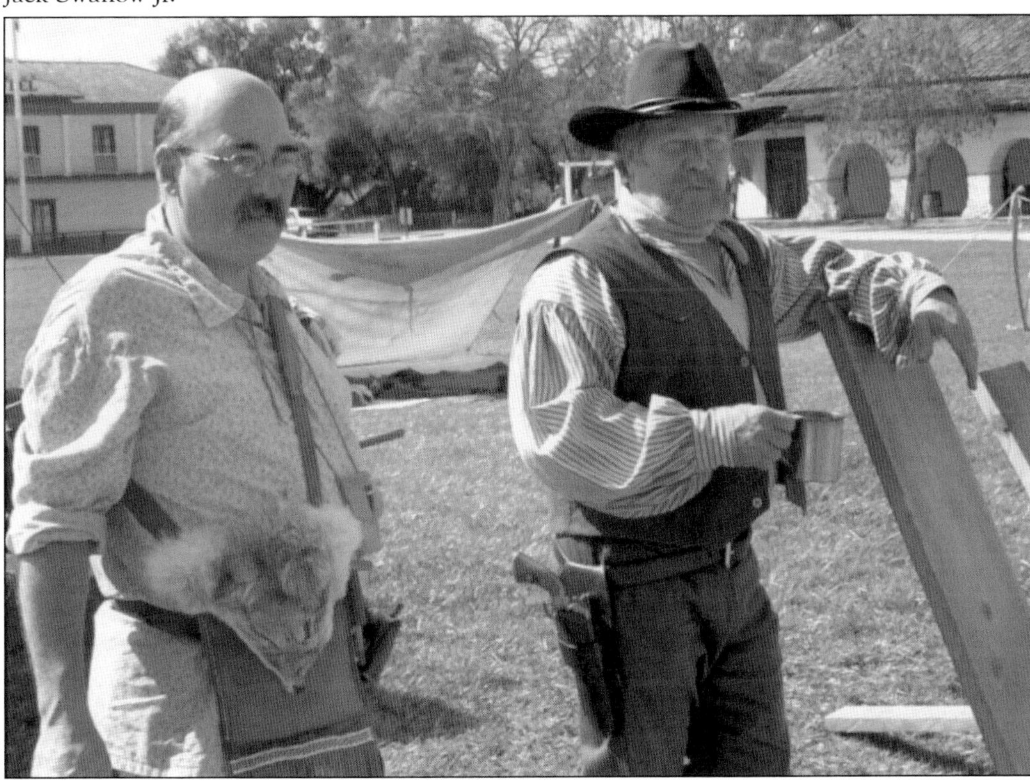

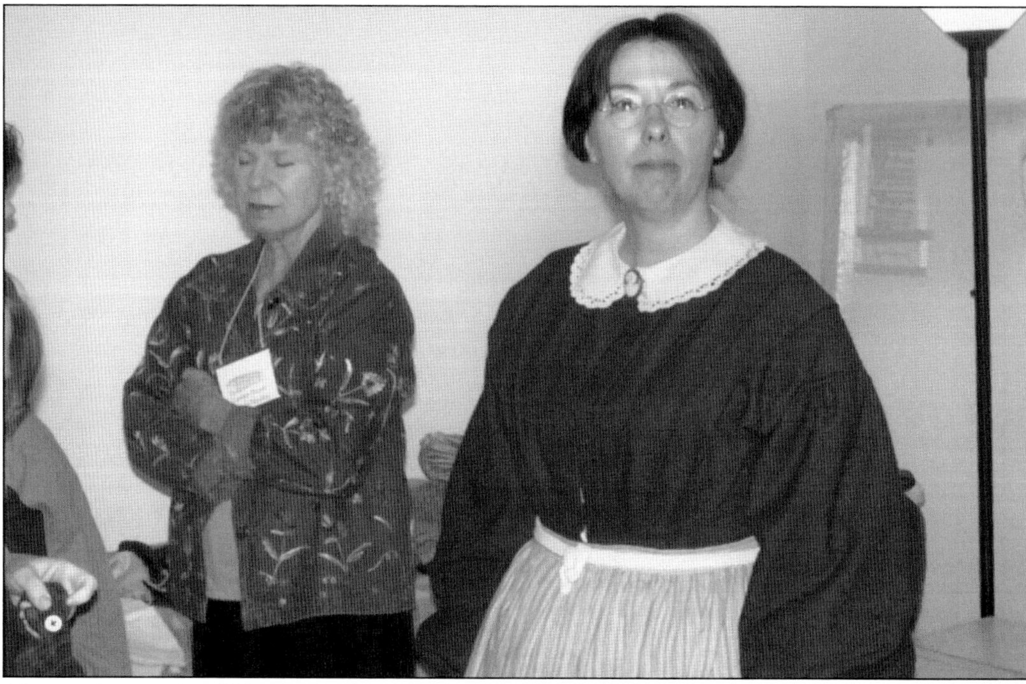

Above, docent Carol Verbeeck shows park guests how a lady dressed in the 19th century. Below, Perry Barrett, another San Juan Bautista State Historic Park docent, holds court in front of the Plaza Hotel.

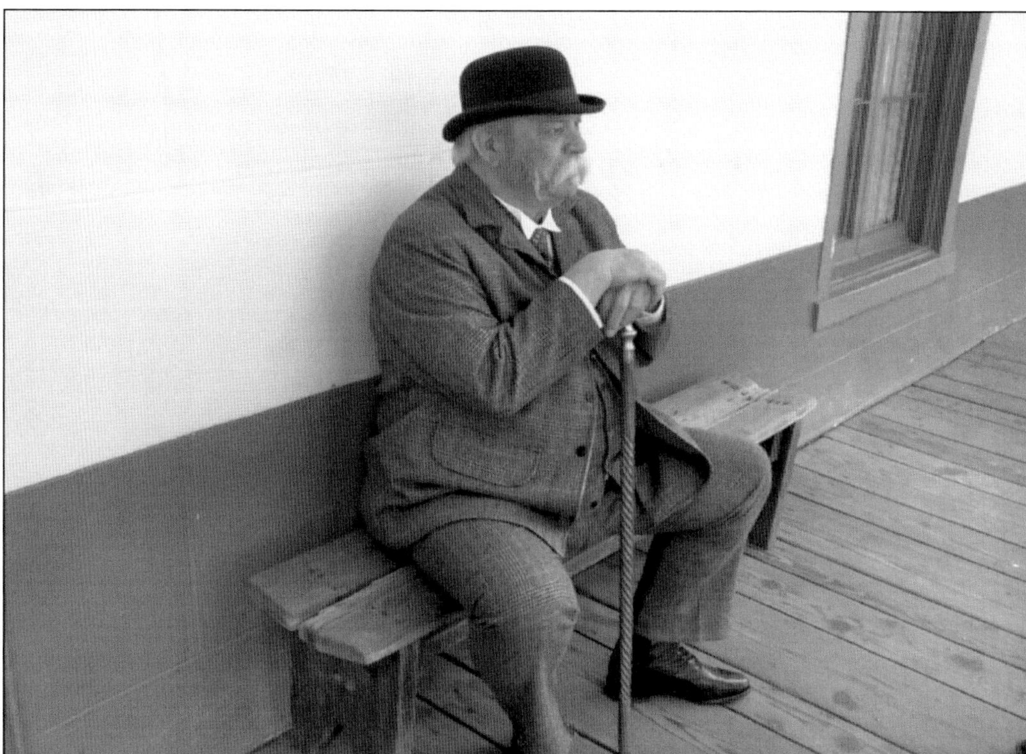

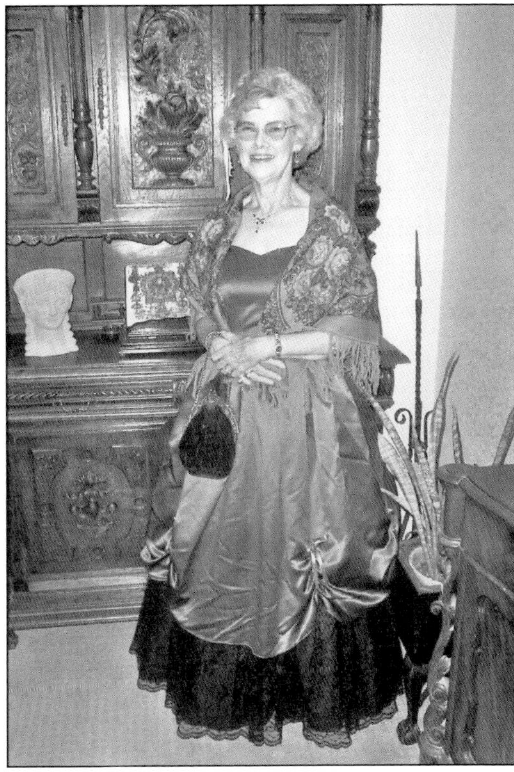

Joseph and Joanna McMahon are dressed in their formal clothes, ready for the Plaza History Association's Grand Victorian Ball.

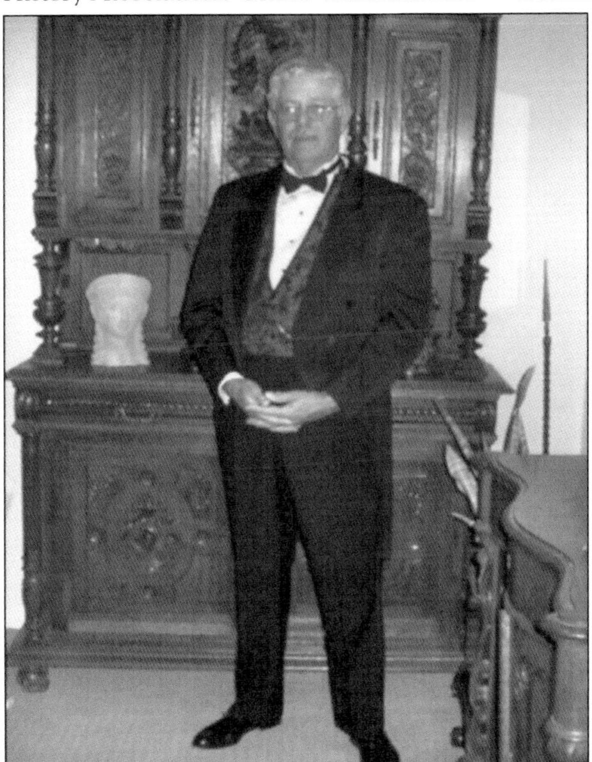